Birnbaum's

Disneyland ®

STEPHEN BIRNBAUM
FOUNDING EDITOR

TOM PASSAVANT
EDITORIAL DIRECTOR

ALICE GARRARD
EXECUTIVE EDITOR

DEANNA CARON
SENIOR EDITOR

GLENN NAKAHARA
ART DIRECTOR

SCOTT RICHTER
CONTRIBUTING EDITOR

TRACY A. SMITH
COPY EDITOR

ALEXANDRA MAYES BIRNBAUM
CONSULTING EDITOR

HYPERION AND HEARST BUSINESS PUBLISHING, INC.

CONTENTS

113 Good Meals, Great Times

From simple snacks to creative multi-course feasts, there are meals to please every palate in (and around) Disneyland. If you venture just a little farther afield —into Anaheim, greater Orange County, or even as far as Los Angeles—you'll find unusual and delicious dining experiences. We've provided a meal-by-meal guide that highlights our picks of the restaurants, tells you where they are, and describes some of their specialties.

133 Sports

Whether you're dreaming of the perfect wave or just want to swim a couple of lazy laps, whether you delight in smashing a serve across a tennis net or love to see your golf ball sail onto the green, chances are you'll be able to fulfill your fondest athletic dream in this land of continuous sunshine. If spectator sports are more your speed, there are professional baseball, football, hockey, and basketball teams to watch, all within an easy drive. These activities perfectly complement a Magic Kingdom visit.

141 Anaheim

Walt Disney chose Anaheim as the home of his Disneyland dream when there was nothing much there but orange groves. Today, it's Orange County's largest city. In addition to Disneyland, Anaheim and its surrounding towns offer a number of appealing attractions and cultural diversions, plus that irresistible Southern California phenomenon—the monumental shopping mall.

149 In All Directions

After you've thoroughly explored Disneyland, a variety of fascinating things to see and do still awaits you in Southern California. And it's so easy to plan a weekend getaway, a week's sojourn, or an even longer tour of the area. Your options are as diverse as the landscape—from the urban sophistication of Los Angeles and star-studded Beverly Hills to desert trails and the spectacular Pacific coastline.

For Steve, who merely made this all possible.

ISBN: 0-7868-8110-0

Printed in the United States of America

Other 1996 Birnbaum Travel Guides

Bahamas and Turks & Caicos
Bermuda
Canada
Cancun/Cozumel & Isla Mujeres
Caribbean
Country Inns and Back Roads
Hawaii
Mexico
Miami & Fort Lauderdale
United States
Walt Disney World
Walt Disney World For Kids, By Kids
Walt Disney World Without Kids

A Word from the Editors

When his two daughters were growing up, Walt Disney often accompanied them to local amusement parks on Sundays. There he observed that the youngsters had no trouble entertaining themselves, but there was nothing of much interest for the adults to do. A park, to his way of thinking, should appeal to the sense of wonder and exploration (and to the child) in everyone, no matter what age. His vision became a reality for all of us when Disneyland opened on July 17, 1955. The inaugural ceremonies were televised live, hosted by Art Linkletter, Bob Cummings, and Ronald Reagan.

While the park has grown over the years, its magic has remained the same. In 1971, some of Tinkerbell's pixie dust settled in Florida as well, when its larger, younger sibling opened, further delighting Disney fans. Yet although certain aspects of these two places are undeniably the same, Disneyland possesses a unique charm, intimacy, and hospitality that can only be experienced at a park of such a manageable size.

This allure endures no matter how many times one visits. Whenever we journey into the Magic Kingdom—for the opening of a new attraction or to revisit some of our old favorites—we are reminded again and again of what a special place Disneyland is.

We've found that the people who visit here fall into two distinct categories: those who live within 100 miles of Disneyland's Anaheim site, and those who come from often very distant points. For those within a short drive of the park, our *Magic Kingdom* chapter may be the primary focus. For those who plan to make their visit to Disneyland part of a vacation encompassing Southern California, our chapters *Anaheim* and *In All Directions* should be of significant value.

In planning your trip, keep in mind that Disneyland is a unique entity, far more complex than most first-time visitors imagine. And the scope of its diversity has only increased with the addition of Mickey's Toontown, adjacent to Fantasyland, and the Indiana Jones Adventure attraction in Adventureland.

It's important to take into account every aspect of the park, not just the attractions (which justifiably receive a lot of attention) but also the appealing shops, glittering shows and other live entertainment, special events, and diverse dining opportunities. (Did you know, for instance, that you can dine by moonlight beside a bayou in the middle of the day, or indulge in a dessert buffet on the balcony of a royal suite Walt Disney designed for himself?)

Knowing the full inventory of what's available at Disneyland—and the best time and the order in which to enjoy it—is essential. Likewise, it's important to place the park in a geographical context—the diverse Southern California region—and to consider all there is to see and do in the area.

In designing this book, we've kept every possible aspect of your trip in mind and have compiled all the information you'll need for a memorable, hassle-free visit in an accessible format. Plus we've added plenty of photos to bring these attractions more vividly to life.

Despite the designation "Official Guide," we must stress that *Disneyland staff members have exercised no veto power whatever over the contents of this book.* Quite the contrary, they have opened their files and explained operations to us in the most generous way imaginable so that we could prepare the comprehensive appraisals, charts, and schedules that are necessary to help visitors understand the complex workings of a complex enterprise.

We daresay there are times when the folks at Disneyland are less than delighted with some of our opinions and conclusions, yet these statements all remain in the guide. Furthermore, we've been flattered again and again by Disneyland staff members who have commented about how much they've learned from the material presented here.

As for our readers, we firmly believe that the combination of our years of experience and independent voice, coupled with our access to accurate, up-to-date inside information from the Disney staff, makes this book uniquely useful. We like to think it's indispensable, but we'll let you be the final judge of that 150 pages from now.

This guidebook owes an enormous debt to the special people who created Disneyland and to those who continue to keep its magic alive. They call themselves "cast members" because each one of them contributes to the incomparable "show" that is Disneyland. Without the extremely forthcoming cooperation of Disneyland personnel on every level, this guide would not be as helpful as it is.

Both in the park and behind the scenes, they've been the source of the most vital factual data.

We hope we're not omitting any names in specifically thanking Tim Runco (Entertainment); Gary Burson and Joanne Hong (Food Administration); Jerry Wright and Alan Niizawa (Finance/Guest Research); Barbara Al-Shammaa, Tracy Montoya, Dave Omel, Gil Scarnecchia, and Jon Storbeck (Operations); and John McClintock and Patrick Alo (Publicity).

In addition, John Hench, Marty Sklar, Tony Baxter, and Ken Anderson (Walt Disney Imagineering) deserve a special tip of the editorial hat for their assistance. To Renie Bardeau, LouAnne Cappiello, and Eva Goulette, all of whom do so much to make our job easier (and often possible), we extend special thanks for their unflagging and extraordinary help.

In the production of this book, we salute Elizabeth Irigoyen and Margaret Casagrande for their typesetting skills, and Laura Vitale for her keen eye in reading the final galleys. A nod especially is due to Shari Hartford, who kept our own cast of characters on schedule, and Susan Hohl, who knows that every picture has its place, even if it gives us the runaround. We'd also like to thank our favorite off-site Disney expert, Wendy Lefkon, who edited these guides for many years and is still instrumental in their publication as executive editor at Hyperion.

Certainly, no list of acknowledgments would be complete without mentioning our founding editor, Steve Birnbaum, whose spirit, wisdom, and humor still infuse the pages of this guide, as well as Alexandra Mayes Birnbaum, who continues to be a guiding light—to say nothing of a careful reader of every word.

Prior to the opening of Disneyland, Walt Disney surveyed his work in progress and remarked that its main attraction was still missing—people. That's where you come in.

Have a wonderful time.

The Editors

DON'T FORGET TO WRITE

No contribution is of greater value to us in preparing the next edition of this book than your comments on what we have written, as well as information about your own experiences at Disneyland. Please share your insights with us by writing to: The Editors, Official Disney Guides, 1790 Broadway, Sixth Floor; New York, NY 10019.

GETTING READY TO GO

Planning is the key to insuring a trouble-free vacation, and a holiday in Southern California is no exception. The geographical area is just too broad and filled with too many attractions to allow a visitor to see even the highlights of all that's available—during a full week (or even two)—without careful preparation.

That doesn't mean that every detail must be decided before departure—just that the major options should be known before leaving home. This helps in choosing just which sights and attractions are simply too good to pass up.

The chapters that follow describe Anaheim's top sites and the other Southern California musts (see *Anaheim* and *In All Directions*). The pages that follow in this chapter are designed to supply all the data necessary to help you decide when to go and how to get there (for the amount of money you have available to spend). It also provides a variety of helpful hints on how to make your Disneyland holiday most enjoyable, relaxing, and free of unexpected problems.

(Unless otherwise noted, all phone numbers are in the 714 area code.)

When to Go

When weighing the very best times to visit Disneyland, the most obvious possibilities seem to be Christmas, Easter, and summer vacation months—especially if there are children in the family. But there are some very good reasons to avoid these periods—the major one being that almost everybody else wants to go then, too. On the busiest of those days, you may encounter lengthy lines at one or more attractions, thus limiting the amount of time spent in pure enjoyment. In general, busy days tend to be the least satisfying.

Other times of the year are more pleasant. The week before Thanksgiving, for example, is notably uncrowded. The week after Christmas Day is frantically busy—but the week before stands out for its peaceful atmosphere, with the additional bonus that the fabulous Christmas decorations and special yuletide activities are all available to be enjoyed. Though most of the summer is very busy (the park's summer season runs from mid-June through early September this year), the period before July 1, the last week in August, and the first week of September are usually less crowded. They also allow a visitor to see the park at its twinkling nighttime best, complete with fireworks, the Main Street Electrical Parade, and Fantasmic!—but without the crowds of most of the rest of the summer. Spring months are lovely because of the abundance of seasonal flowers. So is February, when there are spectacular displays of tulips in the Central Plaza.

Saturday is usually the busiest day of the week year-round. (In summer, Mondays and Fridays are the next busiest, Tuesdays, Wednesdays, and Thursdays slightly less crowded.) If it's necessary to visit the park on a weekend day, try to make it on a Sunday.

When not to go: If you hate crowds, avoid the week between Christmas and New Year's Day, Easter Week, and the weeks from early July through the third week in August.

DISNEYLAND WEATHER

If dry, sunny weather is your ideal, Anaheim may indeed seem like heaven. Rainy days are few and far between, and generally occur between the months of November and April, which also is the coolest time of the year. Santa Ana winds during this season occasionally produce short periods of dry, crisp, warm, desert weather and sparkling clear air that unveils the distant mountains that the smog hides most of the rest of the time.

In summer, Southern Californians are accustomed to thin, low morning clouds that make it wise to plan expeditions to the beach in the afternoon, when the haze burns off and the mercury rises; mornings and nights are generally cool.

	Temperatures (F°)		Rainfall (in.)
	Average high	Average low	Average
January	65	44	3.62
February	67	45	2.09
March	68	46	2.00
April	70	50	1.63
May	72	53	0.29
June	77	56	0.02
July	82	61	0.01
August	83	60	0.04
September	81	59	0.10
October	77	55	0.26
November	72	50	1.01
December	67	46	1.60

Special Events

Disneyland itself sponsors nearly a dozen annual special events during the year, and nearby communities stage as many more, all adding considerable spice to the Southern California scene. For information about other annual activities at Disneyland see the *Magic Kingdom* chapter.

JANUARY

New Year's Eve, Disneyland: There are fireworks and live entertainment on hand for this big end-of-the-year bash, one of the prettiest times to visit the park. A general admission ticket is valid for this event. For more details about this and other Disneyland activities mentioned below, contact Disneyland Guest Relations; 1313 Harbor Blvd.; Anaheim, CA 92803; 999-4565.

Rose Bowl, Pasadena: The annual college football game between the Pac 10 and Big 10 conference champions is a New Year's Day tradition. Rose Bowl; Pasadena, CA; 818-449-7673.

Tournament of Roses Parade: Another New Year's Day tradition in Southern California, the floats in this procession are all made of roses. The parade route follows Colorado Boulevard through Pasadena. Tournament of Roses Parade; Pasadena, CA; 818-795-4171.

FEBRUARY

Dana Point Harbor Festival of Whales: This event, which celebrates its 25th anniversary this year, is held in late February or March (depending on the whale migration itself) and highlights the southward migration of California gray whales. Festival activities include seaside musical performances, Navy and Coast Guard ship tours and rides (weather permitting), displays of whale-related artifacts, a street fair, and a slate of anniversary events. A program for youngsters features children's art exhibits, musical performances, and other entertainment. Whale-watching cruises, offered in the area from January to March, are frosting on the cake. Dana Point is about 35 miles south of Disneyland. Festival of Whales; Box 12; Dana Point, CA 92629; 496-1555 or 800-290-DANA.

Winter Festival, Laguna Beach: At this three-day arts festival, some 100 to 120 specially selected artists are on hand to exhibit and sell pottery, jewelry, macramé, and other

handiwork on the grounds of the Festival of Arts (described in "July," below) at 650 Laguna Canyon Road. Music, poetry readings, mime, and an international food fair round out the festivities. Laguna Beach Chamber of Commerce; Box 396; Laguna Beach, CA 92652; 494-1145.

MARCH

Glory of Easter, Garden Grove: This celebrated pageant at the Crystal Cathedral is best known for its colorful array of costumes, live animals, flying angels, spectacular special effects, and dramatic interpretation of the Crucifixion and Resurrection. Crystal Cathedral; 12141 Lewis St.; Garden Grove, CA 97640; 544-5679.

Fiesta de las Golondrinas, San Juan Capistrano: The townspeople here have been welcoming the March 19 arrival of the celebrated square-tailed cliff swallows (from their wintering grounds in Goya, Argentina) ever since the founding of the community's mission in 1776. But during the last two decades, the birds' return has been celebrated with special fervor, though they have decreased in numbers. The mission hosts folk dances and children's programs, while the Fiesta Association sponsors a "hairiest man" contest and the largest non-motorized parade in the U.S., featuring participants in Native American and Mexican attire. The mission is one of the ten most active archaeological sites in this country, and the chapel is the oldest building still in use in the state (see *In All Directions* chapter). A smaller celebration is held in October to bid farewell to the famous birds. San Juan Capistrano Fiesta Association; Box 532; San Juan Capistrano, CA 92693; 493-1976, or call the Chamber of Commerce, 493-4700.

APRIL

Toyota Grand Prix of Long Beach: A CART (Championship Auto Racing Teams) race using Indy-type cars converts the streets of Long Beach into a racetrack each year during a weekend in April. Grand Prix Association of Long Beach; 3000 Pacific Ave.; Long Beach, CA 90806; 310-436-9953.

MAY

Summer Preview Weekends, Disneyland: Beginning in the spring, the park stays open until midnight on Fridays and Saturdays, and until 10 P.M. on Sundays. The Main Street Electrical Parade and Fantasmic! are presented all three nights, and a fireworks display is an extra bonus during selected nights in May and June. Disneyland Guest Relations; 1313 Harbor Blvd.; Anaheim, CA 92803; 999-4565.

Strawberry Festival, Garden Grove: Between 30,000 and 50,000 holidaymakers show up for each day of this Memorial Day weekend in Garden Grove, not far from Anaheim. The Strawberry Festival Parade of floats, bands, and equestrians is one of the highlights. Gourmands smile at the cutting of an enormous strawberry shortcake, big enough to cover a whole stage and substantial enough to provide most festivalgoers with at least one portion. Radio and TV celebrities are on hand for autographs, and there are plenty of contests—such as the one for redheads that's open to all ages, with prizes for the oldest and the youngest carrottops, and for the longest, shortest, and curliest tresses. Strawberry Festival Association; Box 2287; Garden Grove, CA 92642; 638-0981.

JULY

Orange County Fiesta, Fountain Valley: This four-day-long festival (held around the July Fourth weekend) features a chili cook-off, bluegrass and country music, fireworks, and other entertainment in the Mile Square Park area in Fountain Valley. A carnival is held in conjunction with the festival. Along with a fireworks show on July Fourth, the festival features contests, arts and crafts displays, food stands, and musical entertainment. The park is located on the corner of Brookhurst and Heil streets, Fountain Valley. Chamber of Commerce; 11100 Warner Ave., Suite 204; Fountain Valley, CA 92708; 668-0542.

Festival of Arts and Pageant of the Masters, Laguna Beach: More than half a century old, this well-respected, seven-week-long event—which begins in early July and lasts through August—brings some 160 artists and craftspeople to the tree-dotted grounds of Irvine Bowl Park to display and sell their watercolors, oil paintings, sculptures, tapestries, jewelry, and more in open-air booths on the grounds. Meanwhile, at the popular Pageant of the Masters, models re-create famous works of art on stage in two-hour-long "living pictures," accompanied by narration and the music of a 28-piece orchestra. Seats must be reserved well in advance. Programs for children and other entertainment complete the festival. Traditionally, more than 200,000 people attend the festival. A Sawdust Festival and an Art-A-Fair have grown up nearby in the shadow of this Laguna Beach festival, and make the area

even more lively during this period. Festival of Arts; Irvine Bowl Park; 650 Laguna Canyon Rd.; Laguna Beach, CA 92651; 494-1145.

Flight of the Lasers: This two-hour, one-person sailboat race around a five-mile course in Newport Harbor has been a tradition for over 50 years. Thousands line the shores of Newport Harbor to watch. Prizes are awarded to top finishers. Newport Beach Area Chamber of Commerce; 1470 Jamboree Rd.; Newport Beach, CA 92660; 729-4400.

Orange County Fair, Costa Mesa: Held at the Orange County Fairgrounds, this annual event is a bustling hodgepodge of celebrity entertainment, rodeo events, carnival rides, motorcycle races, a jazz festival, cooking contests, flower and garden shows, arts and crafts exhibitions, commercial exhibits, and more. Orange County Fair; 88 Fair Dr.; Costa Mesa, CA 92626; 708-3247.

AUGUST

Ocean Pacific Professional Surfing Contest, Huntington Beach: Each year, for a week in August, the world's best surfers compete here and draw more than 100,000 spectators. This is a good time to see some terrific wave riding, and the people watching is nearly as good. Huntington Beach Community Services Office; 2000 Main St.; Huntington Beach, CA 92648; 536-5486.

SEPTEMBER

Newport Seafest, Newport Beach: Held annually during the second and third weeks of September, this ten-day extravaganza celebrates the Southern California way of life through approximately 35 marine and related community events. For details and a schedule of events contact: Newport Harbor Area Chamber of Commerce; 1470 Jamboree Rd.; Newport Beach, CA 92660; 729-4400. Major events include: **Taste of Newport:** The Newport Center Fashion Island mall hosts this three-day festival, which features culinary delights and continuous live entertainment. Sample food, wine, and beer offered by more than 40 of the area's top restaurants. **Sand Castle Contest:** Clubs, organizations, families, and businesses vie for trophies by sculpting dragons, castles, cars, and much more intricate creations during this three-hour-long competition. In the past, participants have even gone to the trouble of dyeing their creations an assortment of colors. Not surprisingly, thousands show up at Newport Beach's Corona del Mar State Beach to watch.

Catalina Festival of Art, Avalon: Held annually on the third weekend in September, this festival fills two or three city blocks along Front Street (a.k.a. Crescent Avenue) in downtown Avalon, on Catalina Island, with arts and crafts exhibits. This is a pleasant time of year on the island: The summer crowds have largely dispersed, while the weather is, if anything, more pleasant than ever. Catalina Island Art Association; 310-510-0808.

International Street Fair, Orange: The Plaza Square area is taken over by this event every year from Friday through Sunday of Labor Day weekend. The streets around the square are closed off, and large banners rename them for the duration—American Street, Italian Street, and German, Swedish, Mexican, Vietnamese, and Japanese streets. Local residents in appropriate national costumes dish out savory platters full of foods typical of their countries, and entertainers amuse visitors with music and folk dances. International Street Fair; Box 927; Orange, CA 92666; 532-6260.

Wooden Boat Festival: More than 60 classic and contemporary wooden boats are displayed, both in and out of the water. There also are demonstrations, seminars, a wooden-boat sailing regatta, a boat parade, and a boat-building contest. Wooden Boat Festival; 400 Main St.; Balboa, CA 92661; 673-5258.

DECEMBER

Christmas Festivities, Disneyland: This may be the park's most beautiful season. Main Street is festooned with greenery, and hundreds of poinsettias bloom in Town Square and the Central Plaza, while a 60-foot Christmas tree decorated with 3,000 colorful lights and 2,800 ornaments embellishes the atmosphere further. Carolers in 19th-century English garb stroll the grounds and, two nights early in the season, there's a solemn and impressive candlelight ceremony involving a procession, Christmas music sung by a 1,000-voice choir, and a reading of a Christmas story by a well-known actor or actress. A special holiday parade also is featured. The week before the holiday ranks among the best times of year to visit. The week afterward, however, is one of the busiest, so wise guests will plan accordingly. Disneyland Guest Relations; 1313 Harbor Blvd.; Anaheim, CA 92803; 999-4565.

Glory of Christmas, Garden Grove: This annual nativity pageant features 200 performers and a mini menagerie of animals in a spectacle performed three times daily from November 26 through December 30. Crystal Cathedral; 12141 Lewis St.; Garden Grove, CA 97640; 544-5679

Newport Harbor Christmas Boat Parade, Newport Beach: First held in 1908, this event draws about 200 boats each evening, all of them decked out with Santa Clauses and angels and other holiday characters, and enough Christmas lights to illuminate a score of oversize Christmas trees. Reflecting in the inky waters of Newport Harbor—which hosts the celebration on the seven nights preceding Christmas Eve—all those little colored stars make up a spectacle worthy of the Magic Kingdom. Area waterfront restaurants book reservations for this period up to a year in advance. Newport Harbor Area Chamber of Commerce; 1470 Jamboree Rd.; Newport Beach, CA 92660; 729-4400.

HOW BIG ARE THE CROWDS?

Crowds at Disneyland vary greatly from weekends to weekdays as the charts below illustrate. The information listed should assist in making a decision on when to visit the park. Keep in mind that choosing a least crowded time of year to visit may also mean that some of Disneyland's most entertaining parades and special events (the Main Street Electrical Parade, Fantasmic!, and the fireworks exhibitions, for example) might not be on the schedule. Also, certain attractions may be closed for annual refurbishment. Call 999-4565 for the most up-to-date information.

WEEKDAYS
(Mondays through Thursdays)

Least Crowded	Average Attendance	Most Crowded
1st week in January to Presidents' week	Week after Easter Sunday	Presidents' week
Last week in February to 3rd week in March	Memorial Day week	Week before Easter Sunday
3rd week in March to week before Easter	Labor Day week	Beginning of summer to Labor Day weekend
Two weeks after Easter Sunday to Memorial Day week		Thanksgiving weekend (Thursday to Sunday)
End of Labor Day week to Columbus Day		Christmas Day to New Year's Day
Columbus Day to Thanksgiving		
End of Thanksgiving weekend to week before Christmas		
Week before Christmas		

WEEKENDS
(Fridays, Saturdays, Sundays)

Least Crowded	Average Attendance	Most Crowded
1st week in January to Presidents' week	1st week in February to 3rd week in March	Presidents' week
End of Thanksgiving weekend to week before Christmas	3rd week in March to the week before Easter	Week before Easter Sunday
	Week after Easter Sunday	Two weeks after Easter Sunday to Memorial Day
	Labor Day week	Memorial Day week
	End of Labor Day week to Columbus Day	Beginning of summer to Labor Day weekend
	Columbus Day to beginning of Thanksgiving weekend	Thanksgiving weekend (Thursday to Sunday)
	Week before Christmas	Christmas Day to New Year's Day

Planning Ahead

Although it takes time to plan a trip, the increased enjoyment that results from custom tailoring a vacation to your personal tastes makes the effort worthwhile.

The planning will go more smoothly if it's done in an organized manner. First, collect as much information as you can about the sites and attractions to be visited from the sources of information mentioned below. Then peruse these materials before beginning to make any definite plans. Above all, don't try to see and do too much in too short a period.

INFORMATION: For information about special events and performance times, the latest ticket prices, operating hours, and other Disneyland specifics contact Disneyland Guest Relations; Box 3232; Anaheim, CA 92803; 999-4565.

For other area information, contact the following organizations:

● **Anaheim Area Visitor and Convention Bureau**; Box 4270; Anaheim, CA 92803; 999-8999. It's also possible to stop by in person at the office at 800 West Katella Avenue. For a recorded message detailing current area activities, phone 635-8900.

● **Los Angeles Convention and Visitors Bureau**; 633 West Fifth St., Suite 6000; Los Angeles, CA 90071; 213-689-8822 or 213-624-7300.

● **San Diego Convention and Visitors Bureau**; 401 B St., Suite 1400; San Diego, CA 92101-4190; 619-232-3101.

Inside Disneyland: Park employees can answer questions on just about any subject, and what they don't know they're almost always happy to help you find out. Furthermore, people at both City Hall (on the west side of Town Square) and Bank of Main Street (across the street from City Hall) can field questions about goings-on inside the park.

RESERVATIONS: Scheduling activities down to the tiniest detail is not necessary when planning a vacation in Southern California. For visits during the busy July and August season, however, make lodging reservations as far in advance as possible to get your choice of accommodations—at least six months ahead if you can, since area hotels run 95 to 97 percent full during these months. For visits at other times of year, check with the Anaheim Area Visitor and Convention Bureau (above) to see what conventions are scheduled when you want to travel. Some of these can crowd facilities enough to warrant altering your plans.

WHAT TO PACK: Southern California isn't *so* laid back that you need no more than a bathing suit, but it isn't an environment that

demands formal fashions either. Casual wear will suffice in all but the most formal restaurants, and men usually can wear sports jackets without ties even there. Bathing suits are an obvious must if you plan to take advantage of your hotel's swimming pool (most establishments have them) or go for a walk on one of those long, surf-pounded, Pacific beaches. It's also a good idea to bring along a beach towel. Tennis togs or golf gear may be necessary if you plan to hit the courts or the course. The weather in summer can be hot, but because Southern California air conditioning is usually overefficient, bring a lightweight sweater or jacket to wear indoors.

In winter, warm clothing is a must for evening; during nighttime visits to the park at Christmastime, a heavy jacket may be appropriate. Always pack for unexpected contingencies by including something to keep you comfortable should the weather turn unseasonably warm or cool.

DO YOU NEED A CAR? Southern California is considered America's prime automotive area, but if you're staying in Anaheim for only a couple of days, visiting only Disneyland, and lodging in a nearby hotel, it's not absolutely necessary to have a car. Several airport transportation companies provide service between Anaheim lodging places and the major airports. For details see "To and From the Airports" on page 37. Most hotels have shuttle buses to transport you to and from the park. Many hostelries are within walking distance, and there are connecting sidewalks throughout the area. Local taxis are available when you don't feel like walking.

If you're staying for more than two days, however, you will almost surely want to see a bit more of the area than just a small corner of Anaheim, and although bus transportation does exist, it's far more convenient to have wheels of your own.

SHOULD YOU BUY A PACKAGE?

The wide variety of Southern California vacation packages can confuse even the savviest traveler. Every offering contains so many different components that it's difficult to compare one with another.

Most packages save money over the amount that their various elements would total if purchased separately. Another advantage of packages is the convenience of having all the details and elements arranged in advance.

Finding the very best package is mainly a matter of deciding just what sort of vacation you want, and then shopping around for the package that best fits the bill. The various sections of this book describe many of the Southern California activities and attractions that surround Disneyland in enough detail so

that it should be relatively easy to choose just what you want to add to your Disneyland visit.

Don't select a package that includes elements that don't interest you— remember, you're paying for them. Also remember that the real value of such so-called extras as welcome cocktails, souvenir keychains, and descriptive brochures is negligible.

Disneyland is a component in a wide variety of package tours available from many companies, including Delta Air Lines, the Official Airline of Disneyland, and the Walt Disney Travel Company, Inc. Delta Dream Vacation packages (800-872-7786) can usually save visitors some money on airfares.

The Walt Disney Travel Company (1441 South West St.; Anaheim, CA 92802; 520-5050) offers packages that are particularly good because the company is in the best position to handle any problems that may arise on the spot. Their offices, at the *Disneyland Hotel*, are open Mondays through Fridays from 7 A.M. to 7 P.M.; Saturdays from 8 A.M. to 5 P.M.; and Sundays from 9 A.M. to 4 P.M. The Travel Company often maintains up to 15 percent of the room inventory at the *Disneyland Hotel* and therefore usually has access to hard-to-book accommodations. Other area hotels also are included in Walt Disney Travel Company packages.

Most of the hotels in the Disneyland area also are part of package tours offered by a variety of companies around the country, and by the hotels themselves. This book's comprehensive guide to Anaheim hotels and motels, beginning on page 38, should help you decide which is most appealing. Then contact the hotel directly or a travel agent for package information.

Should You Use a Travel Agent?

Travel agents who know Disneyland and its surrounding area well, and who understand your tastes and vacation goals, can be a great help in planning a trip. Not only will they have a good sense of the various types of Anaheim accommodations, but they also should save you the trouble of shopping around for the lowest airfare, arranging for rental cars, and other travel-related needs.

Look for a travel agent in the same way you'd seek out a doctor, lawyer, or other professional; recommendations from friends who share your tastes and whose judgment

you respect usually go a long way. It's also possible to work directly with the Walt Disney Travel Company (a corporate subsidiary of The Walt Disney Company); its personnel welcome consumers as cheerfully as they work with travel agents, and they are able to book airline tickets and rental cars for you as well as rooms.

It is important to note that the *Disneyland Hotel* and all other major Anaheim hotels pay direct commissions to travel agents, as does the Walt Disney Travel Company, so there are no extra fees to consumers.

Sample Schedules

For those lucky enough to live in the Los Angeles/Orange County area, Disneyland offers the opportunity to return again and again. Nonetheless, there are strategies even area residents use to make every minute count (you'll find them in the "Special Tips" section of the *Magic Kingdom* chapter).

But those travelers making a special trip to Southern California really should spend at least two to three days in and around the Magic Kingdom to experience it fully. Furthermore, if you are planning an extended stay, use some of that extra time to explore other area attractions. The sample schedules below provide possible approaches.

ONE-DAY VISIT: This is far from our most enthusiastic suggestion, but if your itinerary allows only one day in Anaheim, spend the entire time at Disneyland. Get to the park early, by all means, and make the most effective use of your time by following the "Suggested Disneyland Itineraries" on page 112 of the *Magic Kingdom* chapter.

TWO-DAY VISIT: Follow the program outlined above for the first day. On the second day, get to the park early and spend the morning in the Magic Kingdom. Have lunch there, too, but when things look like they're crowding up, head back to your hotel (remember to have your hand stamped before exiting and to keep your Passport), change into golf, tennis, or beach attire and stretch your muscles a bit (see *Sports*). Then luxuriate in a refreshing shower and return to the Magic Kingdom. The evening, especially when the park is open late, is a great time to see some popular attractions that you may have missed during the day—Big Thunder Mountain Railroad or the Haunted Mansion perhaps.

THREE-DAY VISIT: Follow the program outlined above for the first two days. On the morning of the third day you can slow your pace a bit. See any appealing attractions you might have missed, and then revisit your favorite ones. In Pirates of the Caribbean, for instance, the Audio-Animatronics figures are so enticing and the attention to detail so amazing you can't possibly catch it all the first time. Take a break for lunch and then do some shopping in the early afternoon when the shops tend to be least crowded. After you've stored your purchases in lockers at the Lost and Found on Main Street, or made use of the park's package pick-up service, head off to enjoy some live entertainment. End the day with dinner at the *Blue Bayou* restaurant or *Café Orleans* in New Orleans Square and dancing at *Carnation Plaza Gardens* or *Tomorrowland Terrace*.

FOUR-DAY VISIT: Follow the program outlined above for the first three days. On the fourth day bid Disneyland farewell for a morning of sportfishing with the Dana Point fleet (see *Sports* chapter), about 30 miles south of Anaheim. If fishing doesn't appeal, head to Laguna Beach to browse in the galleries and boutiques and, in season, enjoy the popular summer arts festival (described in "When to Go," earlier in this chapter). If there's time left, visit Buena Park's Movieland Wax Museum and Knott's Berry Farm, where Mrs. Knott's chicken dinners became famous (see *Anaheim* chapter).

FIVE-DAY VISIT: This length of stay allows a day for Los Angeles. Start at the Los Angeles County Museum of Art and its next-door neighbor, the La Brea Tar Pit, or visit the Los Angeles Children's Museum, a hands-on, crawl-through sort of place. For lunch, kiosk-hop at the Farmers Market. In the afternoon, visit Universal Studios and have an early dinner there, thus avoiding the rush-hour traffic. Or you could eat at Universal CityWalk (the open-air dining and shopping promenade connecting Universal Studios to the 18-screen Universal City Cinema) and afterward do some shopping, listen to live blues, or see a film.

LONGER VISITS: Once you've become familiar with Disneyland, Anaheim and environs, and Los Angeles, you may be ready to venture even farther afield. Several routes lead to memorable Southern California destinations as diverse as the Hearst Castle in San Simeon and the Carmel mission, both reached via a breathtaking coastal drive; haunting Joshua Tree National Park; and the world-famous San Diego Zoo (see *In All Directions*).

How to Get There

Most visitors who come to Disneyland arrive by car. That's partly because so many visitors drive down just for the day or a weekend, and partly because, for many travelers from distant points, Disneyland is just one stop on a broader tour of California. However, you may want to investigate travel by bus or by train. And if you're traveling any significant distance, it may actually cost less to fly than to drive. Here are the leading transportation alternatives.

By Car

The following are the fastest, most direct routes to Disneyland from 27 major cities (including four in Canada). These are far from the only recommended routings; more scenic and leisurely routes do exist. If you wish to map out something different on your own, assume you'll drive no more than 350 to 400 miles a day—a reasonable distance that won't wear you out so you can't enjoy your stay.

Atlanta: I-20 west to Birmingham, AL, U.S. 78 west to Memphis, I-240 west, I-55 north, I-40 west to Barstow, CA, I-15 south, S.R. 91 west, S.R. 57 south, Katella Ave. west, Harbor Blvd. north to entrance. 2,174 miles (approx. 43 hours).

Boston: I-90 west, I-84 west to Scranton, PA, I-81 south, I-80 west to Youngstown, OH, I-76 west, I-71 south, 270 west and south around Columbus, OH, I-70 west, I-55 south through St. Louis, I-44 west to Oklahoma City, I-40 west to Barstow, CA, I-15 south, S.R. 91 west, S.R. 57 south, Katella Ave. west, Harbor Blvd. north to entrance. 2,991 miles (approx. 60 hours).

Calgary: P.R. 2 south, U.S. 89 south, U.S. 287 south, I-15 south, S.R. 91 west, S.R. 57 south, Katella Ave. west, Harbor Blvd. north to entrance. 1,543 miles (approx. 31 hours).

Chicago: I-55 south through St. Louis, I-44 west to Oklahoma City, I-40 west to Barstow, CA, I-15 south, S.R. 91 west, S.R. 57 south, Katella Ave. west, Harbor Blvd. north to entrance. 2,103 miles (approx. 43 hours).

Cleveland: I-71 south, I-270 west and south around Columbus, OH, I-70 west, I-55 south through St. Louis, I-44 west to Oklahoma City, I-40 west to Barstow, CA, I-15 south, S.R. 91 west, S.R. 57 south, Katella Ave. west, Harbor Blvd. north to entrance. 2,374 miles (approx. 48 hours).

Dallas: S.R. 183 west, S.R. 121 west, I-820 west, I-35W north, U.S. 81/287 west to Amarillo, TX, I-40 west to Barstow, CA, I-15 south, S.R. 91 west, S.R. 57 south, Katella Ave. west, Harbor Blvd. north to entrance. 1,471 miles (approx. 29 hours).

Denver: I-70 west, I-15 south, S.R. 91 west, S.R. 57 south, Katella Ave. west, Harbor Blvd. north to entrance. 989 miles (approx. 21 hours).

Detroit: I-75 south toward Dayton, OH, I-70 west to St. Louis, I-55 south, I-44 west to Oklahoma City, I-40 west to Barstow, CA, I-15 south, S.R. 91 west, S.R. 57 south, Katella Ave. west, Harbor Blvd. north to entrance. 2,372 miles (approx. 51 hours).

Houston: I-10 west, I-410 north around San Antonio, I-10 west to San Bernardino, CA, I-215 south, S.R. 91 west, S.R. 57 south, Katella Ave. west, Harbor Blvd. north to entrance. 1,507 miles (approx. 32 hours).

Las Vegas: I-15 south, S.R. 91 west, S.R. 57 south, Katella Ave. west, Harbor Blvd. north to entrance. 265 miles (approx. 5 hours).

Miami: I-95 north, Florida's Turnpike north, I-75 north, I-10 west, I-12 west around New

Orleans, I-10 west, I-610 north around Houston, I-10 west, I-410 north around San Antonio, I-10 west to San Bernardino, CA, I-215 south, S.R. 91 west, S.R. 57 south, Katella Ave. west, Harbor Blvd. north to entrance. 2,753 miles (approx. 56 hours).

Montreal: P.R. 40 west, P.R. 401 west to Detroit, I-75 south toward Dayton, OH, I-70 west to St. Louis, I-55 south, I-44 west to Oklahoma City, I-40 west to Barstow, CA, I-15 south, S.R. 91 west, S.R. 57 south, Katella Ave. west, Harbor Blvd. north to entrance. 2,913 miles (approx. 58 hours).

New York City: George Washington Bridge west, I-80 west to Youngstown, OH, I-76 west, I-71 south, 270 west and south around Columbus, OH, I-70 west, I-55 south through St. Louis, I-44 west to Oklahoma City, I-40 west to Barstow, CA, I-15 south, S.R. 91 west, S.R. 57 south, Katella Ave. west, Harbor Blvd. north to entrance. 2,793 miles (approx. 56 hours).

Philadelphia: I-76 west, I-70 west, I-55 south through St. Louis, I-44 west to Oklahoma City, I-40 west to Barstow, CA, I-15 south, S.R. 91 west, S.R. 57 south, Katella Ave. west, Harbor Blvd. north to entrance. 2,716 miles (approx. 54 hours).

Phoenix: I-10 west to San Bernardino, CA, I-215 south, S.R. 91 west, S.R. 57 south, Katella Ave. west, Harbor Blvd. north to entrance. 362 miles (approx. 7 hours).

Portland (OR): I-5 south, Harbor Blvd. south to entrance. 988 miles (approx. 19 hours).

Reno: I-80 west to Sacramento, I-5 south, Harbor Blvd. south to entrance. 545 miles (approx. 10 hours).

Sacramento: I-5 south, Harbor Blvd. south to entrance. 409 miles (approx. 8 hours).

Salt Lake City: I-15 south, S.R. 91 west, S.R. 57 south, Katella Ave. west, Harbor Blvd. north to entrance. 683 miles (approx. 13 hours).

San Diego: I-5 north, Harbor Blvd. south to entrance. 80 miles (approx. 2 hours).

San Francisco: I-80 east to Oakland, I-580 east, I-5 south, Harbor Blvd. south to entrance. 418 miles (approx. 8 hours).

Seattle: I-5 south, Harbor Blvd. south to entrance. 1,171 miles (approx. 23 hours).

St. Louis: I-44 west to Oklahoma City, I-40 west to Barstow, CA, I-15 south, S.R. 91 west, S.R. 57 south, Katella Ave. west, Harbor Blvd. north to entrance. 1,818 miles (approx. 36 hours).

Toronto: P.R. 401 west to Detroit, I-75 south toward Dayton, OH, I-70 west to St. Louis, I-55 south, I-44 west to Oklahoma City, I-40 west to Barstow, CA, I-15 south, S.R. 91 west, S.R. 57 south, Katella Ave. west, Harbor Blvd. north to entrance. 2,585 miles (approx. 52 hours).

Tucson: I-10 west to San Bernardino, CA, I-215 south, S.R. 91 west, S.R. 57 south, Katella Ave. west, Harbor Blvd. north to entrance. 478 miles (approx. 10 hours).

Vancouver: P.R. 99 south, I-5 south, I-405 around Seattle, I-5 south, Harbor Blvd. south to entrance. 1,318 miles (approx. 26 hours).

Washington, D.C.: I-66 west, I-81 south, I-40 west to Barstow, CA, I-15 south, S.R. 91 west, S.R. 57 south, Katella Ave. west, Harbor Blvd. north to entrance. 2,944 miles (approx. 53 hours).

AUTOMOBILE CLUBS: Any one of the nation's leading automobile clubs can come to your aid in the event of breakdowns en route, and provide insurance covering accidents, arrest, bail bond, lawyers' fees for defense of contested traffic cases, and personal injury, plus trip-planning services—not merely advice, but also free maps and route-mapping assistance. No two programs are quite the same; fees range from around $12 to $75 annually for the most reputable clubs, which include the following:

● **Allstate Motor Club**; 1500 W. Shure Dr.; Arlington Heights, IL 60004; 800-347-8880
● **American Automobile Association**; 1000 AAA Dr., Heathrow, FL 32746-5063; 800-222-4357
● **Amoco Motor Club**; Box 9046; Des Moines, IA 50368; 800-334-3300
● **CIGNA Road and Travel Inc.**; Box 2637; Virginia Beach, VA 23450-2637; 800-523-4816
● **Ford Auto Club**; Box 224688; Dallas, TX 75222-4688; 800-348-5220
● **Gulf Motor Club**; 6001 North Clark St.; Chicago, IL 60660; 800-633-3224
● **Montgomery Ward Auto Club**; 200 North Martingale Rd.; Schaumburg, IL 60173; 800-621-5151
● **Motor Club of America**; 484 Central Ave.; Newark, NJ 07107; 800-833-3207
● **United States Auto Club Motoring Division**; Box 660460; Dallas, TX 75266-0460; 800-348-5058

ROAD MAPS: Those who aren't members of a travel or automobile club should peruse *Rand McNally's Road Atlas* ($9.95 in bookstores). It also is possible to obtain free maps from individual state tourist boards.

By Bus

Buses make sense if you're not traveling from too great a distance, if you have plenty of time to spend in transit, if there are only two or three people in your party, or if cost is a major consideration.

The Greyhound terminal (999-1256) is located at 100 Winston Road in Anaheim, about one mile north of Disneyland. Taxis can transport you from the terminal to Disneyland or to your accommodation.

Direct buses make the trip from Los Angeles and San Diego, though they stop along the way. Travel from most other destinations will probably require a change of vehicles in Los Angeles.

By Air

Los Angeles International Airport is one of the busiest in the world. There are approximately 1,100 departures and arrivals by nearly 65 commercial airlines each day. Delta Air Lines alone, as the Official Airline of Disneyland, carries more than three million passengers into Los Angeles on nonstop flights from 45 cities, direct flights, and connecting flights from 150 additional cities. Delta also offers The Fantastic Flyer® program for kids. Other major carriers serving L.A. include American, Continental, TWA, United, and USAir. Though Anaheim lies about 45 minutes to the southeast, most Disneyland guests who come by plane arrive at LAX, as this airport is generally known.

Orange County's John Wayne Airport is located considerably closer to Anaheim in Santa Ana. Many airlines offer flights to this convenient airport. Long Beach Airport also is close by, but only a few airlines serve it on a nonstop basis.

Which airport you use and which airline you decide to fly will depend largely on where you live, when you'll be traveling, and which airline can get you there when you want to go—at the best possible price and with the most direct route. It is sometimes possible to find the same fare to John Wayne/Orange County Airport, so the major consideration is whether a nonstop flight is available.

HOW TO GET THE BEST AIRFARE: There was a time when it cost a finite, predictable number of dollars to get from one city to

WHICH AIRLINE FLIES FROM YOUR CITY?

More than two dozen airlines serve Los Angeles Airport, Orange County's John Wayne Airport, and Long Beach Airport from over 100 different cities nonstop. The list that follows was correct at press time. Schedules do change, however, and flights are occasionally dropped or added. So be sure to double-check as close to your departure date as possible. A (2) indicates that the flight lands at John Wayne Airport. A (3) indicates the flight lands at Long Beach Airport.

Albuquerque, NM ....WN
Anchorage, AL.................................AS, PL
Atlanta, GA ....DL
Austin, TX ....CO
Bakersfield, CA.....................DL*, AA*, UA*
Baltimore, MD.....................................FF, US
Boston, MA.................................FF, AA, UA
Bullhead City, AZ/Laughlin, NV ....UA*
Calgary, Alberta ....DL, AC
Cancun, Mexico ....AM, MX
Carlsbad, CA.............................UA*, AA*
Charlotte, NC ....US
Chicago, IL...............FF, TZ, AA, UA, QF*
Chicago, IL(2) ....AA, UA
Cincinnati, OH ....DL
Cleveland, OH ....CO
Colorado Springs, CO.............................W7
Columbus, OH ....UA
Dallas/Ft. Worth, TX.................SQ*, DL, AA
Dallas/Ft. Worth, TX(2) ....DL, AA
Dallas/Ft. Worth, TX(3) ....AA
Dayton, OH ....US

Denver, CO.......................................BF, UA
Denver, CO(2) ....UA
Detroit, MI ....NW
Detroit, MI (2) ....NW
El Centro/Imperial, CA ....DL*, UA*
El Paso, TX...WN
Fresno, CA.............DL, DL*, UA*, US*, AA*, UE, AM*
Guadalajara, Mexico.................DL, MX, AM
Honolulu, HI ....DL, KE, AA, CO, UA, QF, NZ, HA, JN, NW, TZ, TW, GA
Houston, TX...CO
Houston, TX(2)..CO
Indianapolis, IN...................................US, TZ
Inyokern, CA...................................AA*, UA*
Kahului, Maui, HI......................................UA
Kansas City, MO ....US
Lake Tahoe, CA...........................TW*, QQ
Las Vegas, NV ....DL, HP, AA*, WN, UA, HA
Las Vegas, NV(2) ....HP
Leon-Guanajuato, Mexico ....MX
Los Angeles, CA(2)................DL*, AA*, UA*
Los Cabos, Mexico...................MX, JR, AS
Mazatlan, Mexico ....AS
Memphis, TN ....NW
Mexico City, Mexico ....DL, MX, LR, UA, AM, MH
Miami, FL ....AA, UA
Milwaukee, WI ....YX

GETTING READY TO GO

another. No longer. Today, the fare is governed not only by when you go and how long you stay, but also by the airline that transports you. Each one has its own set of restrictions and rules governing who can qualify for the lowest fares. In spite of efforts to structure fares, continuing airfare wars make it important to shop around. Here are some suggestions:

● Find out the names of all the airlines serving your destination, and then call them all (or ask your travel agent to

Minneapolis/St. Paul, MN	NW
Minneapolis/St. Paul, MN(2)	NW
Monterey, CA	DL*, US*, AA*
Monterey, CA(2)	DL*
Montreal, Quebec	AC
Nashville, TN	AA
New Orleans, LA	DL, UA, CO
New York, NY/Newark, NJ	DL, AA, LY, TW, UA, CO, FF, QF*
New York, NY/Newark, NJ (2)	CO
Oakland, CA	UA, WN, AS
Oakland, CA(2)	AS, WN
Ontario, CA	DL*, US*, UA*
Orange County, CA	DL*, AA*, US*, UA*
Orlando, FL	DL, UA
Oxnard, CA	AA*, UA*
Palmdale/Lancaster, CA	UA*
Palm Springs, CA	DL*, AA*, UA* US*, TW*
Philadelphia, PA	UA, US
Phoenix, AZ	HP, WN, UA
Phoenix, AZ(2)	HP
Phoenix, AZ(3)	HP
Pittsburgh, PA	US
Pittsburgh, PA(2)	US
Portland, OR	DL, AS, UA
Portland, OR(2)	AS
Puerto Vallarta, Mexico	DL, AS, AM, MX
Reno, NV	WN, QQ
Sacramento, CA	DL*, WN, UA
Sacramento, CA(2)	HP
St. Louis, MO	TW
St. Louis, MO(2)	TW
Salt Lake City, UT	DL*, WN, DL
Salt Lake City, UT(2)	DL
San Antonio, TX	CO
San Diego, CA	DL, DL*, AA, AA*, YX, NW, UA, UA*, US, US*, TW
San Francisco, CA	DL, UA, US, QF*, WN, TW*
San Francisco, CA(2)	WN, UA, AS UA*, AA*

San Jose, CA	DL*, AS, WN, QQ
San Jose, CA(2)	QQ, WN
San Luis Obispo, CA	DL*, AA*, UA*
Santa Barbara, CA	DL*, US*, AA*, UA*
Santa Maria,CA	DL*, AA*, UA*
Seattle/Tacoma, WA	DL, AS, UA
Seattle/Tacoma, WA(2)	AS
Spokane, WA	HS
Tampa/St. Petersburg, FL	DL
Toronto, Ontario	AC
Tucson, AZ	QQ, DL, WN
Tucson, AZ(2)	VZ,
Vancouver, British Columbia	DL, CP
Washington, DC	AA, US, UA, QF*, FF
Yuma, AZ	UA*, DL*
Zacatecas, Mexico	MX

ABBREVIATIONS—AA: American Airlines. AA*: American Eagle. AC: Air Canada. AM, AM*: Aeromexico. AR: Aerolineas Argentinas. AS: Alaska Airways. BF: Markair. CO: Continental. CP: CP Air. DL: Delta. DL*: Delta Connection. FF: Tower Air. GA: Garuda Airlines, HA: Hawaiian Air Lines. HP: America West Airlines. GA: Garuda Airlines. JN: Rich International Airways. JR: Aero California. KE: Korean Air. KN: Morris Air. KW: Carnival Air Lines. LR: Lasca. LY: El Al. MX: Mexicana. NW: Northwest. NZ: Air New Zealand. QF, QF*: Qantas Airways. QQ: Reno Air. SQ*: Singapore Airlines, TW: Trans World Airlines. TW*: Trans World Express. TZ: American Trans Air. UA: United. UA*: United Express. UE: Air LA. US: USAir. US*: USAir Express. VZ: Arizona Airways, WN: Southwest Airlines. VZ: Arizona Airlines. WR: Royal Tongan Airlines. W7: Western Pacific Airlines: YX: Midwest Express.

Source: *Official Airline Guides*

do so)—more than once if your route is complex. Tell the airline's reservation clerk how many people are in your party, and emphasize that you're interested in economy. Ask if you can get a lower fare by slightly altering the dates of your trip, the hour of departure, or the duration of your stay—or, if you live halfway between two airports, by leaving from one rather than the other or by flying into a different airport.

● Watch your local newspapers for ads announcing new or special promotional fares.

● Fly weekends on routes heavily used by business travelers, and midweek on routes more commonly patronized by vacationers.

● Try for a night flight and ask for low night-coach fares.

● Plan and pay as far ahead as possible. Most carriers guarantee their fares, which means you won't have to pay more if fares have gone up since you purchased your ticket. If, however, you have *not* paid for your ticket, you *will* be required to pay the higher charge. Similarly, if you change dates of travel or flight times and your ticket has to be reissued, you'll have to pay the new fare, plus any penalties that may apply. If fares have come down in price since you paid for your ticket, the difference will be refunded to you by the airline, even if you've already paid the higher fare in full. Be sure to watch the newspaper ads and to call the airline to check for new, lower fares since you have to request the refund.

By Train

Anaheim is a part of Amtrak's network of California stations; the station is located at 2150 East Katella Ave., just two miles from Disneyland's main gate. For reservations and information call 800-USA-RAIL. The *San Diegan*, the train that runs between Los Angeles and San Diego, stops at Anaheim; the train operates eight times daily. Three trains run daily between Santa Barbara (about 80 miles north of Los Angeles) and

San Diego. The *San Diegan* does not offer checked-baggage service.

Union Station in Los Angeles is served by a number of trains from the rest of the state, the South, and the Midwest. To get to Anaheim, it's possible to make a connection with the *San Diegan*, described above. Those preferring to rent a car can use the major car rental agencies' direct-dial phones (to their downtown offices) available at Union Station. Among the trains arriving in Los Angeles are:

● *Coast Starlight*: Originating in Seattle, this train—one of the two most heavily used long-distance trains in the Amtrak system— makes stops in Portland and Eugene, Oregon; and Sacramento, Oakland, and San Jose, California. Daily. Seattle to L.A., about $34^{1}/_{2}$ hours.

● *Desert Wind*: Departing Chicago daily, this train stops in Omaha and Lincoln, Nebraska; Denver, Colorado; Salt Lake City, Utah; and Las Vegas, Nevada. Total trip time from Chicago to L.A. is about $50^{1}/_{4}$ hours; getting to Los Angeles takes about 31 hours from Denver; about $15^{1}/_{2}$ hours from Salt Lake City; and about 7 hours from Las Vegas.

● *San Joaquin*: Four trains daily provide service between the San Francisco Bay area and the San Joaquin Valley, with stops at Emeryville and Fresno. At the terminus in Bakersfield, a bus transports connecting passengers to Union Station in Los Angeles. The trip takes about six hours from San Francisco to Bakersfield.

● *Southwest Chief*: Daily service from Chicago is provided by this train, which stops in Kansas City, Missouri; Topeka, Kansas; and Albuquerque, New Mexico, among other cities. From Chicago to L.A., about 40 hours; $31^{1}/_{2}$ hours from Topeka; and about 16 hours from Albuquerque.

● *Sunset Limited*: Service is provided from New Orleans on Mondays, Wednesdays, and Saturdays, with stops in Houston, San Antonio, El Paso, Tucson, and Phoenix. About 43 hours for the trip from New Orleans to L.A.

How to Cut Travel Costs

Although vacations are not getting any less expensive, scrapping periodic getaways is not the answer. If financial considerations are a primary concern, it's far better simply to prune the vacation budget in these areas:

Lodging: The most important rule is not to pay for more than you need—or can realistically afford. Budget chains don't offer many frills, but they are usually clean and contain all the essentials. The best guide to these economical accommodations is the *National Directory of Budget Motels*, revised annually and available for $6.95, including postage and handling, from Pilot Books; 103 Cooper St.; Babylon, NY 11702; 516-422-2225.

If swimming pools and other such optional amenities are important, you'll probably prefer to stay in less austere chain establishments. You can even save here occasionally by checking the cutoff ages for children—the age at which there is a charge for youngsters sharing their parents' rooms. Most of the hotels and motels in the Anaheim area allow children under 12 to stay free. Some have a cutoff of 17 or 18, so it's a good idea to check when making reservations.

Food: The budget-minded should try to have hot meals in coffee shops or fast-food outlets, which are less costly than establishments with waitress service. If you want to try a fancy place, don't go at dinnertime but at lunchtime, when the same entrées usually cost less. Carry sandwich fixings and have lunches alfresco, when possible. Beach picnics are great in Southern California; Disneyland even has a small picnic area just outside the main gate. You can also save significantly by looking for lodging places that include kitchen facilities. The savings on food, especially where a large family is concerned, may more than cover the additional cost of accommodations. In Anaheim proper, there are a number of establishments that offer refrigerators and/or kitchen facilities. Some hotels and motels also offer a complimentary breakfast. See "Anaheim-Area Motels and Hotels," beginning on page 38. These accommodations rent quickly, so it's a good idea to make your reservations as far in advance as possible.

If there aren't too many people in your family or traveling group, guesthouses and tourist homes may be a very good buy. Since these hostelries generally assess extra charges for more than two people in a room, regardless of age, rooms that are inexpensive for a couple may prove less economical for a whole family. For a list of such accommodations, consult *The Complete Guide to Bed & Breakfasts, Inns & Guesthouses in the United*

States and Canada published by Ten Speed Press ($16.95). For more detailed information, see *Transportation & Accommodations*.

Transportation: It pays to shop around. But when you do, be sure to add the cost of local transportation to your computations. When calculating the cost of driving, consider your car's gas mileage, the current price of gasoline, the distance you plan to cover, and the expense of accommodations and food en route. And when you compare that estimate to the cost of going by bus, train, or plane, don't overlook the cost of getting from the airport or train or bus terminal to your motel, and the cost of renting a car at your destination, if you plan to do that. Be sure to look into packages since they usually include transportation, accommodations, and even a rental car.

Magic Kingdom Club: Members can receive discounts on special Disney vacation packages, park admissions, accommodations, select flights on Delta Air Lines, merchandise in The Disney Stores and The Disney Catalog, car rentals, and more. If you work for a large company, free membership may be offered as an employee benefit. Inquire at your human resources department. Also, individuals can now join the Magic Kingdom Club Gold Card, which provides the same benefits, plus more. The cost is $65 for a two-year membership. Seniors age 55 and over may join the Magic Years Club. The cost is $35 for a five-year membership. For more information or to join either club, call 520-2500. Keep in mind that it takes at least four weeks to receive membership materials.

How to Get

Disneyland was designed by artists who had spent their lives framing scenes in camera viewfinders. So it's not surprising that almost every square foot of the place seems amazingly photogenic. If you find yourself instinctively reaching for your camera while strolling around, it's because the park was especially planned with that in mind. Millions of photographs are snapped here every year. (Look for the "Photo Spot" markers throughout the park and on the map on page 60.)

There are so many terrific images to be snatched that almost every camera in good working order can get a few for you. Still, it helps if you rely on some trusty techniques:

• Don't shoot closer than 4 feet from your subject, and don't try for a flash picture when you're standing more than 12 feet away. The former will turn out fuzzy, and the latter will be dark, since flash light doesn't reach more than a dozen feet away. (Important: Flash photography is prohibited inside all Disneyland attractions.)

• Fill the frame with as much of your subject as possible. Remember, especially when photographing people, that pictures are more interesting when the subject appears large in the picture.

• Hold the camera steady as you squeeze the shutter.

• Don't shoot into the sun. Cameras with electric eyes assume that there is more light on the subject than there actually is and adjust shutter openings accordingly—leaving the subject dark. A better idea is to stand so that the light is falling directly on the object you want to photograph—that is, coming from the side or from behind you.

• Check the camera's batteries and battery contacts regularly. (Pack extra batteries.)

• Be sure to use fresh film. Check the expiration date printed on the film boxes when making film purchases. Keep film as cool as possible—don't leave it in a hot car for a long period of time.

• Blow dust off your lenses or wipe them with soft lens tissues to keep specks off your pictures. Also, blow dust out of the inside of the camera periodically.

• For videotapes, remember that the most effective results are obtained when you have a basic theme, such as "A Walk Through Adventureland," or something similar. Never shoot directly into the sun (for the reasons noted above), and check carefully before you tape to make sure that your subject matter is evenly lighted. When you pan, do it smoothly and slowly; give every image about five seconds. Use a zoom lens sparingly, or it can become too much of a good thing.

RENTAL CAMERAS: Among Disneyland's best bargains are the rental cameras offered at the Main Street Photo Supply Co. The rental fee is $5, plus a refundable deposit from $30 to $95, depending upon the equipment you choose. VHS video cameras also are available for a $40 fee, with a $1,000 refundable deposit. All deposits can be made with cash, American Express, MasterCard, Visa, or The Disney Credit Card (available through The Disney Store or by calling 800-222-1262).

Outside Disneyland, Anaheim Camera Supply (855 South Harbor Blvd., half a mile from the main gate; 778-3115) rents 35mm single-lens reflex cameras and a variety of lenses, VHS video cameras, and some Polaroid cameras. Deposits, payable in cash or by credit card (American Express, MasterCard, Visa, or Discover), are required.

the Best Photos

HOW TO PHOTOGRAPH FIREWORKS: To get acceptable images, it's necessary to have a camera with a manually adjustable shutter speed and aperture. Using color negative film (ASA 400), put the camera on a tripod, or brace it firmly in some other way; set the aperture at f8 and the shutter speed at B, and hold the lens open for three to five seconds at each burst, covering the lens with your hand between explosions.

WHERE TO BUY FILM

Main Street
Emporium, Newsstand, Main Street Photo Supply Co., souvenir stands (at main entrance tunnels), Stroller Shop

Adventureland
Tropical Imports

Frontierland
Frontierland Candy Shop
Davy Crockett Pioneer Mercantile

New Orleans Square
Pieces of Eight

Critter Country
Briar Patch, Crocodile Mercantile

Tomorrowland
Star Trader, Premiere Shop, Hatmosphere

Fantasyland
Character Carrousel (near the Matterhorn, in front of It's A Small World), Small World Gifts, Tinker Bell Toy Shoppe, Kodak Information Kiosk (in front of It's A Small World), Stromboli's Wagon.

Mickey's Toontown
Gag Factory

CAMERA REPAIRS: If the repairs are minor, they can be handled by the Main Street Photo Supply Co. in the Magic Kingdom. For anything more than a simple problem, your best bet is to rent a camera and have a factory-authorized shop do the necessary work on your camera when you return home.

FILM PROCESSING: Same-day processing is available through Fox Photo Film Processing at the *Disneyland Hotel* and the Main Street Photo Supply Co. in the Magic Kingdom. Processing takes two to three hours, so you can take today's photographed memories home tonight.

Helpful Hints

Traveling can be hard work, but a little know-how can smooth the way and make a vacation much more relaxing. Here are some hints for getting the most out of your trip and your visit to Disneyland.

Tips on Traveling with Children

When you tell your kids that a Disneyland vacation is in the works, the response can be overwhelming. It may take all your savvy to keep them relatively calm until you arrive.

PLANNING: By far the best way to cope with excited youngsters is to allow them to participate in some part of the planning of the upcoming Disneyland trip. Not only will it heighten their enjoyment after they arrive, but also it will provide visitors of all ages with a realistic sense of what to expect. Give every child a small part of the trip's preparations as his or her responsibility—what attractions to see in what order, where to have lunch each day, what other activities to include in your Southern California visit, etc. Just writing for brochures can be a very important job for a youngster, and make him or her feel more a part of the general undertaking.

EN ROUTE: Certain techniques can stave off children's tiresome "Are-we-there-yets?" until you walk through the main gate. If you're traveling by car, one ploy is to set up a series of intermediate goals to which they can look forward. Younger kids might anticipate getting to the bottom of a child-size suitcase, stuffed with well-loved toys and games.

Also, be sure to pack snacks to quiet rumbling stomachs at those inconvenient times when there's not a decent restaurant in sight. Most important of all, plan on taking plenty of breaks along the way.

If you're flying, try to time your departure and return flights for off-peak hours and off-seasons, when chances are better that an empty seat or two will be available. During takeoffs and landings, encourage babies to suck on bottles, pacifiers, or even thumbs to keep ears clear, and supply small children with chewing gum or hard candy. As the Official Airline for Disneyland, Delta tries to make flying fun. There is a special program just for kids, ages 2 to 12, who fly on Delta. The Fantastic Flyer® program means that children will receive a complimentary Mickey Mouse visor, a copy of the Fantastic Flyer magazine, with games, puzzles, prizes, and other treats. Ask a flight attendant for details.

IN ANAHEIM: Many Anaheim restaurants offer children's menus. See *Good Meals, Great Times* for a listing.

IN THE HOTELS: During the summer, several hotels offer special kids' programs in sports, arts and crafts, and storytelling at no charge for the children of guests. Some hotels offer babysitting services or babysitting referrals.

INSIDE DISNEYLAND: In the park, the smiles that break out on the faces of the little ones as they greet Mickey, Minnie, and the other characters, or go aloft in Dumbo, or gaze in wonder at all those moving dolls in It's A Small World will repay you a thousandfold for any fuss and bother en route. And no place in the world is more aware of the needs of children (and their parents) than this one.

Favorite attractions: When traveling with young children, you will want to substitute some of the attractions listed in the Disneyland itineraries at the end of our *Magic Kingdom* chapter with a few others. For example, Casey Jr. Circus Train and the Autopia are mainly for young children with their parents; the Storybook Land Canal Boats and It's A Small World charm young children and older folks alike. (Teenagers, however, might be less enchanted.) In Fantasyland, young children delight most in the bright colors and the dazzling special effects. Snow White's Scary Adventures may be too frightening for some youngsters, but the guest waiting area does set the mood, so check your child's reaction before you board. Some youngsters have gotten upset inside the Haunted Mansion, but most kids enjoy both these attractions enormously. Note: Children under age seven must be accompanied by an adult on all attractions.

Strollers: These can be rented for $6 (plus a returnable $5 deposit) at the Stroller Shop, to the right as you enter the main gate. If yours disappears while you're inside an attraction, just show your claim ticket and you can get another. Replacement centers are located at Star Traders, Crocodile Mercantile, and the Gag Factory.

Baby care: The Baby Center has child-size flush toilets that can only be described as cute—and are conveniently functional as well. In addition, there are changing tables, a limited selection of juices, strained baby foods, and diapers for sale at a nominal fee, and facilities for warming both food and bottles. A special room with comfortable chairs is available for nursing mothers. The decor is soothing, and the hubbub of the rest of the park seems a million miles away. A stop here for diaper changing or feeding is a restful break for both parent and child alike—although changing tables are in most womens' and some mens' restrooms as well.

Where to buy baby care items: Disposable diapers and baby bottles are sold at the Emporium on Main Street.

Lost children: When a child suddenly disappears or fails to show up on time, it's reassuring to know that Disneyland's security force and all Disneylanders are carefully trained to follow specific procedures with a lost child. The child is taken to Lost Children, adjacent to Central First Aid, where there are Disney movies and a variety of books to amuse lost youngsters. The child's name is registered in the lost children's log book there, and in the one at City Hall. The telephone number for Lost Children is 999-4210. (If you're calling from inside the park, dial only the last four digits.)

Tips for Older Travelers

Southern California can overwhelm elderly (or any) travelers who are not accustomed to freeways and busy traffic, and even Disneyland can be disorienting with its abundance of sights and sounds. Yet as one newly married nonagenarian, away from home for the first time in her life, exclaimed, "What a beautiful world it is!"

The suggestions below can add to your comfort and to the enjoyment of your trip. For answers to specific questions, contact the Anaheim Senior Citizen Center at 280 East Lincoln Ave.; 533-1981; or 2271 West Crescent Ave.; 535-8210.

● Join a tour. Travel agents can help find one that best suits your interests. Visitors who come in groups should allow plenty of time to return to their buses at the end of a day. One good tactic is to save Main Street's sights—such as The Walt Disney Story featuring "Great Moments with Mr. Lincoln," the Penny Arcade, and the Main Street Cinema—for the end of the day. If you arrive at the main gate too far in advance of the group's meeting time, you can spend the extra minutes at those attractions. Town Square is an easy 10- or 15-minute walk, at most, from the bus parking area.

● Inside the Magic Kingdom, group tours also are a good idea for individual travelers. These guided tours cover the whole park, and the price includes general admission to Disneyland for the day, visits to six of the park's most popular attractions, the services of a guide throughout the three-and-a-half-hour tour, and then the run of the park for the rest of the day. For details, contact Disneyland Guest Relations; 1313 Harbor Blvd.; Anaheim, CA 92803; 999-4565. Reservations are suggested for groups of 15 or more only.

HEIGHT HO!

At attractions with age and/or height restrictions, a parent who waits with a child too young or small to ride while the other parent goes on the attraction can stay at the front of the line and take a turn as soon as the first parent comes off. This is called the "kid switch" policy, and if lines are long it can save a lot of time. Be sure to ask the attendant.

• The week before Christmas and the weekdays in spring and fall are ideal. Remember that Tuesdays, Wednesdays, and Thursdays are generally the quietest days of the week, and that Saturdays are always the busiest. If you must visit on a weekend, choose a Sunday.

• Read Disneyland literature carefully before arrival, so the park's layout is as familiar as possible.

• In the park, don't be shy about asking for advice or directions from Disneyland employees. They're happy to help out.

• Eat early or late to avoid the crowd crunch at mealtimes.

• Protect yourself from the sun. Wear a hat and sunscreen.

• If you do visit in summer, don't allow yourself to get overheated. Take frequent rest stops in the shade, and get out of the midafternoon heat by pausing for a snack in a cool restaurant or snack stand. If you feel faint, speak to a Disney employee or go to a first aid center.

• Don't push yourself. After all, half the fun of Disneyland is just sitting on a park bench underneath some shady tree and watching the people go by.

• Remember that sightseeing takes energy, and only healthy meals can provide it. Don't try to save money by scrimping on food. Prices for meals at Disneyland are quite reasonable. Outside the park, some restaurants offer discounts for senior citizens.

Senior Fun Days at Disneyland: All year long, specially priced Passports are available to those age 60 and up. Be sure to check with Disneyland Guest Relations about exact prices.

Tips for Travelers with Disabilities

Disneyland is more accessible to guests with disabilities than ever before, and as a result makes a very good choice as a vacation destination. But advance planning is still a must: The *Disneyland Guide for Guests with Disabilities*, offering information on accessible restrooms and park attractions, is a good planning tool as well (see "Inside Disneyland," on page 28).

LOST ADULTS

Traveling companions do occasionally get separated. If someone in your party disappears all of a sudden, or fails to show up at an appointed meeting spot, head for City Hall. Here you'll find a message book where members of a group can leave notes for each other during the day.

TOURS: The Society for the Advancement of Travel for the Handicapped (347 Fifth Avenue, Suite 610; New York, NY 10016; 212-447-7284 or fax 212-725-8253) has a number of member travel agents who are knowledgeable about tours for travelers with disabilities and can help arrange individual and group trips. (Send $3 and a self-addressed, stamped envelope to receive a copy of their listings.) In addition, a good travel agent can help you find a tour to suit your needs.

GETTING THERE: Probably the most effective means of assuring a smooth trip are plenty of advance contacts for every phase of your journey.

Traveling by train: All new and rebuilt Amtrak equipment operating in and to California has special facilities to aid travelers with disabilities, including grab bars in the toilets, specially equipped sleeper compartments, and seats with an adjoining empty space for a wheelchair. Wheelchairs or electric carts are available at all major stations, including both the Los Angeles and Anaheim stations. Both stations have wheelchair-lift devices. Many other stations in the western part of the United States have been similarly fitted out.

Passengers with disabilities are entitled to a 25 percent discount on regular one-way fares; companions must pay full fare, however, and most round-trip excursion fares are lower than the discounted fares for the disabled. Service dogs are allowed to ride with passengers at no charge.

Battery-powered, standard-size wheelchairs are permitted in coaches. Fuel-powered and oversize chairs must be stored in the baggage car for the duration of the trip. (Note, however, that not all trains stopping at Anaheim carry baggage cars, so check in advance.) Always be sure to phone the train stations and reservations center well before your departure date to arrange for any special facilities or services you may need.

Additional information about train travel for elderly travelers and passengers with disabilities is included in Amtrak's free "Travel Planner" booklet, which is available by calling 800-USA-RAIL.

Traveling by plane: Fortunately, times have changed in the way that airlines deal with travelers with disabilities. Vacationers are occasionally allowed to board aircraft in their own wheelchairs—provided the chair is narrow enough for the plane's aisles; more often, the passenger is transferred to a narrower airline chair at the loading gate and his or her own is packed away in the luggage compartment. Passengers in wheelchairs are usually helped on board before other passengers, and deplaned after everyone else. If you have a tight connection, it's especially important to notify airline attendants in advance. The use of an airline wheelchair to make these connections also must be arranged ahead of time. Again, don't fail to alert airline personnel at the time you make your reservation of any special needs you may have.

Note that airlines' policies on motorized wheelchairs vary, depending on the type of chair and the carrier. So check well in advance. All airlines now permit service dogs aboard aircraft, though some may require the animal to be muzzled. Canes and crutches, unless collapsible, must be stowed during takeoffs and landings, but will be returned to passengers upon request during the flight. Again, let the carriers know in advance about what's coming.

For more helpful hints on traveling by air, obtain *Access Travel: Airports*, available for free (one copy only) from the National Clearing House of Rehabilitation Training Materials (Oklahoma State University; 816 West Sixth St.; Stillwater, OK 74078-0435; 405-624-7650; include the code number, 265-AT).

Traveling by bus: Vacationers with disabilities and a companion may travel together on Greyhound with a single adult ticket; the only requirement is a written statement from a doctor confirming the necessity for such aid. Ask for the "helping hand" rate. Nonmotorized folding wheelchairs are carried with no extra charge. Motorized chairs are not accepted.

GETTING AROUND ORANGE COUNTY: Avis, Hertz, and National (the official car rental agency of Disneyland and Walt Disney World) have a limited number of hand-control cars for rent in Southern California, most of which are at the Los Angeles International Airport.

Though slightly less convenient, it's also possible to get around by public transportation. Some 40 percent of the buses operated by the Orange County Transportation Authority, the public bus company that serves Orange County, have lifts so that travelers in wheelchairs can board them easily. Many routes pass Disneyland. The company also operates a Dial-A-Ride Service (560-6282).

Sightseeing tour buses are another option. Though none have lifts for wheelchairs, all have storage facilities for collapsible chairs, making this a possibility for travelers who have a companion to help them on and off

the bus. Odyssey Tours (939-1001 or 800-304-1001), Pacific Coast Sightseeing/Gray Line of Anaheim (978-8855 or 800-828-6699), and Tour Connection & Charters (517-6655 or 800-678-9590) offer tours to Hollywood, Universal Studios, Los Angeles, San Diego, and Tijuana, Mexico. Call for specifics or brochures.

ANAHEIM LODGING: Most hotels and motels have rooms equipped for guests with disabilities with extra-wide doorways, grab

TIPS FOR SINGLE TRAVELERS

There's so much to see and do in Disneyland that the park can be as enjoyable for solo travelers as it is for couples, families, and groups. The ambience certainly is conducive to talking with others if you're in the mood, and the attractions are naturally shared events. And it's a lot of fun to talk with the park's outgoing employees, called cast members.

Outside Disneyland, Southern California offers plenty of opportunities for striking up a friendship, or at least conversation. In Anaheim proper, the wood-paneled bar at *El Torito's*, at 2020 East Ball Road (956-4880), is as active as they come. Anyone who likes people watching can have a field day studying who's moving in on whom—and that's true even when the place is nearly empty. *Neon Cactus* in the *Disneyland Hotel*, at 1150 West Cerritos Avenue (778-6600), offers drinks, a good show, live entertainment, country and western dancing, and the opportunity to mix as you choose.

Probably the liveliest areas for singles are Newport Beach, the Balboa Peninsula, and Balboa Island—a half hour's drive to the south. Disneyland employees can often be found here after work at spots like the *Cannery* at 3010 Lafayette Avenue in Newport Beach (675-5777). *Legends Sports Bar & Rib Room*, the restaurant and bar at 580 Anton Boulevard in the South Coast Plaza area of Costa Mesa (966-5338), is frenetically active, especially after performances at the Orange County Performing Arts Center or the South Coast Repertory Theater.

bars in the bathroom for shower or bath and commode, and sinks at wheelchair height, plus ramps at curbs and steps to provide wheelchair access. (See *Transportation & Accommodations* for further information on lodging.)

INSIDE DISNEYLAND: For visually impaired guests, a tape recorder with cassette describing the park is available at City Hall. Service dogs are allowed in almost all places in the park except on extremely active attractions such as Space Mountain, the Matterhorn, and Big Thunder Mountain Railroad.

For hearing-impaired guests, there are volume-control telephones available all around the park. At City Hall and the Bank of Main Street, ask for the descriptive book available to enhance the attractions. Also, there are scripts for some attractions.

When passing through the auto toll plaza, guests in wheelchairs, displaying a "disabled" placard, who request directions from park employees, will be directed to the disabled parking section near the main gate ticket booths. Remember to request the *Disneyland Guide for Guests with Disabilities* at the main gate turnstiles, the Bank of Main Street, or City Hall. It describes accessibility to Disneyland's shops, restaurants, and attractions, and tells where to find the wheelchair entrances. It also can be obtained by writing to Disneyland Guest Relations; Box 3232; Anaheim, CA 92803. Wheelchairs also can be rented at the Stroller Shop just inside and to the right of the main gate turnstiles.

Attractions: Generally speaking, the conventional waiting areas are not accessible and guests in wheelchairs enter attractions at some other point. These entrances are described in the *Disneyland Guide for Guests with Disabilities*. Guests with disabilities may be accompanied by up to six other party members using the special entrance point.

In all cases, guests with disabilities should be escorted by someone who can provide any necessary help. In the list below, the attractions marked (C) are accessible to those who are completely wheelchair bound, while those marked (P) require that the guest be lifted in and out of the wheelchair, and those marked (W) require that the guest be able to walk a few steps. Those marked (I) are inaccessible to guests in wheelchairs.

- **Adventureland:** Enchanted Tiki Room (W), a few steps up a small stairway; Jungle Cruise (P); Swiss Family Treehouse (I); Indiana Jones Adventure (P).
- **Critter Country:** Splash Mountain (W); Davy Crockett's Explorer Canoes (I); Country Bear Playhouse (C); Teddi Barra's Swingin' Arcade (C).
- **Fantasyland:** Snow White's Scary Adventures (P); Pinocchio's Daring Journey (P); Dumbo, the Flying Elephant (P); Casey Jr.

Circus Train (P); Disneyland Railroad (P); Storybook Land Canal Boats (P); It's A Small World (P); Matterhorn Bobsleds (W); Alice in Wonderland (P); Mr. Toad's Wild Ride (P); Peter Pan's light (P); King Arthur Carrousel (P); Mad Tea Party (P).
- **Frontierland:** Frontierland Shootin' Arcade (C); Golden Horseshoe Stage (C); Big Thunder Mountain Railroad (W), about 10 to 15 feet from loading area to seat; *Mark Twain* Steamboat (C); Sailing Ship *Columbia* (W), a few steps up a stairway; rafts to Tom Sawyer Island (I); Mike Fink Keel Boats (P).
- **Main Street:** Disneyland Railroad (W), recommend using the Tomorrowland, New Orleans, or Toontown stations, only certain trains; The Walt Disney Story (C); Main Street Vehicles (P); Main Street Cinema (C); Penny Arcade (C).
- **Mickey's Toontown:** Mickey's House and Meet Mickey (C); Minnie's House (C); Goofy's Bounce House (W); Donald's boat, the *Miss Daisy* (C), required to walk up stairs and slide down slide if access to second deck desired; Chip 'n' Dale's Treehouse (I); Acorn Ball Crawl (P); Gadget's Go-Coaster (W); Jolly Trolley (W); Roger Rabbit's Car Toon Spin (P).
- **New Orleans Square:** Pirates of the Caribbean (P); Disneyland Railroad (P); Haunted Mansion (P).
- **Tomorrowland:** Starcade (C); Space Mountain (W); Disneyland Railroad (W), only certain trains, and locking wheelchair required; Star Tours (P); Captain EO (C); Tomorrowland Autopia (P), need to be able to push the pedals; Submarine Voyage (I); Disneyland Monorail System (C), maximum 26-inch wheelchairs; PeopleMover (I); Rocket Jets (P), World Premiere CircleVision (C).
- **Disneyland Monorail System:** This attraction is accessible to mobility-impaired guests if the wheelchair is less than 26 inches wide. Guests with wheelchairs more than 26 inches wide must be able to be lifted into the train or walk a few steps.

Restaurants: Nearly all food locations are completely accessible to mobility-impaired guests, with the following exceptions and qualifications:
- **Main Street:** The *Plaza Pavilion* has a short flight of steps at the entrance.
- **Frontierland:** At *River Belle Terrace*—otherwise accessible—the stanchions that mark off the cafeteria line are spaced too closely together to permit wheelchair passage. Tom Sawyer Island and consequently the snack stands there are not accessible to guests who use wheelchairs.

Shops: Nearly every shop in the park is completely accessible to mobility-impaired guests. Exceptions include Great American Pastimes on Main Street, which is a bit small to allow easy maneuverability, and One of a Kind Shop in New Orleans Square, which is very cramped.

Other Information

BARBER SHOP: Lord Jim's Barber Shop; 700 West Orangewood, Suite A; 971-5530; about three blocks from Disneyland.

BEAUTY SALONS: The Coral Tree, in the *Marriott* hotel; 700 West Convention Way; 750-6573; and Wolf's Beauty Salon, in the *Anaheim Hilton*, lower level; 777 Convention Way; 750-4321. Besides hair cutting and styling, both offer manicures and pedicures, and they welcome men and women.

CAR CARE: Those who belong to auto and travel clubs should call their club-sponsored towing service in the event of problems. An Auto Club of Southern California office is located at 150 West Vermont Ave., 774-2392. For AAA emergency roadside service call 800-400-4222.

RELIGIOUS SERVICES: One of the most interesting places to attend services (Dutch Reform) is the Crystal Cathedral; 12141 Lewis St.; Garden Grove; 971-4000. Completed in 1980, it is huge—one of the largest houses of worship in the world—but unlike some others it is not oppressive. The entire structure is made of glass, so the sky is visible all around. The pipe organ is the biggest in the western United States and the minister, Robert Schuller, is renowned for his emotional services. One unusual feature of the church is that two 90-foot doors open so people can take part in the service without ever leaving their cars. This has been called a typical California phenomenon, and is a throwback to the days when Schuller began his ministry preaching in a drive-in theater 30 years ago. Services are held on Sundays in the small Chapel-in-the-Sky on the grounds at 8 A.M. In the main cathedral Sunday services are held at 9:30 A.M., 11 A.M., 1 P.M. (Hispanic), and 6 P.M. in the summer (7 P.M. in the winter). See "Special Events" in this chapter for additional information.

Baptist: The Garden Church; 8712 East Santa Ana Canyon Rd. (Anaheim Hills); 282-1899. Services are on Sundays at 8:30 A.M. and 10 A.M.; Sunday school at 9 A.M.; Bible study on Tuesdays at 7 P.M.

Catholic: The Church of St. Boniface; 120 North Janss at Harbor Blvd.; 956-3110; is about two miles from Disneyland. Masses are held on Saturdays at 8 A.M. and 5 P.M. (in English), 6:30 P.M. (Vietnamese), and 8 P.M. (Spanish), and on Sundays at 7 A.M. (English), 8 A.M. (Spanish), 9:30 A.M. and 11 A.M. (English), 12:30 P.M. (Spanish), 5 P.M. (English), and at 7 P.M. (Spanish). Daily masses are held

at 6:30 A.M., 8 A.M., and 5:30 P.M. (English), and at 7 P.M. (Spanish).

Christian Science: The First Church of Christ Scientist; 918 North Citron St.; 535-0631. Services are at 10 A.M. on Sundays and at 7:30 P.M. on Wednesdays. Sunday school is at 10 A.M.

Episcopal: St. Michael's Episcopal Church; 311 West South St.; 535-4654; is about seven blocks from Disneyland. Services are held on Sundays at 8 A.M. and 10 A.M., Wednesdays at 6:30 P.M., and Thursdays at 12:10 P.M.

Jewish: The Temple Beth Emet; 1770 West Cerritos Ave.; 772-4720; a 15-minute walk from Disneyland, has services at 8 P.M. on Fridays, 9:30 A.M. on Saturdays and Sundays.

Lutheran: Prince of Peace Church; 1421 West Ball Rd.; 774-0993; located two miles from Disneyland, has services on Sundays at 8 A.M. and 10:30 A.M. Sunday school is at 9:15 A.M.

United Methodist: The West Anaheim United Methodist Church; 2045 West Ball Rd; 772-6030; about three miles from Disneyland, has Sunday services at 10:30 A.M. Adult Sunday school is at 9 A.M., and children's Sunday school is at 10 A.M.

LIQUOR: Though liquor is served in the Magic Kingdom, don't get the idea that spirituous libations are easy to come by. In an effort to compete more effectively with off-premises restaurants and clubs for corporate gatherings, beer, wine, and champagne are available on Disneyland turf, but only at pre-arranged, after-hours private parties of 500 or more. So, for all intents and purposes, a casual drink is still not available at Disneyland. Liquor may, however, be purchased at the *Disneyland Hotel* lounges and nearby liquor stores, restaurants, and bars. The legal drinking age in California is 21.

LOCKERS: Coin-operated lockers are available just outside the main gate. There are token-operated lockers inside the park at the Lost and Found on Main Street behind the Market House. Tokens cost $1 each. New tokens (or quarters in the case of the outside lockers) must be inserted every time you open and relock one. The easy access of these storage facilities makes it convenient to do your shopping in midafternoon, when the stores are relatively empty and the attractions are busy, and then to stash purchases when you want to return to the attractions, during the less-congested late afternoon or evening hours. Locker availability is limited, and during busy periods, space can sell out before noon.

LOST AND FOUND: At any given time, a survey of the shelves of Lost and Found might turn up cameras, umbrellas, strollers, handbags, lens caps, cigarette lighters, sunglasses, prescription glasses, suitcases, and even hair dryers; once, a wallet containing $1,700 in cash was turned in. Hub caps, false teeth, crutches, radios, and jewelry also have turned

up. If you find something, you'll be asked to fill out a card with your name and address; if the item isn't claimed within 30 days, you have the option of keeping it. Items not claimed by their finders are eventually sold to employees and the proceeds donated to charity. The system has a way of encouraging honesty, so if you lose something, don't fail to check at the Lost and Found office, located on Main Street behind the Market House.

MAIL: Postcards are for sale in gift shops all over Anaheim, and in many Disneyland shops and souvenir stands, including the Main Street Photo Supply Co.—which is, incidentally, a good spot to buy special occasion cards as well. (Don't forget to arrange for your mail at home to be held by the post office or picked up by neighbors while you're on vacation.)

Postage stamps: For sale in the park in postage machines located at the Main Street Photo Supply Co. and the Premiere Shop in Tomorrowland.

Mailboxes: There are 20 of these olive-drab mail depositories inside Disneyland. Cards and letters are picked up and delivered to the post office once a day and postmarked Anaheim.

Post office: The closest U.S. post office is Holiday Station, about three blocks from the park; 1180 West Ball Rd.; Anaheim; 533-8700. It is open from 8:30 A.M. to 5 P.M. Mondays through Fridays.

MONEY: Cash, traveler's checks, personal checks, American Express, Visa, and Master-Card are accepted as payment for admission to Disneyland, for merchandise purchased in shops, and for meals (except for food carts, where only cash is accepted). Checks must be imprinted with the guest's name and address, drawn on a U.S. bank, and accompanied by proper identification—that is, a valid driver's license and a major credit card such as American Express, Diners Club, MasterCard, or Visa, as well as The Disney Credit Card (available through The Disney Store or by calling 800-222-1262). Oil company credit cards and department store charge cards are not acceptable identification for check-writing purposes.

Financial services: You can purchase Disney Dollars at the old-fashioned Bank of Main Street, as well as at City Hall across the street. Disney Dollars are accepted as cash throughout the park, but you may want to keep one as an inexpensive souvenir. There are automated teller machines located at the Bank of Main Street, Frontierland Stockade, and the Premier Shop in Tomorrowland. These machines at the main entrance also accept credit cards for cash advances. Also, at Starcade in Tomorrowland and Penny Arcade on Main Street, attendants can give you a cash advance against a credit card. Check cashing up to $100 also is available here with proper identification.

MEDICAL MATTERS

Blisters are the most common complaint received at Central First Aid, at the north end of Main Street near Carefree Corner, the *Plaza Inn*, and the Baby Center. So be forewarned and wear comfortable, well-broken-in shoes for your Disneyland visit.

If you have a more serious medical problem in the park, contact any Disneyland employee. He or she will get in touch with Central First Aid to make any necessary arrangements.

Those with chronic health problems should be sure to carry copies of all their prescriptions, and before leaving home ask family physicians for the names of Southern California colleagues.

Prescriptions: Try Sav-on Drugs located about two blocks from Disneyland, at 1021 North State College Blvd.; Anaheim; 991-9161. It is open 24 hours every day.

Refrigerator facilities for insulin: At Disneyland, insulin that must be refrigerated can be stored for the day at Central First Aid on Main Street. Outside the park, there are refrigerators in many of the hotels and motels in Anaheim and the surrounding areas. In most cases, if there is no refrigerator in the room, one can be requested at a nominal charge. The hotel or motel also can store insulin in its own refrigerator. Be sure to inquire in advance so there aren't any surprises.

American Express cardmember services: American Express has an Express Cash machine near the *Disneyland Hotel*'s monorail station. American Express cardholders can cash personal checks of up to $1,000 with a personal American Express card (up to $5,000 with a Gold Card) at the American Express Travel Agency in the Main Place Mall; 2800 North Main St., Suite 600; Santa Ana; 541-3318. This American Express office also can exchange foreign currency, can replace lost cards within 24 hours (first call 800-528-4800), as well as lost American Express traveler's checks (first call 800-221-7282), and can arrange emergency fund transfers. Hours are 10 A.M. to 9 P.M. weekdays, 10 A.M. to 1 P.M. and 2 P.M. to 7 P.M. Saturdays, 11 A.M. to 6 P.M. Sundays. There are six Cardmember's Check Dispensers at the Los Angeles airport. To use these, you need a personal identification number, which must be arranged through American Express in advance.

Other major credit cards: Cash advances on Visa credit cards can be arranged through Western Union. The Western Union office in Anaheim, located at 616 North Anaheim Blvd.; 535-2291; is open from 9 A.M. to 6 P.M. weekdays, until 3 P.M. Saturdays, and from 10 A.M. to 3 P.M. Sundays.

To report lost Visa or MasterCard credit cards, guests in the Disneyland area should call 800-556-5678. Among the banks in Anaheim that sell traveler's checks are:

● **Union Federal Savings and Loan**; 511 South Harbor Blvd.; 991-3720

● **Wells Fargo Bank**; 100 North Harbor Blvd.; 480-5000.

PETS: Except for service dogs, animals are not allowed in the Magic Kingdom. Those who are traveling with their family pet can board it for the day in Disneyland's air-conditioned kennel, where there are large, airy, individual enclosures ($10 per pet, per day, including food). Enclosures are disinfected between arrivals. Just outside the kennel, there's a 494-square-foot exercise area. (The lawn here is resodded about every two years.) All pet owners must put their animals into the cages and take them out again, since Disneyland personnel do not handle the animals. Cheetahs, nonpoisonous snakes, ocelots, parrots, guinea pigs, and other animals have been accommodated here, as well as cats and dogs.

Note that in busy seasons there may be a morning rush period, starting about 30 minutes before park opening. You may be subject to some delay in arranging your pet's accommodations.

Outside Disneyland: Some hotels and motels in the Anaheim area accept well-behaved, and preferably small, pets. Keep in mind, however, that most of properties do not allow guests to leave pets in the room unattended. These pet-friendly places include the following:

- **Anaheim Hilton and Towers**; 777 Convention Way; 750-4321
- **Anaheim Marriott**; 700 West Convention Way; 750-8000
- **Hampton Inn**; 300 East Katella Way; 772-8713
- **Residence Inn**; 1700 South Clementine St.; 533-3555

SHOPPING FOR NECESSITIES: It's a rare vacationer who doesn't leave some essential at home, or run out of it mid-trip, so it's always useful to know where to find certain everyday items.

Health aids and toiletries: Gift shops in all the big hotels stock essentials, but they usually cost more than in conventional retail shops, so when it's convenient try to shop elsewhere. One good source is the Sav-on Drugs closest to Disneyland; 1660 West Katella Ave.; 530-0500.

Inside Disneyland, aspirin, suntan lotions, lozenges, and similar sundries are available at the Newsstand at the main gate, at the Emporium on Main Street, at the Davy Crockett's Pioneer Mercantile in Frontierland, at Pieces of Eight in New Orleans Square, and at Star Trader in Tomorrowland. You'll also find a variety of personal items in Fantasyland at Geppetto's Arts and Crafts. Sundries also are available at Mickey's Corner at the *Disneyland Hotel*.

Newspapers: In Anaheim proper, your best bets are hotel gift shops. The *Anaheim Marriott*; 700 West Convention Way; 750-8000; stocks *The Wall Street Journal*, *Barron's*, *USA Today*, and, on Sundays, *The New York Times*, in addition to local papers. The *Grand*; One Hotel Way; 772-7777; and Mickey's Corner in the *Disneyland Hotel*; 1150 West Cerritos Ave.; 778-6600; stock *The Wall Street Journal*, as well as local papers.

For a more varied selection, you'll have to leave Anaheim. Bookstar; 3000 S. El Camino Real; Tustin; 731-2302 carries papers from as many as 38 states, including *The New York Times*, *The Washington Post*, *The Chicago Sun-Times*, and others, plus magazines, paperback books, and foreign periodicals from as far afield as Europe and the Middle East. It's open from 9 A.M. to 11 P.M. daily.

Books: For a better selection of reading matter than is generally found in hotels, try Waldenbooks (836-8433) or Brentano's (835-9688) in the Main Place Mall; 2800 N. Main Street; Santa Ana; and B. Dalton Bookseller in the City Shopping Center off Freeway 22 on City Drive; 634-8603. If you're staying in Costa Mesa, your best bet is the B. Dalton Bookseller (540-2192) in the Southeast Plaza Mall.

TELEPHONE: Local calls from most pay phones in Southern California cost 20¢. However, most hotels in the same area charge 75¢ for local calls made from your room. So make it a point to call from outside your hotel or use a public pay phone whenever possible (you'll find many of them at Disneyland, and they are well marked). For long-distance calls, policies vary from hotel to hotel, but charges are always higher than they would be for direct-dial calls made from a pay phone. It generally makes the most sense to use a telephone credit card when calling long distance.

TIME AND WEATHER PHONE: In Anaheim, call 853-1212 for the exact time. For the best local weather forecast, call the National Weather Bureau, which is based in Los Angeles (310-235-7761).

TIPPING: The standard gratuities around Anaheim are about the same as in any other city of its size. Expect to tip bellboys 75¢ per bag; $1 per bag is considered generous. It's customary to give cab drivers a 15 percent tip, especially on longer trips, and in restaurants, 15 percent to 20 percent is the norm, depending on the establishment.

TRANSPORTATION & ACCOMMODATIONS

Until you've actually been to Southern California, it's not unusual to assume that all of the most appealing attractions are situated within a few short miles of one another. That's only partly true. Although distances may be relatively short, driving time can really add up if destination and route are not planned with care. So it's important to pick a lodging that's convenient to all the sites you want to visit. You may even want to stay in several different places to make your trip more efficient.

This chapter provides a broad overview of the transportation options within Southern California—rental cars, buses, taxis, tours, and, yes, even freeways. And it offers some recommendations on places to stay around the area—not only in Anaheim proper, but also in Buena Park, Newport Beach, Orange, Garden Grove, Los Angeles, and San Diego. We've tried to provide a reasonable variety of styles of accommodations, from contemporary to old fashioned, and we've included some bed-and-breakfast and camping possibilities. We've spanned the spectrum of prices, from quite expensive to strictly no-frills. A careful perusal of the offerings that follow should help save you valuable time and money.

(Unless otherwise noted, phone numbers are in the 714 area code.)

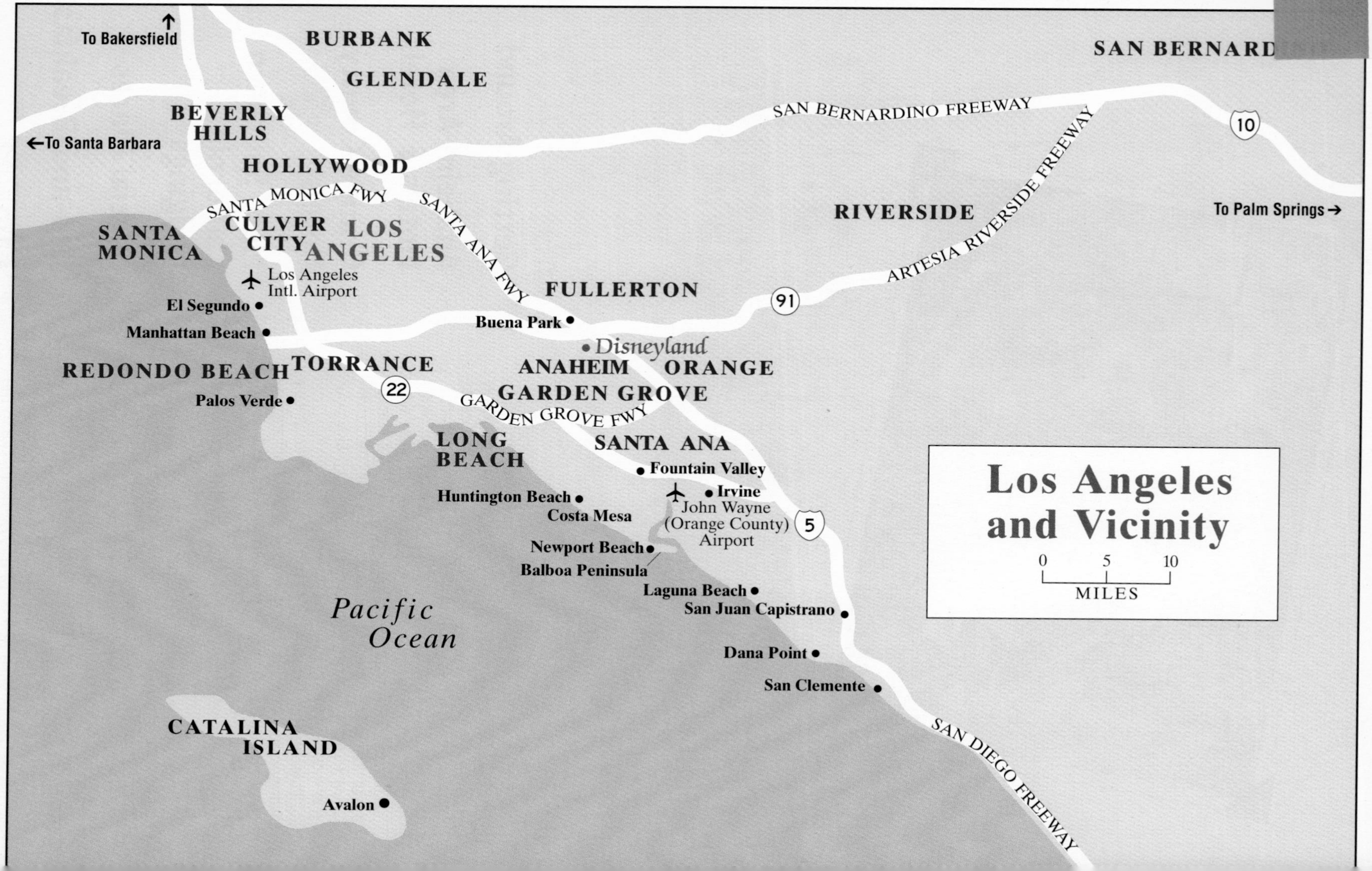

Los Angeles and Vicinity

MILES
0 5 10

SAN BERNARD

To Palm Springs →

10

SAN BERNARDINO FREEWAY

ARTESIA RIVERSIDE FREEWAY

RIVERSIDE

91

FULLERTON

SANTA ANA FWY

Disneyland

ANAHEIM ORANGE

GARDEN GROVE

GARDEN GROVE FWY

SANTA ANA

Fountain Valley

Irvine
John Wayne
(Orange County)
Airport

5

Buena Park ●

22

LONG
BEACH

Huntington Beach ●

Costa Mesa ●

Newport Beach ●
Balboa Peninsula

Laguna Beach ●

San Juan Capistrano ●

Dana Point ●

San Clemente ●

SAN DIEGO FREEWAY

BURBANK

GLENDALE

HOLLYWOOD

SANTA MONICA FWY

CULVER LOS
CITY ANGELES

Los Angeles
Intl. Airport

BEVERLY
HILLS

SANTA
MONICA

El Segundo ●

Manhattan Beach ●

REDONDO BEACH TORRANCE

Palos Verde ●

↑ To Bakersfield

← To Santa Barbara

Pacific
Ocean

CATALINA
ISLAND

Avalon ●

Getting Around

Southern California is a blend of small communities that have grown until their borders touched and their city limits have become irretrievably blurred. Anaheim, for instance, is bordered by Fullerton and Placentia to the north, the city of Orange to the east, Santa Ana to the southeast, Garden Grove to the southwest, and Buena Park to the northwest.

South of Anaheim you'll encounter the communities of Huntington Beach, Costa Mesa, Newport Beach, Irvine, Laguna Beach, San Juan Capistrano, San Clemente, and, about 75 miles (1½ hours) from Anaheim, San Diego. The towns of San Bernardino, Riverside, and Palm Springs lie roughly to the east.

Proceeding west, you'll come to Long Beach, Palos Verdes, Redondo Beach, Torrance, Manhattan Beach, El Segundo, Los Angeles International Airport, and Culver City. Traveling north through Los Angeles are Beverly Hills, Hollywood and West Hollywood, Santa Monica, Glendale, and Burbank. The San Fernando Valley is farther north and a bit inland. Malibu is about the same distance from Anaheim as the San Fernando Valley, but on the coast. Santa Barbara lies about two hours away to the north.

Disneyland is located in the city of Anaheim. Many of the other area attractions are in nearby towns—Garden Grove, Buena Park, Fountain Valley—or even farther away in Los Angeles or along the coast. Most of the driving to be done requires using a combination of surface streets and freeways; but once one is familiar with a few names and numbers, navigating shouldn't be too difficult.

SOUTHERN CALIFORNIA FREEWAYS: Even if you like to drive, driving on the freeways here is not exactly pure pleasure. Still, they are well marked and (in the best of times) quite fast, and driving them is by far the most convenient way to see Southern California.

For a stranger, the best way to get from one spot to the next is to ask directions. Be sure to write them down and trace the route on a road map before heading down the freeway entrance ramp. When making note of the directions, don't fail to get some idea of the distances between one turnoff and the next. Also remember to get both the names and the route numbers of the freeways to be followed. The proper names of most roads change frequently depending on where you are. For instance, I-5—called the Santa Ana Freeway in Orange County—becomes the Golden State Freeway in the Los Angeles area. Once you're on the highway, it can be very difficult to get on track again if you go astray.

It also is useful to have some idea of the overall layout of the freeways. There are several that run parallel to the Pacific coast. These are intersected by other freeways running due east and west. And though this scheme is pretty clear as stated here, it is complicated by still other freeways that seem to squiggle willy-nilly across the map. Nor does it help matters much that the roads' names are sometimes misleading (the San Diego Freeway, for example, does not go to San Diego).

North-south freeways: I-5, which runs from Vancouver, Canada, to San Diego, is the principal inland route. Near Hollywood, it sprouts I-405 (the San Diego Freeway). This road bulges toward the coast and rejoins I-5 at Irvine, south of Anaheim.

East-west freeways: Of the roads that intersect these two principal north-south arteries, one of the closest to Disneyland is Rte. 22, known as the Garden Grove Freeway, which begins near the ocean in Long Beach and runs across the southern border of Anaheim. Rte. 91, which is known as the Artesia Freeway on the west side of I-5 and the Riverside Freeway on the east side, lies about eight miles north of Rte. 22. The next east-west route to the north is I-10, which is called the Santa Monica Freeway from its beginning near the Pacific shore in Santa Monica to just east of downtown Los Angeles. At this point, it makes a jog north and then turns east again, becoming the San Bernardino Freeway. I-10 is located about 12 miles north of Rte. 91. North of I-10—anywhere from two to eight miles depending on your location—is U.S. 101. This comes from Ventura (up north), and then heads due east across I-405. It is called the Ventura Freeway on the west; at a point a few miles beyond the intersection with I-405, it makes a jog south, becomes the Hollywood Freeway, and eventually crosses I-5.

ANAHEIM-AREA SURFACE STREETS: Disneyland is bounded by Harbor Boulevard on the east, West Street on the west, Ball Road on the north, and Katella Avenue on the south. Many of the city's hotels and motels, restaurants, and coffee shops are located on or just off these streets. Slanting through Anaheim, more or less bisecting the city, is the Santa Ana Freeway (I-5). This is the main route north to Los Angeles or south to San Diego. Ball Road, near Harbor Boulevard, is the most convenient place to pick up this freeway going north. Katella Avenue, which runs between Harbor Boulevard and State College Boulevard, is the most convenient entrance to the southbound Santa Ana Freeway.

CAR RENTAL FEES

	AMO	AVIS	BUDGET	DOLLAR	HERTZ	NATIONAL	THRIFTY
	$46.98	$46.99	$45.99	$35.99	$49.99	$42.99	$40.99
	$48.98	$48.99	$48.99	$39.99	$51.99	$44.99	$45.99
...ediate	$51.98	$51.99	$50.99	$45.99	$54.99	$48.99	$55.99
WEEKEND (per day)							
Subcompact	$29.99	$37.99	$33.99	$35.99	$36.99	$34.99	$30.99
Compact	$33.99	$41.99	$35.99	$39.99	$40.99	$38.99	$32.99
Intermediate	$36.99	$44.99	$37.99	$45.99	$43.99	$41.99	$40.99
ONE WEEK							
Subcompact	$215.99	$215.99	$214.99	$205.99	$220.99	$210.99	$200.99
Compact	$232.99	$233.99	$232.99	$222.99	$243.99	$225.99	$210.99
Intermediate	$237.99	$237.99	$234.99	$225.99	$247.99	$229.99	$255.99

- To ensure the best rate, use exact dates and pick-up and drop-off locations when making your reservation.
- Confirm the size and type of car by make and model.
- Review your insurance coverage carefully to determine if any additional insurance is necessary.
- You may be entitled to additional discounts through your credit card or travel club memberships.
- Weekly rates generally require a five-day rental. Weekend rates generally require a three-day rental between noon Thursdays and noon Mondays. Be sure to check when making your reservations.
- Renters must be at least 25 years of age and have a major credit card.
- **Note:** Prices were accurate at press time but are subject to change.

CAR RENTALS: There are at least 20 car rental agencies in the Anaheim area alone, and the prices charged and the selection of cars available vary widely. To get the best deal it's imperative to shop around for the most competitive prices.

Most of the firms offer unlimited mileage programs; some offer special convention rates. It's also important to figure the cost of collision damage waiver (CDW) insurance in all price calculations; it can vary enough from agency to agency to make a difference in the overall cost of longer rentals. (Note that most vacation packages that include a rental car do not include CDW; if you choose not to take it, the agency may require a large deposit.) Also be aware that an increasing number of credit cards offer free collision damage coverage simply for charging the rental to their card, and that some of these may even provide *primary* coverage. That means your credit card company may deal with the rental company directly in the event of an accident, rather than compensate you after your own personal insurance has kicked in. This sort of coverage is a strong incentive to charge your rental to the card that offers the most extensive coverage.

The Anaheim-area car rental firms includes:
- **Alamo:** 800-327-9633
- **Avis:** 800-331-1212
- **Budget:** 800-527-0700
- **Dollar:** 800-800-4000
- **Hertz:** 800-654-3131
- **National:** 800-227-7368
- **Thrifty:** 800-367-2277

To celebrate a special occasion, contact the Luxury Line Rent-A-Car office in Beverly Hills (300 South La Cienega Blvd.; 310-659-5555 or 800-826-7805), one of the few car rental agencies that rent deluxe vehicles to individuals. You can drive around in style in a Rolls Royce, Mercedes sedan or convertible, a Cadillac Seville, a Lincoln Town Car, a Corvette, or a Volkswagen Rabbit convertible. Rates range from $595 a day plus 50¢ a mile for a Mercedes 600 SEL, down to about $70 a day plus 100 free miles per day for a VW Rabbit convertible. On the other hand, if luxury is not important, look into Ugly Duckling Rent-A-Car (2145 Harbor Blvd., Costa Mesa; 642-8733).

MAPS: Most gas stations sell local maps (usually for about $2) detailed enough to show tourist attractions, major roads, and many minor streets. The small maps that car rental companies give out when you pick up a car may also be helpful. If you intend to do enough driving to warrant the investment, buy *The Thomas Brothers' Orange County Street Guide and Directory* ($15.95), or the combined Los Angeles–Orange County edition ($25.95). These books, available at local bookstores and some hotel gift shops, are so detailed that they can provide directions to a specific block.

BUS TRANSPORTATION: Orange County Transit District provides daily bus service throughout the area, but on a limited basis weekends. Several bus lines stop at Disneyland, but keep in mind that all public transportation generally involves considerable

waiting and considerable transferring, and may not prove truly convenient. Exact-change fares are $1, transfers are 5¢. Seniors pay 15¢, except during weekday rush hours (from 6 A.M. to 9 A.M., and from 3 P.M. to 6 P.M.) when the fare is 45¢. Dial-A-Ride (638-9000) is also available. This door-to-door van service, which is designed for short trips within specific neighborhoods, is only available for seniors and people with disabilities; vehicles with wheelchair lifts can be requested. The fare is 90¢.

To get farther afield without your own wheels, the best bet is to sign up for a bus tour. Several companies in the area offer them, including Pacific Coast Sightseeing (978-8855) and VIP Tours (939-6814). Hotel and motel desks can provide information about schedules and prices, sell you the tickets, and notify the sightseeing tour company to pick you up.

TAXIS: Yellow Cab of Anaheim provides 24-hour service. Fare is $1.90 at the flag drop, $1.60 each mile thereafter for one to five persons (535-2211). Cab fare from John Wayne Airport to the *Disneyland Hotel* runs about $35 with tip.

TRANSPORTATION TO THE AIRPORTS:
Los Angeles International Airport is 45 minutes (at the best of times) from Anaheim. Airport Coach buses (491-3500 or 800-772-5299) and Airport Cruiser (761-3345) provide frequent scheduled service between Los Angeles International and Anaheim hotels. Airport Coach and Airport Cruiser buses both stop in front of each airline terminal just outside the baggage claim area. After claiming your luggage, proceed outside the terminal building to the red "bus stop" signs on the center island. Airport Coach buses can be identified by the words "Disneyland/Anaheim" displayed above the windshield. Airport Cruiser buses can be identified by the words "Disneyland/Buena Park" displayed above the windshield.

After claiming your luggage at the John

Wayne Airport (named after Orange County's most famous resident and only 20 minutes from Anaheim), proceed to the red "bus stop" zone outside the baggage claim area. Airport Coach buses can be identified by the words "Disneyland/Anaheim" displayed above the windshield.

To return to the airports, check with your hotel front desk the day before departure for bus schedules and reservation information.

SuperShuttle also serves both airports. At Los Angeles International, proceed to the nearest courtesy phone or pay phone and contact SuperShuttle at 310-417-8988 for pickup. (The courtesy phone has specific dialing instructions.) The van picks up passengers at the outer island within 15 minutes. For guests arriving at John Wayne Airport, 24-hour advance reservations are recommended; call 517-6600. Upon arrival, use a courtesy phone to request pickup. A van will arrive within 15 minutes at the curb outside the terminal.

For passengers returning to John Wayne Airport, check with hotel front-desk personnel for return schedules the day before departure.

TO AND FROM THE AIRPORTS

	Airport Coach Airport Shuttle Airport Cruiser	SuperShuttle
From Los Angeles International Airport to Disneyland	$14 per person $8 per child (ages 3-11)	$13 per person
From John Wayne Airport to Disneyland	$10 per person $7 per child (ages 3-11)	$10 per person

All fares are one-way; round-trip fares are lower; children under 3 ride free.
Prices were accurate as we went to press, but are subject to change.

Anaheim Area Motels & Hotels

There are no accommodations inside Disneyland itself. The *Disneyland Hotel*, however, is owned by The Walt Disney Company, is directly across the street from the park, and is connected to it by monorail. With its large shops selling Disney merchandise and resortwear, its outdoor activities, and diverse dining and nightlife possibilities it feels like an extension of Disneyland.

The only reason not to stay here during a visit to the park would be price. So first, decide how much money you can spend, then check to see which hostelry recommended here offers the most for your dollar.

Disneyland is literally ringed with hotels and motels, ranging from local representatives of national chains to "mom-and-pop" operations, with each one promising that it alone offers the only rooms in the area of any true distinction. Actually, most area lodging places provide predictable U.S. motel fare: two double beds, plush carpet, a color TV set, and a private bath. Most have modest restaurants or are so near to eateries that it doesn't really matter. Most are about equally convenient to Disneyland.

Motels are usually the least expensive. Some in the area were built during the late 1950s, and despite countless refurbishings over the years, still show their age. In recent years, several new motels have been built, and while most simply sell a room with a view of the parking lot, they offer good value. Some motels specialize in suites (often a desirable option for a family). Others may have family units that can be particularly handy if you have small children, since the second bedroom has no outside access at all.

Hotels, with high-rise towers usually cost more, but they also are livelier and offer more of that ephemeral quality called "atmosphere." Their public spaces are better designed and more attractively laid out. The grounds are generally well landscaped, and swimming pools tend to be larger. Many establishments have their own spa facilities, or offer access to other sports facilities—a local health club, for instance. The guestrooms overlook Disneyland or Anaheim, or face the mountains or the ocean. The towels are generally thicker and larger than in most motels, and small complimentary amenities such as shampoo, fancy soaps, and bubble bath are frequently found in the rooms. Hair salons and boutiques, tour desks and concierges, and the like are givens.

When comparing the cost of accommodations, remember to take into consideration any potentially hidden costs, such as parking. Most establishments provide free van or minibus service to the park (a necessity for visitors without their own vehicles and a convenience for everyone else). Most hotels charge for parking and most charge an additional fee when more than two adults occupy a room. The cutoff age at which children are billed as extra adults does vary (some hotels consider 17-year-olds children, and others start charging for them as adults above age 12). Many establishments offer discounts for senior citizens.

Sometimes payment is only according to the number of beds required. Charges for rollaways and cribs vary widely. Most of the time, the extra costs don't seem to amount to much individually, but they can add up over the course of a few days. So before selecting a place to stay, be sure to figure the total charges with your family's specific needs in mind. Keep in mind that meals can significantly add to the cost of any trip; refer to the *Good Meals, Great Times* chapter for both money-saving suggestions and splurges.

In the following selection of some of the most attractive or most advantageously priced Anaheim accommodations, all the establishments accept major credit cards unless otherwise noted. Rates were correct at press time, but are subject to change. "In season" refers to the Christmas and Easter holidays and the months of June, July, and August. Many hotels offer packages, sometimes through the Walt Disney Travel Company; for details see "Should You Buy a Package?" in *Getting Ready to Go*. In the same chapter, "Other Information" tells which places permit pets.

DISNEYLAND HOTEL: This resort hotel owned by The Walt Disney Company would be a destination in its own right, even if it were not located right across the street from Disneyland. Sprawling on 60 acres landscaped so lavishly you hardly suspect you're in the heart of Anaheim, it has a manmade marina where pedal boats can be rented for a pleasant afternoon; a 165-foot-wide waterfall that you can actually walk underneath; a pool full of exotic Japanese koi to feed; a nighttime Fantasy Waters show that combines lights, fountains, and Disney music; a pleasant resort atmosphere; vast convention facilities; the most extensive gameroom of any hotel in the area (it looks like a Monte Carlo casino); and a whole raft of shops, restaurants, entertainment spots, and sports facilities. The hotel also is directly connected to Disneyland—via speedy monorail or tram—an enormous convenience for hotel guests, who can sneak a quick trip to the hotel's swimming pools when the park gets too crowded (don't forget that a Disneyland Passport and a hand stamp are required for re-entry to the park).

The hotel has three swimming pools, all big enough for serious exercise, two with a sandy beach and the other the largest at any Anaheim hotel. The Sierra Pool has special hours just for lap swimming (adults only) from 7 A.M. to 9 A.M. daily. There's also the cove pools for the kids. Hotel guests also can exercise at Team Mickey's Workout facility, which has a variety of weight machines and aerobic exercise equipment.

The hotel has 1,136 rooms and suites located partly in two-story villas that are actually sections of the establishment's original building, and partly in three high-rise towers. Most tower rooms have two double beds and many can accommodate up to five persons (one of them on a rollaway) quite easily. All the tower rooms have small balconies big enough to accommodate a chair, say, to cool off or (from some) to watch the 20-minute Fantasy Waters show. The 11-story Sierra Tower looks toward Disneyland on one side and the colorful hotel marina on the other. The 13-story Bonita Tower and the 11-story Marina Tower have rooms with marina views as well, but only on one side; guests on the opposite side look out over parking lots or city rooftops. The secluded Villas have private patios or sun decks and grassy lawns, and some Oriental Gardens rooms can accommodate six.

Besides the monorail, there is free ground transportation to the main gate of Disneyland via trams that depart from near the *Monorail Café.* The monorail station sells Disneyland passports, but if you are new to Disneyland, you should consider taking the hotel tram the first time you go to the park since the monorail bypasses the impressive main gate at Main Street U.S.A. and travels directly to Tomorrowland.

Airport buses bound for the Orange County and Los Angeles airports make regular stops at the hotel. There are reservations desks for various airlines and bus companies, as well as the Walt Disney Travel Company, which offers a full range of travel services. Auto rentals, babysitter referrals, and safe-deposit boxes also are available through the hotel. Rates in season for doubles are $150 to $185, depending on the room's view and location, plus $15 for each extra adult (no charge for children under 18 staying in parents' room); $15 for rollaways; no charge for cribs. Suites go for $300 and up. Parking is $10 per day for hotel guests; others pay $3 per hour; $15 maximum for 24 hours. *Disneyland Hotel*; 1150 West Cerritos Ave.; Anaheim, CA 92802; 956-6425 (for reservations and information) or 778-6600 (hotel switchboard).

ANAHEIM COMFORT SUITES: This four-story property, located three-and-a-half long blocks south of Disneyland, offers good rates for its 100 suites. There are petite suites (one room with separate living and sleeping areas), two-room suites with separate living and sleeping rooms, and honeymoon suites with in-room spas. Nonsmoking guest quarters are available, and some suites are equipped for travelers with disabilities. Amenities include refrigerators, microwave ovens, coffeemakers, remote-control color television sets with movie channels, and clock radios. There are also a heated pool and spa. Complimentary continental breakfast is served daily, and there's a free shuttle to Disneyland and the Convention Center. Transportation to the airports is provided by various airport bus companies. Rates for petite suites range seasonally from $69 to $79; two-room suites cost $89 to $94; family suites sleep eight and run $119 to $129. (Inquire about special rates.) *Anaheim Comfort Suites*; 2141 South Harbor Blvd.; Anaheim, CA 92802; 971-3553 or 800-526-9444.

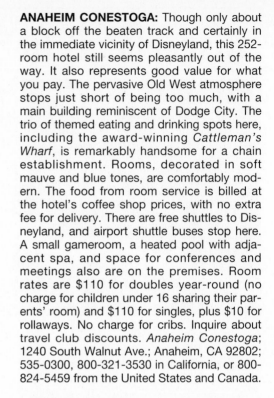

ANAHEIM CONESTOGA: Though only about a block off the beaten track and certainly in the immediate vicinity of Disneyland, this 252-room hotel still seems pleasantly out of the way. It also represents good value for what you pay. The pervasive Old West atmosphere stops just short of being too much, with a main building reminiscent of Dodge City. The trio of themed eating and drinking spots here, including the award-winning *Cattleman's Wharf*, is remarkably handsome for a chain establishment. Rooms, decorated in soft mauve and blue tones, are comfortably modern. The food from room service is billed at the hotel's coffee shop prices, with no extra fee for delivery. There are free shuttles to Disneyland, and airport shuttle buses stop here. A small gameroom, a heated pool with adjacent spa, and space for conferences and meetings also are on the premises. Room rates are $110 for doubles year-round (no charge for children under 16 sharing their parents' room) and $110 for singles, plus $10 for rollaways. No charge for cribs. Inquire about travel club discounts. *Anaheim Conestoga*; 1240 South Walnut Ave.; Anaheim, CA 92802; 535-0300, 800-321-3530 in California, or 800-824-5459 from the United States and Canada.

ANAHEIM HILTON: The three-story atrium lobby brings the outdoors into this hotel, and its 14-story modern glass exterior reflects the Anaheim Convention Center, just steps away. This is Southern California's largest hotel, with 1,600 rooms, including 100 suites. The rooms and suites on the upper floor comprise the Towers Concierge Class level, which has more elaborate decor and furnishings, its own concierge, VIP check-in and check-out, and a special VIP lounge and bar. Tower guests also receive complimentary continental breakfast, and in-room amenities include soaps, lotions, robes, electric shoe buffers, and scales. The hotel's fifth floor is a rooftop recreation center featuring a heated swimming pool, four spas, and acres of sun decks and rose gardens. Provisions for travelers with disabilities include 46 specially fitted guestrooms and suites, reserved parking, and phones for the

hearing impaired. There are good convention facilities here, a café open 18 hours a day, three specialty restaurants, a sports bar, plus a nightclub with recorded music, videos, and a large dance floor. Other services include beauty and barber shops, gift shops, foreign currency exchange, a self-service post office, and a business center. The 25,000-square-foot Sports and Fitness Center has exercise equipment and weight machines, an indoor pool, spa, basketball gym, aerobics classes, co-ed sauna, steam baths, and massage. There also is an outdoor driving range. Rates for a double room range from $135 to $245 (inquire about special packages), plus $20 per extra adult (no charge for children, regardless of age, when sharing their parents' room); no charge for cribs or rollaways. Self-parking costs $6 per day, valet parking $8. Pets are permitted. *Anaheim Hilton and Towers*; 777 Convention Way; Anaheim, CA 92802; 750-4321 or 800-222-9923.

ANAHEIM MARRIOTT: This newly redecorated hotel, opposite the Anaheim Convention Center, is a delightful place—well kept, stylish, comfortable, and well run. Most of the 1,039 rooms located in the two towers (one 17 stories, the other 19 stories) and the two 4-story wings have balconies. Rooms facing Disneyland provide views over Big Thunder Mountain, the Matterhorn, and Space Mountain. The hotel restaurants are some of the best in Anaheim, and for a quick bite there is a *Pizza Hut* on the property. The large, roughly key-shaped pool, part indoor and part outdoor, is palm shaded, surrounded by lounge chairs, and equipped with a hydrotherapy pool. The outstanding facilities for guests with

disabilities include wide doors, grab rails, hand-held shower heads, and elevator buttons low enough for people in wheelchairs to reach. The hotel, located a couple of long blocks from Disneyland, provides complimentary shuttle transportation to the park on a green trolley-on-wheels that kids love. Airport Coach service to the Orange County, Long Beach, Ontario, and Los Angeles airports is available, and the concierge can book tours and tickets and answer just about any question. Rooms, which come with either one king-size bed or two doubles, cost $165 to $185 (from $310 to $425 for suites) for two year-round; no charge for children under 18 sharing their parents' room, plus $10 per additional adult. Rollaways are complimentary. Special packages and discounted weekend rates are available. Self-parking costs $6 per day, valet parking $12. Pets are allowed on the ground floor. *Anaheim Marriott*; 700 West Convention Way; Anaheim, CA 92802; 750-8000 or 800-228-9290.

CANDY CANE INN: There's a lot to like about this moderately priced, two-story New Orleans-style motel, located just down the street from Disneyland's main entrance. It's well designed and nicely landscaped, and the 172 rooms offer ceramic-tiled bathrooms with separate dressing and vanity areas. Add to that a gift shop, guest laundry and valet services, a swimming pool, a kids' wading pool, and a gazebo-covered spa. Complimentary continental breakfast is served. Sightseeing services are available, and transportation to local airports can be arranged. Some rooms are equipped for guests with disabilities. Rates for a double with two queen-size beds range from $69 to $99 (according to season), plus $10 for rollaways; no charge for cribs. *Candy Cane Inn*; 1747 South Harbor Blvd.; Anaheim, CA 92802; 774-5284 or 800-345-7057.

CASTLE INN: This 200-room, four-story property resembles a castle with all its turrets, towers, and heraldic symbols. A drive inside the entrance reveals a more standard motel layout (guestrooms surround and overlook the parking lot). Still, it's a good value and less than a block from Disneyland. Rooms contain either a king- or two queen-size beds, and such amenities as a VCR, color television, and refrigerator, and some rooms have in-room spas. Suites are available. A heated pool and whirlpool are outside, along with a children's pool. Valet service is available, and there's a laundry as well as a one-hour photo developing service. Some rooms are equipped for travelers with disabilities. Rates range seasonally from $68 to $78 for a regular room, and from $88 to $108 for a two-room family suite with three queen-size beds; add $10 for rollaways, $6 for cribs. *Castle Inn*; 1734 South Harbor Blvd.; Anaheim, CA 92802; 774-8111 or 800-521-5653.

DOUBLETREE: Located in the city of Orange near the Crystal Cathedral, this 454-room high rise is a little over two miles from Disneyland. The hotel's lobby is spacious and inviting; its restaurants include the new *City Club*, which serves a variety of steak and seafood dishes, and there are two bars. The hotel also has a complete exercise facility, and outside, a nicely landscaped pool and spa area, with two lighted tennis courts adjacent to the pool. Three of the five business floors provide additional amenities such as bathrobes, iron, coffeemaker, mini-bar, daily newspaper, and other conveniences. Some rooms are equipped for guests with disabilities. The hotel provides complimentary shuttle service to Disneyland. The City Shopping Center, with 100 stores and restaurants, is nearby. Rates for doubles range from $65 to $170, plus $10 for rollaways; no charge for cribs or for children under 18 sharing their parents' room. Parking is $4 per day. *Doubletree*; 100 The City Drive; Orange, CA 92668; 634-4500 or 800-528-0444.

GRAND HOTEL: The big square lobby features antique-white furniture upholstered in soft aqua hues, while the 242 rooms have queen- or king-size beds. Guests prefer rooms with park views. Kids like the video-game enclaves which, though located just off the main corridor to the meeting rooms, still seem discreetly out of the way. There are two whirlpool spas, a swimming pool, and an exercise room, as well as a playground designed primarily for small children (who should be accompanied by a parent). A 20-passenger minibus takes guests to Disneyland free of charge. The hotel is a terminal for airport shuttle buses, which provide scheduled transportation to the major airports. Eight rooms are specially equipped for guests with disabilities. Rates are $90 to $135 for doubles, depending on the season and the room's location, plus $10 for rollaways. No charge for cribs or for children under 18 sharing their parents' room. *Grand Hotel*; One Hotel Way; Anaheim, CA 92802; 772-7777 or 800-421-6662.

HAMPTON INN: This five-story, 136-room property is located about a mile from Disneyland. The interior is modern and comfortable, and complimentary continental breakfast is served in the well-designed lobby. Local phone calls, an in-room movie channel, parking, and transportation to Disneyland and the Convention Center also are complimentary. Nonsmoking rooms are available, as is one hospitality suite (a guestroom with added space and facilities to accommodate a small meeting). Some rooms are equipped for guests with disabilities. There is a pool. This is one of the accommodations in the area that allows pets (call ahead, though). Year-round rates (for up to four people in a room)

range from $77 for a room with two double beds to $82 for a "king study" with a king-size bed and queen-size sofa bed, plus $10 for rollaways; no charge for cribs. Ask about Disneyland packages. *Hampton Inn*; 300 East Katella Way; Anaheim, CA 92802; 772-8713 or 800-426-7866.

HOLIDAY INN ANAHEIM AT THE PARK: Situated about half a mile north of Disneyland's main entrance, this five-story, 258-room establishment has one of the best landscaped pool areas in Anaheim, and the pool is open 24 hours. Other facilities and services include complimentary transportation to Disneyland, Knott's Berry Farm, and many other local attractions, and airport shuttle service; free in-room movies, car-rental service, free parking, tour service, a gift shop, a restaurant, and a lobby bar. Eight rooms are specially equipped for travelers with disabilities. Meeting rooms accommodate from 20 to 180 persons. Rates for doubles are $89 in season, $79 the rest of the year, plus $10 for each extra adult (no charge for children under 18 sharing their parents' room), $10 for rollaways; no charge for cribs. Ask about Disneyland vacation packages. Senior citizen discounts are available. Pets are welcome, but there is a $10-per-day charge; no security deposit is required. *Holiday Inn Anaheim at the Park*; 1221 South Harbor Blvd.; Anaheim, CA 92805; 758-0900 or 800-545-7275.

HYATT REGENCY ALICANTE: The towering 17-story atrium (the largest in the western United States) connects the hotel to the adjoining Plaza Tower office complex. It encloses palm trees, fountains, and greenery, and houses *Café Alicante*, *Papa Geppetto's* Italian restaurant, the *Atrium Bar*, and specialty shops. The hotel also has a lounge with occasional live entertainment. Travelers bound for Disneyland should note that although the hotel's address is Garden Grove, it is situated at the corner of Harbor Boulevard and Chapman Avenue, just a mile from the park. The hotel has 400 renovated guest-rooms, decorated in a pale peach and gray-green color scheme, available with either a king-size bed or two double beds. Imported marble and oak furnishings complement the rooms' modern interior design. Each of the 17 spacious suites has a living room, dining room, wet bar, entertainment console, and balcony overlooking the gardenlike atrium courtyard. The hotel's recreational facilities (located on its attractively landscaped, 25,000-square-foot, third-story roof) include a pool, a raised spa, two tennis courts, a game-room, and an exercise room. There are 12 rooms specially equipped for travelers with disabilities. Many room phones are designed for hearing-impaired guests. There are 47 business-plan rooms equipped with an in-room fax machine, coffeemaker, iron, and hair dryer. Complimentary transportation to Disneyland is provided for guests, and airport shuttle service is available. Rates are $130 for business-plan rooms, $155 for doubles (with a weekend rate of $89), $225 to $895 for suites, plus $25 for each additional adult (no charge for children under 18 occupying their parents' room); no charge for rollaways or cribs. Self-parking is $4 per day, valet parking $8. *Hyatt Regency Alicante*; 100 Plaza Alicante; Harbor Boulevard and Chapman Avenue; Garden Grove, CA 92640; 971-3000, 750-1234, or 800-972-2929.

JOLLY ROGER INN: Another surprising place that represents particularly good value, the property occupies one corner of what is probably Anaheim's busiest intersection, but it has a secluded air. This is accomplished mostly by the positioning of the public buildings as buffers for the worst of the noise. There are 238 rooms, some of which are equipped for travelers with disabilities. There are two out-door pools, a kids' wading pool, and a whirlpool. A convenient coffee shop serves

breakfast, lunch, and dinner; a dining room decorated with marine antiques, usually is open for lunch and always for dinner; and a lounge features live entertainment and dancing. A beauty salon and a gift shop are also on the premises. And there's a courtesy shuttle to Disneyland and to an airport transportation bus stop. Best of all, the staff is friendly and the atmosphere definitely family oriented. Rates for a room occupied by up to four people range seasonally from $60 to $70 for the Courtyard building and from $78 to $98 for the Bali Hai and Harbor buildings; plus $10 for rollaways; no charge for cribs. *Jolly Roger Inn*; 640 West Katella Ave.; Anaheim, CA 92802; 772-7621 or 800-446-1555.

PAN PACIFIC, ANAHEIM: Two high-rise towers—one 15 stories, one 14 stories—are slightly juxtaposed to create a central atrium where the lobby is located. The 502 recently renovated rooms (including 12 suites and 26 rooms equipped for travelers with disabilities) all have two extra-long double beds or a king-size bed plus a fold-out twin sofa bed in the sitting area, making it a particularly comfortable place for families. Nonsmoking rooms are available. It's just across the street from Disneyland and a short walk from the monorail and tram at the *Disneyland Hotel*. On the third floor, a huge landscaped recreation deck includes a split-level sun deck, swimming pool, whirlpool, children's play area, and snack bar. The hotel also has a children's activity center, which features arts and crafts, Disney movies, and more. On the ground floor are the hotel's two restaurants and bar. Rates for doubles are $125 to $185 (ask about special rates), plus $10 per extra adult. Small refrigerators are available for $10 for the entire stay. No charge for cribs or for children under 17 sharing their parents' room. Self-parking is $7 per day, valet parking $10 per day. *Pan Pacific, Anaheim;* 1717 South West St.; Anaheim, CA 92802; 999-0990 or 800-327-8585.

PARK INN INTERNATIONAL: Anaheim's newest hotel, it is directly across the street from Disneyland and has 121 charming rooms and suites set in an atmosphere of Old World country charm. Each room has a refrigerator and coffeemaker. The hotel offers complimentary transportation to Disneyland (even though it is well within walking distance), complimentary continental breakfast, and complimentary parking. The establishment also has a pool (with a great view of Disneyland), a gift shop, and guest laundry. Although there is no in-house restaurant, many fine eateries are within walking distance, including *Millie's Country Kitchen*. Doubles are $79 to $129 year-round and suites range from $149 to $189. *Park Inn International*; 1520 South Harbor Blvd., Anaheim, CA 92802; 635-7276 or 800-828-4898.

PEACOCK SUITES: This all-suite establishment, located just a couple of blocks from Disneyland, is possibly the best deal in town. The four-story complex has 143 suites and although the grounds themselves are small, amenities abound. There is a heated pool and two whirlpools, rooftop sundeck, fitness center (which has stationary bikes, and treadmills), gameroom, gift shop, and snack center. The hotel also has a coin laundry and offers overnight dry cleaning. Complimentary transportation to Disneyland is available, and tours to other area attractions can be booked through the concierge. Although the hotel doesn't have its own restaurant, complimentary continental breakfast is served every day. The hotel's spacious one- and two-bedroom suites are handsomely decorated in a green and mauve color scheme and are comfortably furnished with all the conveniences of home. Each has a separate living room with a sofa bed, microwave, refrigerator, two television sets with VCRs, safe, hair dryer, and coffeemaker. One-bedroom suites start at $79, two-bedroom suites start at $139; no charge for additional adults. Nonsmoking suites are available, and some units are equipped for travelers with disabilities. There is a $6 charge for cribs. *Peacock Suites*; 1745 South Haster Street; Anaheim, CA 92802; 535-8255 or 800-522-6402.

QUALITY HOTEL AND CONFERENCE CENTER: There are 284 recently renovated guestrooms at this light brown, nine-story high rise opposite the Anaheim Convention Center, two long blocks south of Disneyland. The lobby is furnished in French Provincial style, and the guestrooms are decorated in rich and soft pastels with light pine furniture. Some of them are designated nonsmoking rooms. Studio suites also are available, each equipped with a mini-refrigerator and coffeemaker. All rooms except studio suites have balconies, and those on the higher floors have fine views. Some rooms and suites are equipped for guests with disabilities. The hotel has a café, a restaurant, and an adjoining lounge that is open nightly. There also are a swimming pool, a salon, a gift shop, and, for the kids, a video-game area. Valet laundry service is available, as well as a coin-operated laundry room. Free shuttles take guests to Disneyland, and airport shuttles are available. So are conference facilities. Room rates run $75 to $95 for doubles in season, $67 to $87 the rest of the year (no charge for children under 18 sharing their parents' room), plus $10 for additional adults and $10 for rollaways; no charge for cribs. Studio suites range from $89 to $105. Parking is $5 per day. *Quality Hotel and Conference Center*; 616 Convention Way; Anaheim, CA 92802; 750-3131 or 800-231-6215.

RAMADA MAINGATE: This handsome, reasonably priced 465-room establishment is located across from Disneyland on Harbor Boulevard. Rooms are located in two towers (one of nine stories, the other eight stories high). Each room has a refrigerator, coffeemaker, and in-room safes are available for $5 (for entire stay). The hotel is served by a wonderful family-style restaurant called *Millie's Country Kitchen*. Other facilities include a pool and spa, a gameroom, and a gift shop; parking is free. Rental car service is available, as are room service, babysitting referrals, complimentary shuttle service to Disneyland, and airport shuttle service. The hotel has meeting and banquet facilities for up to 300. Many of the rooms are designated nonsmoking, and seven are equipped for travelers with disabilities. Rooms may be occupied by up to five people, and rates range from $69 to $109; plus $10 for rollaways. *Ramada Maingate*; 1460 South Harbor Blvd.; Anaheim, CA 92802; 772-6777 or 800-447-4048.

RESIDENCE INN: This delightful, renovated 200-suite lodging, owned by Marriott, is on a side street about two blocks from Disneyland. At first glance, the two- and three-story, stucco buildings with red-tile roofs might be mistaken for a condominium complex. The grounds are beautifully maintained and landscaped with hibiscus, bougainvillea, and park-style benches, and a court is available for tennis, basketball, or volleyball. Inside, the lobby is spacious and inviting, with comfortable couches, chairs, cocktail tables, a fireplace, and a television. Complimentary continental breakfast is served. Facilities include an attractive swimming pool, kids' pool, and whirlpool, as well as a guest laundry. Because this hotel is designed for long-term (as well

as short-term) guests, suites are spacious and feature a breakfast bar, and a fully equipped kitchen with a dishwasher. Several floor plans are available. Special features and services include safe-deposit boxes, valet service, meeting rooms for up to 50 people, free shuttle to Disneyland and the Convention Center, and free hors d'oeuvres Mondays through Thursdays from 5 P.M. to 7 P.M. A single studio starts at $169; a one-bedroom suite starts at $179; a multi-room family suite starts at $199. There's no charge for cribs, but a rollaway costs $10. Lower long-term rates are available. Nonsmoking suites are offered, and some suites are equipped for travelers with disabilities. Some pets are accepted, but it'll cost you: a $275 deposit is required, $75 of which is nonrefundable. *Residence Inn*; 1700 South Clementine St.; Anaheim, CA 92802; 533-3555 or 800-331-3131.

SHERATON-ANAHEIM: With its turrets, towers, and Tudor design, this 490-room hotel looks a bit like a fortress, surrounded by grounds that include two courtyards, a rose garden, a fish pond, and a waterfall. The hotel's 464 rooms and 28 suites are decorated in soft colors, and 190 rooms are exclusively for nonsmoking guests. The rooms—all large, with two queen-size beds or one king—have cable television. Among the suites, one of the most intriguing is the Turret Suite, located in a round tower and furnished with a king-size bed, plus a wet bar. There is a concierge level with the VIP Le Club that offers personalized services such as airline and restaurant reservations, charge phones, a selection of periodicals and games, and a wide-screen television. The hotel has a swimming pool, room service, valet service, laundry facilities, and conference rooms. The ground-transportation system includes transfers to Los Angeles International Airport and John Wayne Airport and a shuttle that pro-

vides free transportation to Disneyland throughout the day. Summer rates are $110 to $160 for doubles and $220 for the Turret Suite; $105 to $145 for doubles and from $175 for the suite the rest of the year (no charge for children under 18 sharing their parents' room), plus $15 for rollaways; no charge for cribs. *Sheraton-Anaheim*; 1015 West Ball Rd.; Anaheim, CA 92802; 778-1700 or 800-331-7251.

STOVALL'S BEST WESTERN HOTELS: *Stovall's* properties are well known locally for their topiary gardens—bushes and trees wired and trimmed in the forms of camels, elephants, bears, and rabbits. Most of the inns provide free shuttles to Disneyland, and some offer coupon savings for Southern California attractions. Airport shuttle buses stop at all the properties, including the two properties described below.

Park Place Inn: This three-story, 199-room establishment is just across the street from Disneyland. The lobby is large and fashionably decorated in Southwestern furniture, wall hangings, and desert hues of beige and pink. Just off the lobby is a gift shop with Disney souvenirs. There's also a pool with an adjacent whirlpool. Room service is available (with food supplied by the restaurant next door), and there is a laundry room. Some rooms are equipped for guests with disabilities. Rates for doubles in season are $75 to $85 for a room with a king-size bed and pull-out sofa or two queen-size beds; and from $70 to $80 for two double beds. There's no charge for children under 18 sharing their parents' room; no charge for cribs; rollaways cost $8. *Park Place Inn*; 1544 South Harbor Blvd.; Anaheim, CA 92802; 776-4800 or 800-854-8175.

Stovall's Inn: The one Stovall property with a bar, it also has two swimming pools, each with an adjacent spa, 290 rooms (several equipped for guests with disabilities), and a banquet room that holds 50. Rates are $70 to $80 for doubles in season, $50 to $60 the rest of the year (no charge for children under 18 sharing their parents' room), plus $8 for rollaways; no charge for cribs. *Stovall's Inn*; 1110 West Katella Ave.; Anaheim, CA 92802; 778-1880 or 800-854-8175.

TRAVELODGE MAINGATE: There are 254 rooms here with either one king-size or two double beds. Two outdoor swimming pools, a guest laundry, and in-room coffeemakers are among the amenities. Nonsmoking rooms are available and there are some rooms designed for travelers with disabilities. Complimentary shuttle service to Disneyland is available. This property doesn't have a restaurant, but an *International House of Pancakes* is right next door. Rates are $55 to $70 for a double; suites are $70 to $85. *Travelodge Maingate*; 1717 South Harbor Blvd.; Anaheim, CA 92802; 635-6550 or 800-826-1616.

Orange County Hotels

Of the cities other than Anaheim where you might lodge while visiting Disneyland, one of the most obvious choices is Buena Park, situated just northwest of Anaheim and accessible via the Santa Ana Freeway (I-5). That's because of its proximity to so many other area attractions.

For upscale accommodations, lodging in Orange County's coastal areas is a good idea. Note: Since coastal hotels do not generally offer the kind of regularly scheduled shuttle service available around Anaheim and Buena Park, it's advisable to have your own car when you stay there.

Here's a selection of some of the better accommodations in both areas. Rates, which were current at press time, are for two adults unless otherwise noted.

BUENA PARK: Located just behind Knott's Berry Farm, this nine-story high-rise hotel has 350 guestrooms decorated in peach tones. Rooms have balconies (albeit small ones), and there's a good-size swimming pool that's nicely landscaped with shrubs and trees, and surrounded by chaise lounges and umbrella-shaded tables. The hotel has a coffee shop, a specialty restaurant, a nightclub called *Shoe Bops* that features 1950s and 1960s music, and a top-floor banquet room with a fine view of Orange County. There's also a gameroom and gift shop. Year-round rates are $85 to $95 for standard doubles, $95 to $105 for Executive Service doubles (no charge for children under 12 sharing their parents' room), and $12 for rollaways; no charge for cribs. *Buena Park*; 7675 Crescent Ave.; Buena Park, CA 90620; 995-1111; 800-422-4444 from California; 800-854-8792 from the rest of the United States; and 800-325-8734 from Canada.

DANA POINT RESORT: The 350 rooms at this Cape Cod Victorian-style resort have a picture-perfect setting high on a bluff overlooking the 2,500-slip Dana Point Yacht Harbor, the Pacific Ocean, and Doheny State Beach. Surrounding the resort are 42 lushly landscaped acres of park and lawn and an abundance of flowers. The hotel's lobby and other public areas are noteworthy for the truly artistic, exotic floral arrangements created by in-house florist Michael Berbae. The ocean views from the guestrooms, the restaurant, and the two lounges are splendid. Guestrooms are decorated in tropical peach, mauve, blue, and green hues. Amenities include terraces, twice-daily maid service, live plants, two phones, and lounging robes. Some rooms are equipped for guests with disabilities. There

are 17 suites. Recreational facilities include two pools, three whirlpools, a health club and Nautilus gym, massage, croquet, kite flying, bicycle riding, and lawn games. Basketball courts, par-course jogging trails, and a playground are just steps away. Dana Point is the perfect spot for whale watching (in season), parasailing, deep-sea fishing, sailing, and windsurfing. The concierge can help guests arrange activities. Club Cowabunga, for children ages 5 through 12, offers day and evening programs, including arts and crafts. The daytime program, which costs $35 per child, runs from 10 A.M. to 4 P.M. and includes lunch. The evening program, which costs $15 per child, runs from 6:30 P.M. to 9:30 P.M. and includes dinner. Children's programs are offered daily during the summer and on weekends year-round. There's complimentary transportation to the San Juan Capistrano Amtrak depot, where you can get a train to Anaheim. Rates for doubles are $189 to $239 (inquire about money-saving packages, which include whale watching, tennis, and more); no charge for children under 16 sharing their parents' room; $20 per extra adult. *Dana Point Resort*; 25135 Park Lantern; Dana Point, CA 92629; 661-5000 or 800-545-7483.

EMBASSY SUITES: This hacienda-style hotel, located just one block north of Knott's Berry Farm, has several features that make it attractive to family travelers. All 202 rooms are actually suites with a bedroom (one king or two double beds) and a separate living room with a double hide-a-bed. There's a telephone and a color television in each room. Also, all rooms offer galley-type kitchen facilities and conference-dining tables. Rooms are arranged attractively around an open-atrium courtyard with Spanish-style fountains, swimming pool, and whirlpool. There is a gift shop and a restaurant that is open for lunch and dinner. The hotel hosts two hours of free cocktails (and billiards) nightly in the lounge, and provides complimentary, American-style, cooked-to-order breakfasts. One of the nicer aspects: The hotel maintains a no-tipping policy. There are three suites with special facilities for travelers with disabilities. Shuttle service is available to the Los Angeles and Orange County airports, and the hotel's courtesy limousine will take guests to Disneyland and Knott's Berry Farm. Rates are $137 for a double year-round, $15 for each additional adult. Children under 13 stay free in their parents' room. There is no charge for cribs. Ask about special packages and weekend rates. *Embassy Suites*; 7762 Beach Blvd.; Buena Park, CA 90620; 739-5600 or 800-362-2779.

FOUR SEASONS: Set on about five acres of landscaped gardens overlooking Newport Harbor and the Pacific Ocean, this luxurious, 285-room, high-rise hotel is across the street from the Newport Center Fashion Island shopping complex. The property is managed by Four Seasons, the same company that manages such elegant hostelries as San Francisco's *Clift* hotel and the *Pierre* in New York. From its lovely beige lobby to its extra-spacious, luxuriously appointed guestrooms (all with balconies), this hotel is marked by a refined California elegance. Antiques and fine works of art fill the public areas. Outdoors, you can dine casually by the beautifully land-scaped pool and whirlpool area, or enjoy a game of tennis on one of two lighted courts; the hotel also boasts *Pavilion*, a first-rate restaurant. Other facilities include another restaurant, lounge and cocktail bar, and a health club. Guestrooms come with such amenities as twice-daily maid service, bath-robes, and a spacious vanity/dressing area separate from the bath. There are nonsmok-ing floors, as well as rooms for guests with disabilities. Rates for doubles are $245 to $285 (no charge for children under 18 sharing their parents' room), plus $30 per extra adult; no charge for cribs or rollaways. Suites start at $335 and offer partial ocean and mountain views. Parking costs $13.50 per day. *Four Seasons*; 690 Newport Center Dr.; Newport Beach, CA 92660; 759-0808 or 800-332-3442.

HYATT NEWPORTER: This renovated local landmark resort hotel was built on what was a family-owned ranch until the early 1960s. The hotel's rose-beige exterior has French doors and windows that embody the Califor-nia-Mediterranean theme. The resort has 410 guestrooms in several distinctive room set-tings: Some rooms surround a courtyard and have views of the golf course and Newport Bay; terrace rooms surround the lower pool and garden, and have views of the bay; rooms in the main building have convenient access to the hotel's public areas and upper pools; and rooms in the Balboa Building overlook the golf course. For true luxury, there are four villas, each equipped with three bedrooms, three baths, a fireplace, and a pri-vate yard with swimming pool. Recreational opportunities abound: There's a nine-hole golf course, a jogging trail, three large swim-ming pools, three whirlpools, volleyball and shuffleboard courts, a health and fitness cen-ter, and about 26 acres of landscaped grounds. Guests also have privileges at the adjoining private John Wayne Tennis Club, which has 16 courts lighted for night play. The hotel has several shops and an entertain-ment lounge. Its restaurant offers indoor din-ing as well as outdoor patio service and serves traditional American cuisine during the day. At night, the eatery shifts gears and fea-tures Northern Italian cuisine and entertain-ment in the form of singing waiters and wait-resses. There is complimentary transporta-tion to Balboa Island, to Fashion Island, and to the John Wayne (Orange County) Airport, where you can take a shuttle bus to the *Dis-neyland Hotel*. Rates are $129 for singles, $144 for doubles; weekend rates are $115 for both; $300 to $450 for suites (no charge for children under 18 sharing their parents' room), plus $15 per extra adult; no charge for cribs or rollaways. *Hyatt Newporter*; 1107 Jamboree Rd.; Newport Beach, CA 92660; 729-1234 or 800-233-1234.

NEWPORT BEACH MARRIOTT: The charms of this 520-room establishment are many, but foremost are the views of Balboa Bay and the Pacific Ocean, the eight tennis courts (lighted for night play), two good-size swimming pools and two spas, and the location across the street from Newport Center Fashion Island, with its 150 boutiques, department stores, and restaurants. The hotel also boasts a fine restaurant with an open-air terrace, plus a pleasant bar. A concierge is available to help with reservations for airlines, car rentals, tours, and other travel plans. The hotel also offers a gift shop, free transportation to the John Wayne Airport, complimentary under-ground parking for 600 cars, and a health club with saunas (free to hotel guests). Guestrooms are located in two towers (one has a top-story cocktail lounge with a fabulous view of the Pacific Ocean), and in two low-rise wings; they come with double, queen-, or king-size beds. Some rooms are equipped for travelers with disabilities, and small pets are permitted. Rates are $149 to $169 for doubles and $250 and up for suites; no charge for children under 13 sharing their parents' room or for cribs or rollaways. *Newport Beach Marriott*; 900 New-port Center Dr.; Newport Beach, CA 92660; 640-4000 or 800-228-9290.

More Southern California Lodgings

Some truly world class places to stay await you just outside Orange County. The following are especially worth checking into—literally—when you leave the Disneyland area for forays into other parts of Southern California.

Around Los Angeles

BILTMORE: Named a historical landmark by the city's Cultural Board in 1969, this four-star grand old hotel is quite spectacular. In the main galleria, recessed lighting illuminates the vaulted ceiling and friezes designed by Italian muralist Giovanni Smeraldi in the 1920s. The lobby features a working marble fountain, tapestries, silks, overstuffed furniture, and antique tables. Three distinctive trompe l'oeil murals were commissioned for the lobby and the court café. There are 683 extra-spacious guestrooms and all are luxuriously appointed with traditional and French furnishings, writing desks, armoires, plush carpeting, and matching tile. The hotel, which overlooks gardenlike Pershing Square in downtown Los Angeles, has some fine restaurants on the premises including *Bernard's*. There also is a health club with an indoor pool. Some guest quarters are equipped for travelers with disabilities. There is SuperShuttle service ($12 per person) to the Los Angeles Airport, and Shuttle Columbia buses bring guests to Disneyland ($62 for adults, including admission to the park). Rates are $215 to $275 for doubles, and $325 to $2,000 for suites year-round (no charge for children under 18 sharing their par-

ents' room), plus $30 per extra adult (charge includes rollaway); no charge for cribs. Ask about special weekend packages starting at $89 per night. *Biltmore*; 506 South Grand Ave.; Los Angeles, CA 90071; 213-624-1011 or 800-245-8673.

CENTURY PLAZA: This Westin hotel is the centerpiece of Century City, an ultramodern city-within-a-city built on property that once was Tom Mix's ranch and, later, Twentieth Century-Fox Studio's back lot. The tall buildings of this development west of Beverly Hills, between Olympic and Santa Monica boulevards, stand like great exclamation marks against the West Los Angeles skyline. The hotel is actually comprised of two buildings connected by an elegant marble corridor that houses a portion of the hotel's $4 million art collection. One is a half-moon-shaped edifice, 19 stories high, with 750 rooms with king-size or double beds, oak armoires concealing a television, and large, private balconies. The other building, a 30-story tower, has 322 extra-spacious, 570-square-foot guestrooms. Tower rooms have marble baths, wet bars, and private balconies. There is a special children's program for Tower guests, including a box of welcome toys at check-in and milk and cookies at bedtime. For $15 per day, guests can rent a VCR, including videos and a Nintendo game system. The hotel boasts several good restaurants, and two good-size outdoor

swimming pools, with an adjacent landscaped sundeck. There is a mini-fitness room and guests have access to the facilities of a nearby health club for a nominal fee. Oskar J's tours to Disneyland ($63, including transportation and admission; $59 for children 3 to 11) are available as well. Across the street, and accessible via an underground passageway, is the ABC Entertainment Center, home of the Shubert Theater, a handful of dining spots, and four movie houses. The *Century Plaza* is a popular spot for conventions. Double rooms cost $225 in the main building, $280 in the tower. Suites are $250 to $3,000. No charge for children under 18 sharing their parents' room; no charge for rollaways. *Century Plaza;* 2025 Ave. of the Stars; Los Angeles, CA 90067; 310-277-2000 or 800-228-3000.

HYATT REGENCY LONG BEACH: Located 15 miles south of downtown Los Angeles and 30 minutes from Disneyland, it has 521 newly renovated rooms with great views of the beach or the harbor. There is a large pool with an adjacent ten-foot whirlpool. Fifteen rooms are designed for travelers with disabilities, with oversize bathrooms, grab rails, and wide entrance doors. Rates are $79 to $164 for doubles year-round (no charge for children under 18 occupying their parents' room); no charge for rollaways or cribs. *Hyatt Regency Long Beach*; 200 South Pine Ave.; Long Beach, CA 90802; 310-491-1234 or 800-233-1234.

MIKADO BEST WESTERN: This 58-room, two-story establishment is located between Laurel and Coldwater canyons in one of the most scenic sections of Los Angeles. Rooms are nicely decorated, and have two double beds or a single king- or queen-size bed. The tiled, kidney-shaped swimming pool is quite handsome, and a whirlpool is nearby. Other facilities include a steakhouse, sushi bar, and cocktail lounge. Breakfast is complimentary for all guests. Rates are $85 to $90 for doubles, plus $10 per additional person (no charge for children under 12); there's a $10 charge for rollaways or cribs. There are no rooms equipped for guests with disabilities. *Mikado Best Western*; 12600 Riverside Dr.; North Hollywood, CA 91607; 818-763-9141; 800-826-2759, 800-528-1234 for central reservations, or 800-433-2239 in California.

SAFARI INN: While not particularly convenient to Disneyland, this establishment in Burbank is a good bet if you're planning to visit the Burbank studios, and the spacious location in the valley gives a feeling of openness that is not found in many other properties discussed here. There are 103 rooms in a two-story main building and another three-story structure with an elevator, plus a swimming pool, whirlpool, cocktail lounge, and restaurant. Rates range from $48 to $80 year-round, plus $10 per additional person (no charge for infants); a $10 charge for rollaways, $5 for cribs. There are no rooms equipped for travelers with disabilities. *Safari Inn*; 1911 West Olive Ave.; Burbank, CA 91506; 818-845-8586 or 800-782-4373.

SHERATON UNIVERSAL: Location is the reason to stay in this 442-room hotel on the grounds of Universal Studios: When you lodge here, you're at the official hotel of Universal Studios, and you're well positioned for forays into downtown Los Angeles, Westwood, and the suburbs on the northern end of metropolitan Southern California—that is, Beverly Hills, Santa Monica, Malibu, and the like. You're also a stone's throw from Universal City Walk, an outdoor mall, which features fun shops, restaurants, and movie theaters. (Disneyland, however, is about an hour away by freeway.) Rooms in the 20-story tower have views of the San Fernando Valley and the Hollywood Hills; those in the three-story Lanai Wing are close to the pool, the whirlpool, and the nearby sauna and gameroom. All guestrooms are fitted out with irons and ironing boards, coffeemakers, mini-bars, and small safes, and a full-service concierge is located in the hotel lobby. There are rooms equipped for travelers with disabilities. The hotel has a guest laundry, valet service, various shops, and several eating and drinking

spots. Transportation is available to the Los Angeles Airport via SuperShuttle (about $13 per person), and Starline-Grayline tour buses will take you to Disneyland. The fare, which includes park admission, is about $63 for adults and $54 for children 3 to 11. There is free transportation to Universal Studios. Room rates are $180 to $195 year-round, depending on the type of bed and the floor you occupy (no charge for children under 17 sharing their parents' room), plus $20 per extra adult, $20 for rollaways; no charge for cribs. Parking is $9.50 per day. *Sheraton Universal*; 333 Universal Terrace Pkwy.; Universal City, CA 91608; 818-980-1212 or 800-325-3535.

UNIVERSAL CITY HILTON: This 24-story glass tower, designed by architect William Pereira, is located next to Universal Studios. Appointments in the 456 guestrooms and suites are luxurious and include marble baths. Some rooms are equipped for travelers with disabilities. Other facilities and services include a heated outdoor pool, an exercise room, a whirlpool, a transportation and tour desk, valet service, concierge service, a parking garage, a gift shop, and a cocktail lounge. The hotel's restaurant, *Café Sierra*, is housed under a beautiful glass-domed pavilion. SuperShuttle provides service to the Los Angeles Airport. Rates for doubles year-round are $125 to $145 (children under 18 stay free when sharing their parents' room), plus $20 per extra adult, $20 for rollaways; no charge for cribs. *Universal City Hilton*; 555 Universal Terrace Pkwy.; Universal City, CA 91608; 818-506-2500 or 800-HILTONS.

Beverly Hills, Bel Air, & Santa Monica

BEL-AIR: The belle of fashionable Bel Air, this exclusive hideaway, just north of UCLA, has attracted movie stars—Gary Cooper, Grace Kelly, and Sophia Loren among them—since it opened in the 1920s. The 92 lavishly decorated rooms fill one- and two-story mission-style buildings and bungalows spread across 11½ impeccable acres. A member of Relais & Chateaux, the hotel has a restaurant, dining terrace, and bar, as well as a swimming pool and 24-hour fitness center. It's hard to imagine a more luxurious—or secluded—getaway in the middle of a big city. Rates range from $315 to $435 for doubles and $495 to $2,500 for suites year-round; no charge for rollaways or cribs. Parking is $12.50 per day. Facilities

designed for guests with disabilities are available; although there are significant distances to traverse on foot to get around the hotel grounds, all of these areas are accessible to wheelchairs. *Bel-Air*; 701 Stone Canyon Rd.; Los Angeles, CA 90077; 310-472-1211 or 800-648-4097 from outside California.

FOUR SEASONS BEVERLY HILLS: Located in a quiet residential neighborhood, this 285-room hotel is a blend of casual Southern California and elegant Beverly Hills. Designed in the style of a grand European manor house, it is surrounded by flower gardens. *Gardens* restaurant offers California cuisine with a French influence. Afternoon tea is served at *Windows,* and *The Café* is an informal restaurant. The outdoor pool and whirlpool are perched on a beautifully landscaped terrace. The health club features exercise equipment and personal trainers, and the hotel also offers massages. Each guestroom has French doors that open onto a private balcony. Complimentary use of fax machines, VCRs, and cellular phones is available if requested when your reservation is made. Other amenities include multi-line phones, voice mail, twice-daily maid service, and terrycloth bathrobes. Ten rooms are designed for guests with disabilities. Rates start at $295 for doubles year-round; $450 to $3,000 for one- to three-bedroom suites; rollaways are $30. Weekend packages are available. *Four Seasons Beverly Hills*; 300 South Doheny Dr.; Los Angeles, CA 90048; 310-273-2222, 800-332-3442 from the United States, or 800-268-6282 from Canada.

HOLIDAY INN BAYVIEW: With 309 rooms, this is one of the nicest Holiday Inns in Southern California, and is located just a block from the beach, and near some of Santa Monica's most popular shopping and dining spots. Many of the rooms offer breathtaking ocean views, and the hotel also features two pools and whirlpools, a gift shop, newsstand, full service beauty salon, a restaurant, and lobby bar with pool service. Rates for doubles range from $113 to $163 (plus $10 for each additional adult over 18); suites are $250 per night. *Holiday Inn Bayview*; 530 Pico Blvd., Santa Monica, CA 90405; 310-399-9344 or 800-Holiday.

PENINSULA BEVERLY HILLS: European marble, polished wood, sumptuous antiques, and local artwork are just some of the impressive refinements here. This property—with 195 rooms, suites, and villas—is among the newest in Beverly Hills, situated in meticulously landscaped gardens with fountains. Suites are equipped with a private fax machine, a VCR, and a CD player. Sixteen rooms and suites are located in five villas, some of which offer private terraces and fireplaces. The *Living Room*, a lobby lounge, serves traditional afternoon tea; the *Club Bar* serves drinks and hors d'oeuvres; and the *Belvedere* is a topnotch continental restaurant. A health spa features a weight room, lap pool, whirlpool, steamroom, sauna, sundeck, and massage. There also is a terrace dining room as well as 12 poolside cabanas equipped with telephones. The business center offers secretarial services, A/V equipment, photocopiers, and computers. On every floor, a 24-hour room attendant is at guests' beck and call. Express checkout is available. Room rates range from $300 to $330; suites are $350 to $3,000. *Peninsula Beverly Hills*; 9882 Santa Monica Blvd.; Beverly Hills, CA 90212; 310-273-4888 or 800-462-7899.

SHUTTERS ON THE BEACH: This 198-room, five-star hotel hugs the beach in Santa Monica and is within walking distance of the city's most popular sights. The hotel has 24-hour concierge and room service, an on-premises laundry and dry cleaning and twice-daily maid service. There also are a pool, sundeck, fitness center, two oceanfront restaurants, and a bar that features live jazz music Thursday through Saturday nights. Rates for doubles range from $270 to $450 (plus $50 for each additional person over 6; children under 6 free); suites start at $625. The hotel doesn't have rollaways and cribs are $35. Valet parking is $16 per day (there's no self-parking). *Shutters on the Beach*; One Pico Blvd., Santa Monica, CA 90405; 310-458-0030 or 1-800-334-9000.

Around San Diego

HANALEI: Centrally located in the Hotel Circle area and convenient to Sea World, this contemporary eight-story high-rise, on ten acres landscaped with palm trees, succulents, and waterfalls, has 400 cheerful rooms and 12 suites, decorated in Hawaiian floral design. Twelve of the rooms can accommodate guests with disabilities. The hotel has a heated pool, a whirlpool, a laundry facility, and a trio of wining-and-dining spots on the premises.

Six tennis courts and two golf courses are next door, and guests can enjoy visitors' privileges at the nearby Mission Valley Health Center for $7 per day. The club has racquetball and tennis courts, a weight room, a masseur and masseuse, and a pool large enough for swimming laps. In July and August, an authentic Hawaiian luau is held nightly. Starline-Gray Line and other tour bus services go to Disneyland, and the fare for adults is about $60 (including admission to the park). Room rates are $109 to $140 for doubles year-round (no charge for children under 18 sharing their parents' room), plus $10 per additional adult, $10 for rollaways, and no charge for cribs. *Hanalei*; 2270 Hotel Circle North; San Diego, CA 92108; 619-297-1101 or 800-882-0858.

HUMPHREY'S HALF MOON INN: This low-slung, Polynesian-style hideaway on Shelter Island has 182 rooms, many with private patios or balconies and fine views over the bay or a marina full of sleek boats; there are 30 suites with kitchens. The heated, Olympic-size pool (and the adjacent whirlpool) are focal points of activity, but the complex also has lush gardens, a restaurant, a putting green, bicycles, Ping-Pong, and a three-slip marina. Sportfishing facilities are within walking distance. Three rooms are equipped for travelers with disabilities. Transportation to the airport, train station, and bus depot is provided. Starline-Gray Line tour buses also provide transportation to Disneyland; the fare, about $60 for adults, includes park admission. Room rates for two people range from $89 to $249 year-round (no charge for children under 17 sharing their parents' room), $119 to $249 for suites;

$10 for rollaways; cribs are free. *Humphrey's Half Moon Inn*; 2303 Shelter Island Dr.; San Diego, CA 92106; 619-224-3411 or 800-542-7400.

LA VALENCIA: This graceful dowager of a Spanish-style hotel, all pink stucco and Spanish archways and located in the jewellike coastal community of La Jolla (part of the city of San Diego, though 12 miles north of it), has drawn Hollywood's elite for generations. Rudolf Valentino stayed here, and so did Greta Garbo, Lillian Gish, Ramon Navarro, and, more recently, Dustin Hoffman and others. The hotel has 103 guestrooms and 11 suites. Though it isn't on the ocean per se, it does command a glorious view of La Jolla Cove and the Pacific. The lobby, which occupies the seventh floor—the hotel is built into a hillside—is the kind of room that encourages lingering, and many guests do. You can sit with a glass of premium California wine, listen to piano music, and gaze out through the large windows at one of those incomparable Pacific sunsets. The hotel also has a swimming pool, sundeck, whirlpool, a small health spa with exercise equipment and a sauna, and a handful of spots where you can have cocktails or a leisurely meal; the *Whaling Bar* reputedly serves the best Bloody Marys in San Diego; the *Tropical Patio* is great for lunch; and the tenth-floor *Sky Room*, which has a wonderful

ocean view, is perfect for a romantic dinner. Rates are $160 to $190 year-round for doubles, plus $10 per additional adult; suites range from $375 to $600. *La Valencia*; 1132 Prospect St.; La Jolla, CA 92037; 619-454-0771 or 800-451-0772.

SAN DIEGO MARRIOTT: The major asset here is the 26-acre waterfront location, overlooking San Diego Bay and adjacent to the San Diego Convention Center. The two 25-story elliptical mirrored glass towers hold 1,355 guestrooms, most of which have fine bay views. All 681 rooms in one tower have balconies. Sixty-nine suites are available, and several rooms are equipped for guests with disabilities. An especially nice feature is the landscaped pool area. Guests who arrive by boat can tie up at the full-service, 446-slip marina, where telephone and cable television hookup, room service, laundry, and valet services are all available. Other recreation facilities include tennis courts and a health club. There are three restaurants, and extensive conference and convention facilities. Starline-Gray Line tour buses go to Disneyland ($60 per adult, including park admission). Rates for doubles are $175 to $200; suites range from $325 to $2,200. There is no charge for additional persons in the same room; no charge for rollaways or cribs. *San Diego Marriott*; 333 West Harbor Dr.; San Diego, CA 92101-7709; 619-234-1500 or 800-228-9290.

U.S. GRANT: Opened by the son of the 18th president of the United States in 1910, this elegant 220-room and 60-suite hotel has the distinction of being listed on the National Register of Historical Places. Ulysses S. Grant, Jr. even lived here for ten years until his death in 1929. Other notable guests have included Albert Einstein and JFK. The hotel's rooms are furnished with stately 18th-century reproductions and feature beautiful mahogany beds. Ten rooms are equipped for guests with disabilities. The *Grant Grill* is the establishment's popular restaurant, with an adjacent lounge. Afternoon tea is served in the lobby Tuesdays through Saturdays. The hotel also has a fitness center with a great view of downtown and offers access to the San Diego Athletic Club, as well as golf and tennis privileges at the Singing Hills Country Club. Rates are $155 to $175 for doubles year-round; suites start at $245. There is a $15 per person charge for each additional adult (no charge for children under 18 occupying their parents' room). Rollaways and cribs are $10; so is parking. *U.S. Grant*; 326 Broadway, San Diego, CA 92101; 619-232-3121 or 800-237-5029.

Special Places

Even in Southern California, that stronghold of look-alike hotel towers, it's possible to find half a dozen unique hostelries worth traveling the distance to experience.

BEVERLY HILLS HOTEL: The city's legendary Pink Palace reopened its doors in June 1995 after a 2½ year, $100 million restoration that left it looking 83 years younger (much as it did when it first opened, though there is air-conditioning now). A combination of California's Mission Revival architecture outside and late Art Deco inside, it sits on 12 lush acres at the top of Rodeo Drive. The posh lobby has two working fireplaces, curved walls and ceilings, towering plants, and alcoves filled with overstuffed chairs and chaises in pink, green, peach, and apricot hues. The 194 rooms, suites, and bungalows are larger now (there used to be 253 of them) and feature a sitting area, mini-bar, stereo system, at least three telephones (and everything else necessary to clinch a major movie deal), two TVs, Ralph Lauren bed and bath linens, a butler-service button, granite and marble baths, and a walk-in closet. Some have a balcony, terrace, patio, or fireplace. Amenities include 24-hour room service, an extensive video and CD library, and concierge and laundry service. Guests enjoy exclusive use of a competition-size pool, 21 private cabanas, a whirlpool, and a poolside café; two lighted tennis courts supervised by a tennis pro; a fitness center; and jogging trails. Dining possibilities include the world-famous *Polo Lounge*, the new *Polo Grill*, and the informal *Fountain Coffee Shop*. For afternoon tea, drinks, or the chance to see a fabulous hand-painted gold-leaf piano, there's the *Tea Lounge*. Rates for a double room range from $300 to $350; suites start at $595. There are rooms for guests with disabilities. Nonsmoking rooms are available. The drive from Disneyland takes an hour to an hour and half on I-405. An irresistible bit of trivia: Elizabeth Taylor has honeymooned here with six of her seven husbands (the exception was Nicky Hilton). *Beverly Hills Hotel*; 9641 Sunset Blvd.; Beverly Hills, CA 90210; 310-276-2251 or 800-283-8885.

DEL CORONADO: Boasting both the gracious look of the last century and many of the amenities of the present one, this sprawling oceanside establishment, on the Coronado Peninsula just across a bridge from San Diego, is a National Historic Landmark. Twelve U.S. presidents have been guests here, and legend has it that Edward, the Duke of Windsor, met Wallis Simpson here. You will recognize the place immediately by its red roof, turrets, cupolas, and ornate jigsaw-cut wooden trim—all the rage back in 1888, when the hotel first opened its doors. There are all sorts of intriguing touches inside. For instance, just outside the *Prince of Wales Room* is one of the old fire hoses that protected the building before the installation of sprinklers in the early 1900s. The *Crown Coronet Room*, whose Sunday brunch is locally cherished, has an Oregon pine ceiling put together with wooden pegs instead of nails. And the lobby, paneled in dark woods and lighted by a Bavarian crystal chandelier, has an old-fashioned Otis birdcage elevator that still functions. There are enough similar points of interest in the hotel to fill up an informative audiocassette, which you can rent in the lobby gift

shop for $5. Better yet, the hotel offers guided tours on Thursdays through Saturdays for $10 per person. A historian will take you throughout the grounds and main building, including the hotel's majestic turret. The "Hotel Del" also has all kinds of sports facilities, including two huge swimming pools, whirlpools for men and women, and six lighted tennis courts on the premises, plus pedal boats and sailboats for rent on Glorietta Bay right in front of the hotel. Golf is available half a mile away. Guestrooms total 700—more than half of them in the original building, the others in the modern seven-story Ocean Towers and the three-story Poolside Wing. Several are specially equipped for guests with disabilities. Each room in the main building is unique, with decor and furnishings in the Queen Anne and Victorian styles. Rates are $169 to $199 for doubles, depending on the room's size, location, and view; suites range from $309 to $649; plus $25 per extra person (no charge for children under 16; no charge for cribs). One-bedroom apartments are available for $889 per night and two-bedroom apartments are $1,600 per night. Guest parking is $10 per day. The hotel is a 90-minute drive south from Disneyland. *Del Coronado*; 1500 Orange Ave.; Coronado, CA 92118; 619-522-8000 or 800-HOTEL-DEL.

INDUSTRY HILLS SHERATON: Though just 25 miles and 35 minutes north (nestled between the San Bernardino and Pomona freeways, in the City of Industry) by car from Disneyland, this resort is a world away. The multi-level atrium is beautiful, and the guestrooms, which were recently renovated, are large and well appointed and look less like hotel rooms than bedrooms at home. They all have private balconies with spectacular views of the San Gabriel Mountains and Valley. The real lure, however, is an array of sporting facil-

ities varied enough to warrant all sorts of accolades beginning with "paradise for the sports lover." The resort boasts two 18-hole golf courses, one of them ranked by *Golf Digest* in the top 25 public courses in the United States (see *Sports*); additionally, there's a lighted putting green laid out on a hillside. There also are 17 lighted tennis courts (including a center court with room for 2,000 spectators), plus a hitting net and facilities for videotaping (see *Sports*), an equestrian center, a warm-up pool plus an Olympic-size pool with a 33-foot-high diving platform, a whirlpool, steamrooms, and locker facilities. Considering the facilities, the prices are not out of line—$130 to $140 for a double room year-round, $160 to $325 for suites (no extra charge for children under 17 sharing their parents' room), plus $15 for any rollaways you might require, plus whatever fees you incur for use of the sporting facilities, few of which are included in the basic room rates. Cribs are free. Several package deals are available. *Industry Hills Sheraton*; One Industry Hills Pkwy.; City of Industry, CA 91744; 818-965-0861 or 800-524-4557.

RANCHO VALENCIA: Twenty-five miles north of San Diego and only five minutes by car from the seaside communities of Del Mar and La Jolla, *Rancho Valencia* sits on 40 lush acres filled with flowering plants and citrus groves overlooking the San Dieguito Valley. Spanish and Mediterranean in design, this resort, a member of Relais & Chateaux, harks back to the grand old Southern California estates from the 1920s and 1930s. It has 43 suites in 21 casitas. Each suite has whitewashed beams, tile floors and counters, a cathedral ceiling, Berber carpets, ceiling fan, wood-burning fireplace, and private garden patio; modern accoutrements include telephone, television, video player, mini-bar, refrigerator, coffeemaker, a large bathroom, and a walk-in closet. Choose from a Del Mar suite (with the bedroom raised above the living room) or a Rancho Santa Fe suite (with a separate bedroom). The resort's dining room specializes in Mediterranean-California cuisine and serves three meals a day, plus Sunday brunch, inside or alfresco (a children's menu is always available). Poolside and in-room dining also are available, and a carafe of fresh-squeezed juice and a newspaper are delivered to your door each morning. Tennis enthusiasts will find 18 tennis courts (free to guests), not to mention eight tennis pros, assorted clinics, and even private classes for kids. Other facilities include two outdoor heated pools (one's a lap pool), three whirlpools, championship croquet, bikes, and hiking trails. The fitness center has workout equipment (free to guests), personal training, and nutritional consultation. Separate spa facilities for men and women offer everything from Swedish or shiatsu massage and reflex-

ology to aromatherapy treatments to manicures and pedicures. Golf privileges are honored at three nearby courses. Suites range from $315 to $450; no extra charge for an additional person, rollaway, or crib. Ask about tennis, golf, or romantic-getaway packages. It is a one-hour drive southeast of Disneyland. Exit I-5 at Villa de la Valle and head east to El Camino Real, then south to San Dieguito Rd.; from here travel east again and follow the signs. *Rancho Valencia,* 5921 Valencia Circle; Rancho Santa Fe, CA 92067-4126; 619-756-1123 or 800-548-3664.

RITZ-CARLTON, LAGUNA NIGUEL: Located on the southern Orange County coast, this magnificent Mediterranean villa-style resort hotel sits high on a bluff overlooking the Pacific Ocean. The view from the lounge and from many of the 362 guestrooms and 31 suites (all of which have French doors and balconies) is sensational; on a clear day it is possible to see Catalina Island, some 37 miles away. The hotel's marble floors, handwoven area carpets, 19th-century English crystal chandeliers, and 18th-century Belgian tapestries make a visit worthwhile even if you don't plan to stay overnight. In addition to a lovely two-mile stretch of beach (which is open to the public), there are two pools and two whirlpools; an 18-hole golf course designed by Robert Trent Jones, Jr.; several tennis courts; a fitness center (with classes, lockers, sauna, whirlpool, steamroom, exercise room, massage, and personal-care salons); and a volleyball court. The *Dining Room* is one of Orange County's finest restaurants. Rates for doubles range from $215 to $415, depending on location and view, plus $50 per extra adult (no charge for cribs or for children under 18 sharing their parents' room). Suites start at $500. Twelve rooms are equipped for guests with disabilities. The hotel is a 35-minute drive southeast from Disneyland. *Ritz-Carlton, Laguna Niguel*; 33533 Ritz-Carlton Dr.; Dana Point, CA 92629; 240-2000 or 800-241-3333.

SEAL BEACH INN AND GARDENS: Ranked by *Country Inns* magazine as one of the top country inns in the United States, this place is an utter delight, all 23 rooms of it—full of Victorian antiques, old prints, oriental carpets, and vibrant colors. There are brass chandeliers from an old house in New Orleans and stained-glass windows from Scotland. The grounds are ornamented with a red telephone booth from England, lampposts that stood on the streets of nearby Long Beach in the 1930s, a 300-year-old iron fountain from France, a tiny swimming pool and three whirlpools, and gardens that bloom profusely throughout the year. In the *Tea Room*, a lavish complimentary breakfast, prepared by the inn's chef, is served on tables covered with lace cloths. And in the library

next door, you can play chess, checkers, or Scrabble. Most guestrooms have built-in bookcases and kitchens that are fully equipped, right down to teacups. Some of the larger rooms can accommodate more than two people. Rates are $118 for cottage rooms, which face the street. The 12 Royal Villas, most of which have fireplaces, cost $155 to $165. These are charming suites with handcarved tables, satin bedspreads, and lace curtains. King suites are $185 and the penthouse costs $255. For a real treat, inquire about the inn's Chocolate Love-in or Gondola Getaway packages. Extra family members, regardless of age, cost $10 each; non-family members are $20 each. Children are welcome, but given the value of the antiques, it's probably not a good place to bring curious toddlers. The inn is located a short walk from the beach, the town's fishing pier, and several shops and restaurants; it is a 25-minute drive southwest from Disneyland. *Seal Beach Inn and Gardens*; 212 Fifth St.; Seal Beach, CA 90740; 310-493-2416.

Bed-and-Breakfast

Bed-and-breakfast accommodations have become increasingly popular in the United States, and anyone who has stayed in one knows how convenient they can be. For they not only provide a comfortable room, but also prepare you to meet the day with at least a continental breakfast under your belt. Sometimes these private quarters are furnished with antiques, or they have fireplaces or fabulous sea views. Some have private baths; some can accommodate a couple alone, while others welcome whole families. The common denominator is homey, personal ambience not available in even the best hotels. Here are some of our Southern California favorites.

BELLE BLEU INN BY THE SEA: Located on scenic Ocean Avenue in Santa Monica, this quaint, 20-room bed-and-breakfast has the feel of being off the beaten path, though it is smack in the middle of Santa Monica. The rooms are spacious and some have access to a common kitchen, which is separate from the actual rooms. The establishment also provides a morning meal that is more than continental fare but less than a full breakfast. Rates for doubles are $65 to $85 (plus $5 for each additional person, including children). There also are three suites, which have kitchens and start at $85; *Belle Bleu Inn by the Sea*; 1670 Ocean Ave.; Santa Monica, CA; 90401; 310-393-2363.

CHANNEL ROAD INN: Just a hop, skip, and a jump from the beach in Santa Monica, this charming 14-room hideaway appears to be a large country house at first glance. Indeed, it was built in 1910 on nearby Second Street, and was moved to its present location in the 1980s when it became a bed-and-breakfast. Each room is unique and features a variety of late 19th-century antiques. Although the inn does not have a restaurant, there's a dining room, where a full breakfast is served daily, as well as a library where wine and cheese are served from 5 P.M. to 7 P.M. each evening. The inn also features a whirlpool. Rates for doubles range from $85 to $200 year-round

(no charge for children under 18 sharing their parents' room), plus a $15 per person charge for each additional adult. *Channel Road Inn*; 219 Channel Road, Santa Monica, CA 90402; 310-459-1920.

THE COTTAGE: This establishment offers accommodations for up to three people in a quaint, two-bedroom cottage, as well as in the Garden Room of the main house, which sits at the end of a cul-de-sac. Just outside of the cottage, you'll find an herb garden and birdbaths. The cottage itself—which has its own private entrance and patio—is filled with antiques and features a living room (with a queen-size sofa bed), kitchen, and bedroom (with a king-size bed). The Garden Room can accommodate two. Guests are treated to a daily breakfast along with a newspaper. Rates for the cottage range from $75 to $85 (plus $10 for a third person) and from $55 to $65 for the Garden Room. *The Cottage*; 3829 Albatross Street; San Diego, CA 92103; 619-299-1564.

MALIBU COUNTRY INN: This romantic, 16-room bed-and-breakfast just over an hour from Disneyland, is set on an idyllic bluff above one of Malibu's most beautiful beaches. Each of the rooms in this three-acre property contains an array of amenities, including a refrigerator, coffeemaker, television, and snack basket. A complimentary continental breakfast is served daily in a breakfast room by the pool. The inn also has a restaurant, which is open for breakfast and lunch daily. Many off-site recreational activities also can be arranged through the inn's reception desk, including golf, tennis, windsurfing, and horseback riding. Doubles range from $95 to $135 year-round; mini-suites range from $120 to $155. There is a $10 per person charge for additional guests over age 7. *Malibu Country Inn*; 6506 Westward Beach Road; Malibu, CA 90265; 310-457-9622.

B&B LINES

For information about a wide range of bed-and-breakfast accommodations in Southern California, contact Eye Openers Bed & Breakfast Reservations (818-797-2055; fax 818-798-3640), which visits each property it recommends. The State of California Division of Tourism can also supply information; 800-862-2543.

Camping

In a city the size of Anaheim (pop. 285,500), it's surprisiing—but true—that you can park a recreational vehicle or pitch a tent less than a mile from Disneyland. Not only do you save money on lodging by doing so, but you're close enough to walk to the park from your campsite.

Nearly all the Anaheim-area campgrounds offer full hookups, convenience stores, and other camping facilities, but few provide much in the way of planned activities. However, the managements are accommodating and usually will arrange with local tour companies for sightseeing tours outside Disneyland if you're interested.

Here's a selection of some of the best in the area. Unless otherwise noted, the campgrounds mentioned here accept major credit cards and offer full hookups, and reservations are suggested. "In season" refers to Christmas and Easter vacation periods and the summer months of June, July, and August.

ANAHEIM KOA: In this campground, less than a mile from the *Disneyland Hotel*, shade trees and shrubbery separate the sites, all of which are paved. There are two pools (one a wading pool for kids, the other a semicircular adult pool) plus a whirlpool, a recreation room that boasts almost two dozen games, including pinball and Pac-Man, and a 24-hour laundromat. The sandy playground has swings and heavy-duty climbing equipment. There's also a good bathhouse setup. In addition to conventional women's and men's shower stalls, there are ten family-size showers large enough for a parent to bathe small fry. The 221 RV sites are divided almost evenly between back-in and pull-through spaces. Rates for two run about $36.95 in season and $24 the rest of the year, plus $5 per additional

adult over age 18. KOA discount cards are available for $8. Tents are allowed. So are pets, but they must be leashed when outside vehicles. This campground is well equipped for travelers with disabilities, with huge roll-in showers with grab bars, and no curbs. *Anaheim KOA*; 1221 South West St.; Anaheim, CA 92802; 533-7720.

DISNEY'S VACATIONLAND CAMPGROUND: Just a short walk from the *Disneyland Hotel* and a monorail ride into the park, this well-kept campground offers 385 paved, full-service RV slots, with shrubbery between them to buffer sounds and afford some privacy. There also are 60 tent spaces on a grassy area at the back of the park near a group of picnic tables and built-in barbecues. Amenities include a good-size pool (but with steps across one end that make it difficult for lap swimmers) and separate carpeted recreation rooms for adults and teenagers. The adult lounge has couches, chairs, and tables that are convenient for cards and board games, plus a pool table. The teens' game room has pinball, plus just about every electronic game imaginable. There's also a children's play area with a slide and merry-go-round. The laundry room is equipped with 22 washers and 11 dryers. Rates are $33 in season for vehicles under 23 feet long; $23 off season. For vehicles over 22 feet long the rates are $38 in season and $28 off season. *Disney's Vacationland Campground*; 1343 South West St.; Anaheim, CA 92802; 533-7270 or 778-6600, ext. 1256.

ORANGELAND: This 212-site campground is located on eight acres of an orange grove with an abundance of trees for shade and plenty of grass around the sites. It's only three miles from Disneyland and half a mile from Anaheim Stadium. Facilities include a pool, whirlpool, laundromat, gameroom, and a grocery store. No tent camping. Rates for two run about $27 and reservations are recommended. *Orangeland*; 1600 West Struck; Orange, CA 92667; 633-0414.

TRAVELERS WORLD: Occupying some acreage roughly three-quarters of a mile from Disneyland, this 300-site park is large and open, and has some shade trees. All the sites are paved. Tents are permitted, and there's a coin-operated wash rack for cars and RVs, and a small gameroom. Rates for two run about $20 in season and $18 the rest of the year for back-in units; pull-throughs are $2 extra; plus $2 to $3, depending on the season, per additional person age three and over (or for a pet). *Travelers World*; 333 West Ball Rd.; Anaheim, CA 92805; 991-0100.

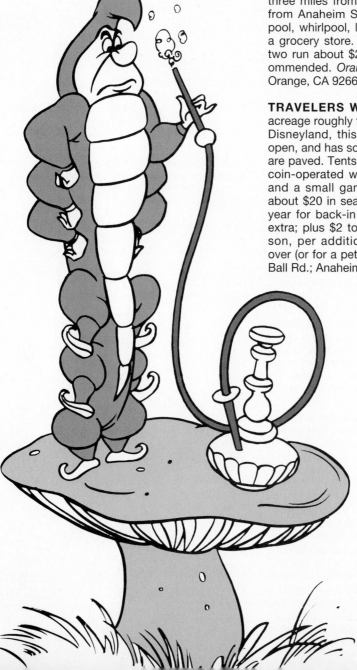

THE MAGIC KINGDOM

Every day is a holiday at Disneyland. Children giggle and grin, and parents not only enjoy their offsprings' glee, but are hard pressed to contain their own pleasure. No one seems immune to the magic of Sleeping Beauty Castle, rising majestically at the end of Main Street, and even the most cynical hearts instinctively respond to the sound of the marching bands that play here every day. Even visitors who have toured this wonderland dozens of times still react with uncamouflaged delight.

What may be the most extraordinary fact of all is that this enjoyment has remained constant for 41 years. Attractions have come and gone, whole new "lands" have been added, and young musicians who began performing here during the 1950s have now grown to middle age. But a visitor who originally came here as a first-grader returns with his own children to find the Disneyland of his memory unchanged in spirit and appeal. The "magical little park," for which Walt Disney borrowed on his life insurance, is still one of America's greatest success stories.

Be aware, however, that part of Disneyland's charm is its abundance, and it's all too easy to miss the best of the Magic Kingdom unless you prepare for your visit. This chapter should help you make the decisions that can keep you on track, so read it carefully before embarking on your own Disneyland adventure, and keep it with you during your stay.

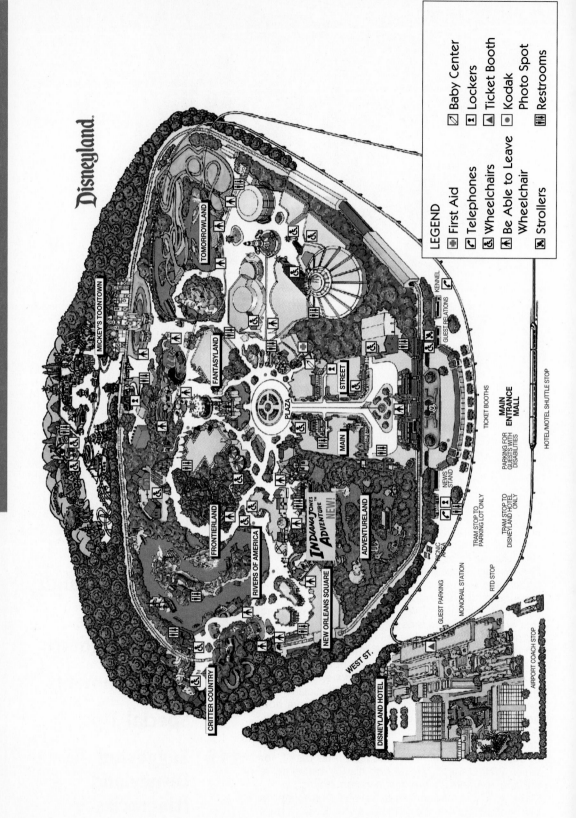

Disneyland.

LEGEND

Baby Center
First Aid
Lockers
Telephones
Ticket Booth
Wheelchairs
Kodak
Be Able to Leave
Photo Spot
Wheelchair
Restrooms
Strollers

MICKEY'S TOONTOWN
TOMORROWLAND
FANTASYLAND
PLAZA
MAIN STREET
FRONTIERLAND
RIVERS OF AMERICA
INDIANA JONES ADVENTURE NEW!
ADVENTURELAND
NEW ORLEANS SQUARE
CRITTER COUNTRY

KENNEL
GUEST RELATIONS
NEWS STAND
TICKET BOOTHS
MAIN ENTRANCE MALL
PARKING FOR GUESTS WITH DISABILITIES
HOTEL/MOTEL SHUTTLE STOP
TRAM STOP TO PARKING LOT ONLY
TRAM STOP TO DISNEYLAND AND HOTEL ONLY
PICNIC AREA
GUEST PARKING
MONORAIL STATION
RTD STOP
WEST ST.
DISNEYLAND HOTEL
AIRPORT COACH STOP

Getting In & Around

Many Anaheim hotels and motels are within walking distance of Disneyland, or at most a short drive away. Many provide shuttle-bus service. If a bus is available, you're well advised to take it to avoid the bother of parking and retrieving your car in the enormous Disneyland parking lot.

If your accommodation offers no shuttle service and you're too far away to walk, driving becomes the most convenient alternative. Here are directions from nearby points. Driving times are given for optimal conditions; rain or rush-hour traffic could double the duration of the trip.

FROM POINTS NORTH

From downtown Los Angeles: Santa Monica Freeway (I-10) east, then Santa Ana Freeway (I-5) south to the Harbor Boulevard exit. About 45 minutes.

From Santa Monica: Santa Monica Freeway (I-10) east, then Santa Ana Freeway (I-5) south to Harbor Boulevard exit. About an hour.

From Beverly Hills: Santa Monica Freeway (I-10) east, then Santa Ana Freeway (I-5) south to Harbor Boulevard exit. About an hour.

From Century City: Santa Monica Freeway (I-10) east, then Santa Ana Freeway (I-5) south to Harbor Boulevard exit. About an hour.

From Los Angeles Airport: San Diego Freeway (I-405) south to Garden Grove Freeway (Rte. 22) east. Take Harbor Boulevard exit and go north about two miles to Disneyland. About an hour.

From the San Fernando Valley: San Diego Freeway (I-405) south to Santa Monica Freeway (I-10) east, Santa Ana Freeway (I-5) south to Harbor Boulevard exit. About 90 minutes.

From Long Beach: Long Beach Freeway (Rte. 710) north, then Rte. 91 east, then Santa Ana Freeway (I-5) south. Alternative: Long Beach Freeway (Rte. 710) north to San Diego Freeway (I-405) south, then Garden Grove Freeway (Rte. 22) east to Harbor Boulevard exit and north about two miles to Disneyland. About 45 to 50 minutes.

FROM POINTS SOUTH

From Newport Beach: Newport Freeway (Rte. 55) north, then Santa Ana Freeway (I-5) north to Harbor Boulevard exit. Turn left and you're a block away. About 30 to 35 minutes.

From San Diego: Santa Ana Freeway (I-5) north. Exit at Harbor Boulevard. Turn left and you're a block away. About two hours.

PARKING: Disneyland has a sizable parking lot—about 110 acres, or enough space to accommodate approximately 15,000 cars. The lot opens one hour before the park and is divided into sections, each of which is named for a Disney character. When passing through the Auto Toll Plaza (where visitors driving regular passenger vehicles pay the $6 parking fee, or $12 for preferred parking, based on space availability, closer to the park entrance; larger vehicles are subject to higher rates), you'll receive a small leaflet that includes a map of the parking lot. *Before leaving your car, carefully mark its location on the map.* Then be sure to take the leaflet along.

If the parking lot is full: There is an additional lot across from the *Disneyland Hotel*. A more expensive alternative is to park in the large lot at the hotel itself ($15) and take either a Disneyland tram (free) to the front gate (preferable for first-time visitors for the magic of it) or the monorail (ticket required) from the hotel directly to Tomorrowland. The trams run from about half an hour before Disneyland opens until about half an hour after it closes. The monorail runs during park hours.

Note that during busy periods Harbor Boulevard and the freeway leading up to the exit are both often backed up with traffic. So it's a good idea to take the Katella Avenue exit from the Santa Ana Freeway (I-5), even though it's a little farther from Disneyland and may mean a slight detour for those arriving from the north. This alternative route does allow easy access to Disneyland's Katella Avenue entrance, which is used on peak days.

Parking for recreational vehicles: Ample space is available in the Eeyore section, close to the small picnic area.

Lost cars: Contact security. If you can remember approximately when you arrived, parking lot personnel can usually provide a general location of the car to an officer, who will then comb the aisles on a small scooter.

Tips on Times & Tickets

HOURS: Disneyland is open daily. Weekday hours are generally from 10 A.M. to 6 P.M., with extended hours during the summer. Hours on Saturdays vary, but are generally 9 a.m. to midnight. Hours on Sundays are generally 9 A.M. to 10 P.M. For the exact opening and closing hours that will be in effect during your stay contact Disneyland Guest Relations; Box 3232; Anaheim, CA 92803 (714-999-4565).

When to arrive: Especially during the busy summer and Christmas holiday seasons, it's wise to arrive first thing in the morning so you can get to all the popular attractions before the queues build up outside. In fact, if you get there too late, the parking lot may be closed. This happens frequently—on such dates as July 4, during the third week in August, and the last week in December. For more details, see the "Special Tips" section of this chapter.

ALL ABOUT TICKETS: An admission ticket is called a Passport. This one-price ticket includes admission to the park and unlimited use of all attractions except the arcade for the number of days the Passport is valid. There are one-, two-, and three-day Passports. Two types of annual Passports also are available. A Basic Annual Passport is valid for 338 days a year. It excludes Saturdays March through June and certain holidays and holiday weekends. A Premium Annual Passport is valid every day and includes preferred parking.

Where to buy tickets: Disneyland Passports are available at the main gate ticket booths and at the monorail station at the *Disneyland Hotel.*

Tickets by mail: Passports and tickets for special events are available by mail at no extra charge. Just send your check or money order for the exact amount. Please specify what kinds of tickets you need and how many. Allow ten *business* days for processing. Send your check and ticket request to Disneyland Admissions Office; Box 3232; Anaheim, CA 92803.

Tickets by phone: Orders may be charged to Visa, MasterCard, American Express, or The Disney Credit Card by calling 714-999-4043. (Magic Kingdom Club discounts are not valid.) Allow four to five days for delivery; ten days during the Christmas holidays.

The Disney Stores: West Coast Disney Stores sell Disneyland tickets, including one at the Main Place Mall in Anaheim.

How to pay for tickets: Cash, traveler's checks, personal checks, American Express, Visa, MasterCard and The Disney Credit Card are all accepted as payment for Disneyland Passports. Personal checks must be

NON-HOLIDAY HOURS

The following are Disneyland's normal operating hours during non-holiday periods. At these times, you will note, schedules vary. Though the seasonal hours are usually as listed below, it's always wise to phone ahead (999-4565) for verification since changes in operating hours frequently occur.

| | WEEKDAYS | | WEEKENDS | |
	Monday to Thursday	Friday	Saturday	Sunday
January	10 A.M. to 6 P.M.	10 A.M. to 6 P.M.	9 A.M. to midnight	9 A.M. to 10 P.M.
February	10 A.M. to 6 P.M.	9 A.M. to 7 P.M.	9 A.M. to midnight	9 A.M. to 10 P.M.
First 2 weeks of March	10 A.M. to 6 P.M.	9 A.M. to midnight	8 A.M. to midnight	9 A.M. to midnight
Last 2 weeks of March	9 A.M. to 7 P.M.	9 A.M. to midnight	8 A.M. to midnight	9 A.M. to midnight
April	9 A.M. to 7 P.M.	9 A.M. to midnight	8 A.M. to midnight	9 A.M. to 10 P.M.
May	9 A.M. to 7 P.M.	9 A.M. to midnight	8 A.M. to midnight	9 A.M. to 10 P.M.
First 3 weeks of June	9 A.M. to 10 P.M.	9 A.M. to midnight	8 A.M. to midnight	9 A.M. to midnight
Balance of June	8 A.M. to 1 A.M.	8 A.M. to 1 A.M.	8 A.M. to 1 A.M.	8 A.M. to 1 A.M.
July	8 A.M. to 1 A.M.	8 A.M. to 1 A.M.	8 A.M. to 1 A.M.	8 A.M. to 1 A.M.
First 3 weeks of August	8 A.M. to 1 A.M.	8 A.M. to 1 A.M.	8 A.M. to 1 A.M.	8 A.M. to 1 A.M.
Balance of August	9 A.M. to midnight	9 A.M. to midnight	8 A.M. to midnight	9 A.M. to midnight
First week of September	9 A.M. to 11 P.M.	9 A.M. to 11 P.M.	9 A.M. to midnight	9 A.M. to 10 P.M.
Balance of September	10 A.M. to 6 P.M.	10 A.M. to 6 P.M.	9 A.M. to midnight	9 A.M. to 10 P.M.
October	10 A.M. to 6 P.M.	10 A.M. to 6 P.M.	9 A.M. to midnight	9 A.M. to 10 P.M.
November	10 A.M. to 6 P.M.	10 A.M. to 6 P.M.	9 A.M. to midnight	9 A.M. to 10 P.M.
December	10 A.M. to 6 P.M.	10 A.M. to 6 P.M.	9 A.M. to midnight	9 A.M. to 10 P.M.

imprinted with your name and address. You also must present a driver's license or a major credit card.

GUIDED TOURS: Disneyland's 3½- to 4-hour guided walking tour is a great way for a first-timer to get to know the park with a minimum of fuss and bother. Your guide can answer questions along the way, and visits to (and rides on) several major attractions are included on the itinerary. Tour tickets cost $12 for adults and $10 for children; they are available at the main gate ticket booths or at City Hall once you have entered the park. **Note:** Tours are offered on availability of guides and only in the morning, usually about 10:30 A.M.

MONEY MATTERS: Cash and traveler's checks are accepted at all food and merchandise locations throughout Disneyland. American Express, MasterCard, Visa, and The Disney Credit Card can be used to pay for charges at all the shops, cafeterias, fast-food eateries, snack bars, and waitress-service establishments. Only cash is accepted at snack wagons. As payment for merchandise and meals, personal checks are also accepted under the conditions outlined above. Guests also may want to purchase Disney Dollars, available in $1, $5, and $10 denominations from the Bank of Main Street. Disney Dollars are accepted at all Magic Kingdom restaurants, shops, and food stands, as well as at the *Disneyland Hotel*, and can be redeemed for real currency at any time. Many visitors, however, take at least one home as an inexpensive souvenir. When purchasing tickets at Disneyland, guests can request Disney Dollars as change.

TICKETS IN BRIEF

	Adults	Children (3 through 11)
Passports	$ 33	$ 25
2-Day Passports	$ 57	$ 44
3-Day Passports	$ 79	$ 60
Basic Annual Passport	$ 99	$ 99
Premium Annual Passport	$199	$199

These prices are subject to change.

EXTENDED HOLIDAY HOURS

New Year
January 1	9 A.M. to 10 P.M.
January 2	9 A.M. to 10 P.M.

Martin Luther King, Jr. Birthday weekend
January 13	9 A.M. to midnight
January 14	9 A.M. to 10 P.M.
January 15	9 A.M. to 7 P.M.

Presidents' weekend
February 17 & 18	8 A.M. to midnight
February 19	9 A.M. to 10 P.M.

Easter season
March 29 through April 13	9 A.M. to midnight
April 14	9 A.M. to 10 P.M.

Memorial Day weekend
May 25 & 26	8 A.M. to midnight
May 27	9 A.M. to 10 P.M.

Independence Day
July 4	8 A.M. to 2 A.M.

Labor Day weekend
August 31	8 A.M. to midnight
September 1	8 A.M. to midnight
September 2	9 A.M. to 11 P.M.

Thanksgiving week
November 25, 26 & 27	10 A.M. to 6 P.M.
November 28 (Thanksgiving)	9 A.M. to midnight
November 29 and 30	8 A.M. to midnight
December 1	9 A.M. to 10 P.M.

Christmas season
December 21 through 23	8 A.M. to midnight
December 24	8 A.M. to 7 P.M.
December 25 through 30	8 A.M. to midnight
December 31	8 A.M. to 3 A.M.

Lay of the Lands

Disneyland's layout is so simple that getting around is quite easy. However, the numerous nooks and crannies, bends and curves, and small alleyways can be confusing until you're sure of your way. The many entrances to each shop or restaurant, and the often irregular placement and architecture of many of the buildings, don't always help orientation. To get the most out of your experience in the Magic Kingdom, it's essential to understand the organization *before* arriving.

There are eight sections, or "lands," in the Magic Kingdom—Main Street, U.S.A.; Adventureland; Frontierland; New Orleans Square; Critter Country; Fantasyland; Mickey's Toontown; and Tomorrowland. The area just inside the main gate is known as Town Square; that in front of Sleeping Beauty Castle is known as the Central Plaza, or, more aptly, the Hub. From it, avenues extend into the various lands like the spokes of a wheel. The first bridge to your left as you face the Castle takes you to Adventureland; the next, to Frontierland and New Orleans Square. To your right, the first walkway leads to Tomorrowland, and the next—known as Matterhorn Way—goes directly into Fantasyland, and then on into

Mickey's Toontown. If you cross the Castle's moat and walk through the archway, you'll also end up in Fantasyland. Critter Country occupies its own cul-de-sac extending from New Orleans Square. In addition, connecting the spokes of the wheel to each other are a number of avenues around the perimeter. The Big Thunder Trail connects Frontierland and Fantasyland. Another meandering walkway links Tomorrowland and Fantasyland. The Disneyland Railroad circles the outer edge of the park, just inside the berm that insulates Disneyland from the rest of the world.

A glance at the park map in this book and inside the front cover of the Disneyland Souvenir Guide (available at no charge at City Hall or Bank of Main Street in Town Square) help clarify Disneyland's layout.

Note: To get your bearings in Disneyland, remember that when you stand at the Magic Kingdom entrance and face Sleeping Beauty Castle, you're looking north. Main Street is straight ahead, with Fantasyland and Mickey's Toontown beyond the Castle. Adventureland, Frontierland, New Orleans Square, and Critter Country are all to the west. Tomorrowland lies to the east (refer to map on page 60).

Main Street, U.S.A.

This pretty thoroughfare represents Main Street at the turn of the century—you know, life in "the good old days." Instead of the traffic, blasting horns, and garish commercial buildings found on so many American small-town Main Streets nowadays, Disneyland's version offers the gentle clip-clop of horse hooves on pavement, the melodic ringing of streetcar bells, and nostalgic old tunes like "Bicycle Built for Two" and "Old Gray Mare." There are the sounds of brass bands, barbershop quartets, and ragtime piano. An old-fashioned steam train huffs into a handsome brick depot as elaborately embellished with frills and furbelows as a Victorian wedding gown. And an array of picturesque buildings with mansard roofs, dormer windows, and wrought-iron accents lines the street. The gaslights flicker once more at sundown in the ornate lampposts lining the walkways, and the storefronts, painted in all the pastels a sophisticated palette might offer, couldn't be more inviting. To make the buildings appear taller, a set designer's device called forced perspective was employed. The first floor is seven-eighths scale (so guests can enter comfortably), the second story is five-eighths, and the third is half size. The dimensions of the whole are small enough that the place seems intimate and comforting, and the proportions appear correct. (Forced perspective also was used to make the Matterhorn and Sleeping Beauty Castle, the park's visual centerpiece, seem taller than they actually are.)

Although there are only a few specific attractions along Main Street, and they're not as compelling as some of those in the other lands, there's hardly a guest who passes through the entrance tunnels who doesn't find something of interest in at least one of the shops. Few can manage to stroll the entire avenue without lingering over some treasure.

Maintenance and housekeeping are superb, both inside and out. White-suited custodians whisk stray candy wrappers into dustpans at remarkable speed, and shovel up droppings from the horse-drawn streetcar just as quickly. The pavement here, like that in the rest of the park, is washed down with high-pressure hoses every night (a 5½-hour job). There also are Disneyland staffers whose job it is to scrape up every bit of squished gum. The sole job of one crew is to change the tiny white lights that edge every roofline, while another spends its time painting woodwork. Another keeps the brass door handles gleaming, and another keeps the window sills dusted. Still another crew—three workers in all—washes windows. The horse-shaped hitching posts, which one youngster once mistook for funny-looking parking meters, are touched up daily and get a complete sanding, washdown, and new coat of paint about once a month. Even professional painters never fail to marvel at the quality of the work they see at Disneyland.

The landscaping also is outstanding, since this section of the park boasts more flowering annuals than any other. First there's the showy Mickey planter face at the entrance, which just happens to be one of the most-photographed spots in the park. *Zoysia tenuifolia* (variety emerald) gives the carpet effect around the park perimeter. Pansies, petunias, and snapdragons brighten the scenery elsewhere. In winter, some 6,000 poinsettias splash the townscape with scarlet, while in spring the Central Plaza blossoms with tulips and Easter lilies. The Chinese elms that once shaded the streets had grown so large and leggy over the years that they dwarfed the Castle and the avenue. After great debate they were replaced in late 1981 with West Coast live oaks, the same type found along Main Street in Walt Disney World's Magic Kingdom in Florida.

The trees in the Central Plaza have been kept for the shade they provide—particularly great on a summer afternoon. The focus of the Central Plaza is the Walt and Mickey Partner's Statue. This wonderful life-size bronze statue is surrounded by smaller statues of Pinocchio, Dumbo, Pluto, Minnie Mouse, Donald Duck, Chip 'n' Dale, the White Rabbit, and Goofy.

While strolling down the street, be sure to see the window displays in the Emporium—elaborate, unusually animated, and usually related to the latest Disney movie release. Also note the names emblazoned on the second-floor windows. This was Walt Disney's way of acknowledging the contributions of the people from whom he had learned and with whom he had worked. Elias Disney, whose name can be seen above the door to the Emporium, was Walt's father. Wally Boag, identified nearby, played Pecos Bill and the traveling salesman in Frontierland's former Golden Horseshoe Revue (now the Golden Horseshoe Stage) for more than two decades until his retirement in 1982. Above the New Century Timepieces and Jewelry Shop, there's the name of Gunther Lessing. He was the head of the Walt Disney Company's legal department for many years and was noted for having been Pancho Villa's lawyer. Bruce Bushman, whose name can be seen nearby, helped design the Mr. Toad cars and worked closely on the King Arthur Carrousel, among other attractions. Ken Anderson, an art director for the film *Snow White*, was a key figure in the design of the Haunted Mansion, Storybook Land, and the original Fantasyland. Edward T. Meck, who was editor-in-chief of *Disneyland News*, was an early Disneyland publicity director. Emile Kuri, honored above the Market House, was another longtime art and set designer. He designed the Below Decks museum at Frontierland's *Columbia* and was Walt's own interior decorator. The names near the Main Street Photo Supply Co. are those of Herbert Ryman, who drew the first overall plan for the park, and of art directors John Hench and Peter Ellenshaw.

Now some advice: Before you head toward Sleeping Beauty Castle, stop at the information desk at City Hall or Bank of Main Street and find out when and where you'll be able to catch up with the singers and musicians who perform all over the park. Schedule your time and direction to intersect with them wherever possible. Do your shopping in the morning or early afternoon, rather than at the end of the day when stores are so mobbed you can't really enjoy looking at the merchandise. You can store your purchases in the lockers located at the Lost and Found (halfway down Main Street, behind Market House, next to the *Main Street Cone Shop*), and just outside the main entrance (to the right when leaving the park). Have your hand stamped on the way out, hold onto your Passport, and you'll be able to re-enter freely on the same day.

The following Main Street attractions are listed in the order in which you'll encounter them while walking from the Main Entrance to the Central Plaza and Sleeping Beauty Castle.

DISNEYLAND RAILROAD: The four narrow-gauge steam trains circle the park through Adventureland, New Orleans Square, Critter Country, Frontierland, Toontown, Fantasyland, and Tomorrowland in a 20-minute round-trip. Walt Disney so loved trains that he actually built a one-eighth scale model, the *Carolwood Pacific*, in the backyard of his Carolwood Drive estate in Holmby Hills. Not only did he relocate

power lines in the process, but he also surrounded his track with a berm (covered with special shrubbery) so he wouldn't disturb his neighbors.

It was only natural that Disney's park should include at least one railroad. The only question was how big it should be—this was easily calculated after it was determined that the cars needed six-foot doors. The four locomotives now serving the line are enough alike that it's easy to think they're identical. But according to the engineers, each has its own personality, its own sound, and its own feel. And each has its own history. Both the *C. K. Holliday* and

the *E. P. Ripley*—the original pair, named for the founder of the venerable Santa Fe Railroad and an early president—were designed and assembled at Walt Disney Studios, using parts from outside contractors. The *C. K.* has a diamond stack, the kind of smokestack found in the mid-19th century on the first transcontinental locomotives. The *E. P.*, modeled on more recent engines, has a capstack.

A third engine, the *Fred G. Gurley*, is named for the man who was chairman of the Santa Fe Railroad board at the time. The locomotive was built by the Baldwin Locomotive Works in 1894, and once hauled sugarcane from three plantations over the Lafourete Raceland and Longport Railway to shipping docks in New Orleans.

The fourth of the quartet—named for Ernest S. Marsh, the Santa Fe's president at that time—was originally built in 1925, also by the Baldwin Works, and had been used at a lumber mill in New England. All of these iron horses are powered by oil-fueled steam boilers and have to stop several times a day to take on water. The engineers and the firemen have to keep constant watch on the gauges, keep the fires up, and watch the water levels. All the cars the locomotives pull are open-air.

The original passenger train has been stored away for the last few years, since the small-windowed cars—reproductions of those used around 1890—offered only a limited view of the Grand Canyon Diorama and the Primeval World attractions. What remains of this train today is the *Lilly Belle*, the erstwhile observation car, which has been transformed into a sumptuous, private VIP caboose with live palms, silk roses, brass fixtures, stained-glass skylights, elaborate woodwork, and chairs and a settee upholstered in burgundy velvet.

The Grand Canyon Diorama and Primeval World: Taking his guests through jungles (in Adventureland), a gracious city (New Orleans Square), Northwestern-type pine woods (in Critter Country), a deciduous forest that resembles those in the Midwest (Frontierland), the Neverland that is Fantasyland, and the sleek world of Tomorrowland wasn't enough for Walt Disney, so he added the Grand Canyon, a $435,000 diorama that depicts this natural wonder as it appears from its South Rim. It was created on a seamless, handwoven canvas 306 feet long and 34 feet high, and required 300 gallons of paint. Deer, a mountain lion, a golden eagle, wild turkeys, skunks, porcupines, desert mountain sheep, quaking aspens, and piñon and ponderosa pines (also real and treated with preservatives), plus a snowfall, a storm, a sunset, and a rainbow make up the scenery. The music is the "On the Trail" section of Ferde Grofé's *Grand Canyon Suite*.

The Primeval World diorama, opened in 1966 after an interim stop at the Ford Pavilion at the New York World's Fair, consists of a series of misty swamps, deserts, rain forests, and erupting volcanoes inspired by the 1940 film *Fantasia*. In this diorama, the Audio-Animatronics process brings to life some 46 prehistoric creatures: a pair of edaphosauruses (the fin-backed dinosaurs munching tropical vegetation and shellfish seen early in the trip); a brontosaurus (the creature breakfasting on water plants in a shallow lake nearby); pteranodons (the vulture-like creatures perching atop rugged cliffs not far away); triceratops (the horned dinosaurs watching their young hatch from eggs in the next scene); ornithomimuses (the "ostrich dinosaurs" gathered around a watering hole in the desert layout); a stegosaurus (an armored sort of dinosaur); and a tyrannosaurus (the fierce one that is 22 feet high, who is clawing and growling at the stegosaurus).

Where to board: Although the Disneyland Railroad makes stops in Frontierland, Toontown, and Tomorrowland, lines are usually shortest at the Main Street station, a composite of the railroad depots that American travelers encountered at the turn of the century. The handcar on the spur track adjoining the station was a gift to Walt from the Kalamazoo Manufacturing Company of Kalamazoo, Michigan.

THE WALT DISNEY STORY FEATURING "GREAT MOMENTS WITH MR. LINCOLN": The theme of this 15-minute attraction, housed in the Disneyland Opera House, is the life and accomplishments of Walt Disney. His formal and working offices from the Burbank studio (which he used for 26 years) are on display, along with considerable Mickey Mouse memorabilia and a number of letters from such notables as Joseph Kennedy, Mary Pickford, Dwight D. Eisenhower, and Richard Nixon.

The real star of the show, however, is the Audio-Animatronics version of our 16th president, which is the most technologically advanced figure of its kind. After a brief slide show depicting the Civil War, Mr. Lincoln stands up and discourses on liberty, the American spirit, the dangers facing the country, respect for law, faith in Divine Providence, and duty. All the while, he's nodding and gesturing, turning, and shifting his weight in a realistic fashion.

The Lincoln figure in the show was completely reprogrammed in 1984, following a jointly funded, three-year research project at the University of Utah. The university, a leader in the development of artificial limbs, was consulted by the Disney organization in its ongoing interest in improving the realism of the movements of Audio-Animatronics figures. The result—the Compliance System—allows Lincoln to shift his body weight as naturally as a human and enables him to sense when he is near another object. Incidentally, the speech is composed of excerpts from talks that Lincoln actually delivered—in Baltimore at the Sanitary Fair (April 18, 1864); in

Edwardsville, Illinois (September 11, 1858); in Springfield, Illinois, for the Young Men's Lyceum (January 27, 1858); in a eulogy honoring Henry Clay (July 6, 1852); and at New York City's Cooper Institute (February 27, 1860).

The Fifth Freedom Mural: Measuring 53 feet in width and 5½ feet in height, this oil painting in the exit hallway of the Walt Disney Story portrays likenesses and vignettes of the contributions of Alexander Graham Bell, Thomas Edison, iron-and-steel magnate Andrew Carnegie, Wilbur and Orville Wright, Henry Ford, Pulitzer Prize-winning novelist Pearl Buck, agricultural chemist and educator George Washington Carver, communications executive David Sarnoff, rocket propulsion pioneer Robert H. Goddard, Albert Einstein, and Walt Disney—all of whom rose to greatness through the free enterprise system, the "fifth freedom" to which the mural's name refers. The first four freedoms—freedom of speech, freedom of worship, freedom from want, and freedom from fear—were described in a 1941 speech by President Franklin D. Roosevelt. The fifth freedom was highlighted in one of Lincoln's own addresses: "I believe each individual is naturally entitled to do as he pleases with himself and the fruit of his labor so far as it in no way interferes with any other man's rights." This quote is reproduced on a brass plaque on the pillar in the middle of the room.

MAIN STREET VEHICLES: Main Street, U.S.A., wouldn't be Main Street without its motorized fire wagon, its horseless carriages, and its horse-drawn streetcars—Disneyland's main thoroughfare bustles with them all day long. The motorized fire engine—which, like all the vehicles, was designed and built by the Disney organization—is modeled after those that might have been found on an American Main Street around the turn of the

century, except that there are seats where the hose would have been carried. The bell is authentic.

As for the streetcars, they are modeled after those in 19th-century photographs. Each carries 30 passengers. A double track half-way down its 1,830-foot-long route, and circular tracks at each end permit cars to pass each other. Most of the horses that pull them are

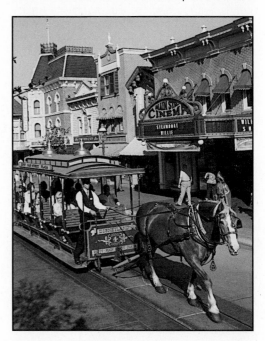

Belgians (characterized by their white manes and tails and lightly feathered legs) and Percheron draft horses. Each horse weighs about two tons and stands 17 to 18 hands tall (68 to 72 inches at the shoulder). They wear shoes coated with polyurethane to give them better traction (it also helps make a neat clip-clop sound as they travel down Main Street). The farrier comes every week to trim their hooves and see to their shoes, and shods the horses with new shoes every six to eight weeks. The animals work two to four-hour shifts, three to five days a week.

MAIN STREET CINEMA: Ironically, one of the best things about this prominent Main Street attraction is that most visitors rush right by it on their way to Tomorrowland's Star Tours and Space Mountain, Frontierland's Big Thunder Mountain Railroad, and the other well-known and most popular thrill-a-minute shows and attractions. This traffic flow headed off to other diversions means that the movie house is never very crowded—even though it's blissfully dark and blessedly air conditioned—making it one of the perfect places to rest and regroup on a scalding summer afternoon in Southern California.

There's more here than cool air, however, since six short, silent film cartoon classics play continuously. Remember, these are the original animated cinema attractions that founded Mickey's monumental reputation— even though he wasn't even named Mickey at the start. Everything that contemporary folks think about when the name "Disney" is mentioned began with these short subjects. The specific historic cartoon films change from time to time. At present the sextet of cinematic showings includes *Plane Crazy*, *Mickey's Polo Team*, *The Moose Hunt*, *Traffic Trouble*, and *Dog Napper*, in addition to the father of them all, *Steamboat Willie*, the early talkie that introduced a spindly legged little mouse. The scene in which this Disney-drawn, musically inclined mouse plays "Turkey in the Straw" on a pig's udder drew one of the film's biggest laughs at its November 1928 release. For film historians and modern moviegoers alike, this is a must.

PENNY ARCADE: Even that Cadillac among arcades—Tomorrowland's blipping, bleeping, and squeaking Starcade—is no match for this turn-of-the-century version with its blinking chaser lights. Among the quainter of the antique amusements found here are the World Soccer mechanical football game, the restored Kentucky Derby, and the Electric Shock (circa 1920), which delivers a reduced version of the jolt with which the brave were zapped before Disney engineers modified the mechanisms. The Uncle Sam strength test used to bear the picture of a scantily clad female, but the arcade wizards took care of that one, too. The funniest is the one with the Egyptian theme, to the left as you face the large band organ at the arcade's entrance, and the best surprises are the vibrating machines—a Massage-o-Matic chair, often found in old penny arcades and along boardwalks, and the early 1940s Vibrant Foot-Ease, which sets the body to tingling from feet to eyeballs when a dime is deposited.

In general, the machines closest to the street cost a penny and date from 1900 to 1920, while those in the rear of the room to the left date from 1920 to the present. Occupying center stage in the street area of the arcade are the Mutascopes and the Cail-o-Scopes. The former, first introduced around 1900, require a penny and feature hand-cranked moving pictures such as *Miracle Rider*, in which Tom Mix is shot off his horse by a truck driver; the *Absent-Minded Janitor*, which depicts a balletic Charlie Chaplin, an artist, and a pretty dancing model; *Outlaws' Getaway*, featuring a gun battle and an ambush; *In the Bag*, an exercise in animation that conveys some impression of just how sophisticated the Main Street Cinema's *Steamboat Willie* really was; *Bounced on the Bean*, featuring Chaplin's Tramp as a baker; *The New Sheriff*, a vignette featuring the lawman, the lawman's daughter, and the handsome bandito; more Chaplin, in *The Dough Fight*; *Stage Coach*, about an attempted

abduction; still more Chaplin, in *Dizzy Racket*; and *Galloping Fury*, perhaps the best of all, in which the cowboy with the white hat gets the girl and gallops off into the sunset. The Cail-o-Scopes, which appeared about a decade after the Mutascopes, give a slightly three-dimensional picture that moves mechanically. All of them offer a few minutes' pleasant diversion, but some are really good. For example, there's the *Painless Dentist*, featuring a hammer, saw, pliers—and a very sorry young boy; *Big Beauty Buster*, starring Bull Montana, tells of a ruffian and a weakling boxer who is caught hiding a hammer in his glove; *Forbidden Sweets*, has a terrific sequence in which father catches son pigging out on a stolen pie and smashes it in his face; and *A Wee Bit O' Scotch*, in which a Playmate of yesteryear takes a nip.

While you're looking, you can be feeding dimes to the arcade's big music boxes. There are two. The Wurlitzer Orchestrion Style L, purchased by Walt Disney in 1953, was introduced around 1921 and probably used to entertain guests in a restaurant or speakeasy until the juke box came along in the 1930s. It combines a piano with 38 violin pipes and an equal number of flute pipes, orchestra bells, a bass drum, a snare drum, and a triangle. The larger Welte Style 4 Concert Orchestrion, which has called the Penny Arcade home since 1955, was built around 1905 in the German city of Freiburg. Its more than 300 pipes, plus a triangle, bass drum, and cymbals, are activated by an electric motor developed around the turn of the century. Change for all these diversions is available at the cashier's booth at the rear of the arcade.

Adventureland

For someone who grew up in Marceline, Missouri, around the turn of the century, the very idea of the Amazon and the South Seas must have seemed terribly exotic. So it's not surprising that when Walt Disney was planning his new park, he designated one segment—Adventureland—to telescope all the far-off and mysterious destinations of the armchair traveler's world into one compact area.

No single piece of architecture here comes directly from Polynesia, Southeast Asia, or the Caribbean, but every structure has a few characteristics of each of these areas, and travelers in Adventureland get a definite feeling of being in a place that's nowhere in particular, but is unquestionably exotic and undeniably foreign. The landscaping is remarkable, and the botanically minded should have a field day trying to identify them all.

Attractions here are described as visitors encounter them when walking from east to west through Adventureland.

ENCHANTED TIKI ROOM: Introduced in 1963, this was the first of the Audio-Animatronics attractions and the precursor of more elaborate renditions (such as "Great Moments with Mr. Lincoln"). This 17-minute show housed in a vaguely Polynesian complex at the entrance to Adventureland, is now a bit dated but is vintage Disney. Inside, you'll meet four feathered emcees (José, Michael, Pierre, and Fritz), a sextet of pastel-plumed, long-eye-lashed parrots (Collette, Fifi, Gigi, Josephine, Mimi, and Susette), and a chorus of 54 orchids, 4 carved wooden tiki poles, 12 tiki drummers, 24 singing masks, 64 bird-of-par-

adise flowers, 7 birds of paradise, 8 macaws, 12 toucans, 9 fork-tailed birds, 6 cockatoos, and several others. The 225 performers all sing and whistle and drum up a tropical storm with such animation that it's hard to resist a smile. The music includes a special arrangement of the "Barcarole" from Jacques Offenbach's opera *Tales of Hoffmann*; "In the Tiki, Tiki, Tiki Room," the show's theme song; "The Hawaiian War Chant"; "Let's All Sing"; and "Aloha to You." The courtyard waiting area holds a few surprises. It's presented by Dole Pineapple.

JUNGLE CRUISE: The spiel delivered by the skipper on this eight-minute adventure trip has its share of corny jokes, and the average boatman does have to repeat the same ones over and over again during his working day. But every once in a while, when your navigator turns out to be one of the handful of natural comics who do the job, the presentation can be genuinely funny. As jungle cruises go, this one is as much like the real thing as Main Street, U.S.A., is like Marceline, Missouri—long on loveliness (plus you get a glimpse of the Temple of the Forbidden Eye from the Indiana Jones Adventure) and short on the visual distractions and minor annoyances that constitute most of the rest of human experience. There are no mosquitoes, no Montezuma's Revenge. And the Bengal tiger and the trio of king cobras at the ancient Cambodian ruins, the great apes, the gorillas, crocodiles, alligators, elephants, hippos, and lions in the water and along the shores represent no threat—though, according to maintenance crews, they're almost as much trouble as real ones.

Movie buffs should note that Bob Mattey, who helped develop the creatures, also worked on the man-eating plants of many Tarzan movies, the giant squid from *20,000 Leagues Under the Sea*, and the mechanical shark in *Jaws*.

The large-leafed upright tree in the Cambodian ruins section of the attraction is a *Ficus religiosa*, an example of the tree under which the Buddha received enlightenment in India many centuries ago. .

INDIANA JONES ADVENTURE: TEMPLE OF THE FORBIDDEN EYE: Mysteriously hidden deep within the dense jungles of India, the Temple of the Forbidden Eye was built long ago to worship the powerful deity Mara. According to legend, Mara could "look into

your very soul," and then grant the "pure of heart" one of three magical gifts: unlimited wealth, eternal youth, or future knowledge. However, legend also issues a stern warning: "A terrible fate awaits those who gaze upon the eyes of Mara!" Dr. Jones would only comment, "Records indicate that many have come, but few have returned."

Now you can take an expedition through the ancient temple ruins in this attraction based on the George Lucas/Steven Spielberg film trilogy; the whole experience, including the pre-show takes about an hour, though the ride itself lasts an action-packed 3½-minutes. You follow the jungle path through Dr. Jones' cluttered encampment, then enter the temple via the path marked by his initial expedition team. A code will help you decipher the hieroglyphics on the walls. In the queue area, a newsreel tells of Indiana Jones' latest expedition. What it does not reveal is that he has entered the temple and disappeared.

Following in his footsteps, you will see warning signs that indicate there still may be some booby traps that have not yet been disarmed. (The fun actually is in paying no heed to the warnings; let the spikes fall where they may.) Once inside the temple, guests board 12-passenger off-road vehicles reminiscent of 1930s troop transports; one person takes the wheel and serves as the driver for the expedition, and everyone is securely fastened in their seats for the twists and turns ahead. Hold on to your belongings!

The search for Indiana Jones is on, and an encounter with the fearsome Mara unavoidable. The trip takes you into an underworld of screaming mummies, glowing fires, falling lava, snakes, and poisonous darts. Surprises lurk around every bend, and escape is only temporary (just like in the movies), as you suffer an avalanche of creepy crawlies, traverse a quaking suspension bridge, and, best of all, come face to face with a gigantic rolling ball that threatens to flatten everyone. At the end of the ride, Indy himself is waiting for you, with a flippant parting remark like "That wasn't so bad" or "Next time you're on your own."

Thanks to the wizardry of the Disney Imagineers, no two rides are exactly alike, so each time you enter the Temple of the Forbidden Eye the experience will be slightly different.

Note: You must be at least 48 inches tall and at least three years old to ride this attraction. The lines can be extremely long, with waits of 1½ hours or more during the week and 3 hours on weekends and throughout the summer, so go first thing in the morning.

SWISS FAMILY TREEHOUSE: The Disney studios' 1960 film version of the 1813 Johann David Wyss classic novel, *The Swiss Family Robinson*, provided the inspiration for what must be one of the three best treehouses on earth (the others being this same attraction at Walt Disney World in Florida and Disneyland Paris). It's well fitted out with real antiques (muskets, an 18th-century barometer, a ship's wheel and gimbal lights, and a sewing basket), and with an organ, beds, tables, and bookshelves built by Disney artisans. It even has running water in all the rooms—thanks to a waterwheel at the base of the tree, a rushing brook, and a series of bamboo buckets on pulleys. "Everything we need right at our fingertips" was how John Mills, who played the father in the film, described the prototype for this arboreal home, which he and two of his three sons had built after the wreck of the *Recovery* on its way to New Guinea. It's such an ingenious construction that it's not hard to understand why, several adventures later when they got the chance to leave the island, all the family members except one son decided to stay on.

Unofficially christened *Disneyodendron semperflorens grandis* (that is, "large everblooming Disney tree"), the tree itself is another intriguing bit of Disney artifice. The 62 roots, which reach 42 feet into the ground, are made of concrete; the limbs, which extend 80 feet across, are of steel; and the more than 300,000 leaves, shaped like those of a banyan tree and grafted onto 1,000 manzanita branches ranging in length from two to six feet, are pure plastic. The treehouse towers 70 feet in the air, high above the rest of Adventureland. Fluttering at the top—visible from almost everywhere in the park—is the Swiss national flag.

New Orleans Square

Though New Orleans Square did not figure in the Disneyland layout until 1966, it's certainly among the park's most evocative areas. This would be true even if it were home only to the superb Haunted Mansion and Pirates of the Caribbean. But there's also its picturesque site on the shores of the Rivers of America, not to mention the architecture—a pastiche of wrought iron, pastel stucco, French doors, polished brass, shutters, and gleaming glass. Not to be missed are the pleasant open-air dining spots; the lovely *Blue Bayou* restaurant overlooking the romantic moonlit lagoon section of the Pirates of the Caribbean; the assortment of shops, some of the best in the park; and the good music—performed on selected days by the Side Street Strutters, who play lively jazz and Dixieland, and by the Royal Street Bachelors and the Brass Brothers, who strum and tootle in the traditional New Orleans style. As you sit here on a summer evening and snack on fritters and hot chocolate, preconceptions of Disneyland-as-amusement-park tend to vanish altogether. Just as Main Street makes Disneyland a great place for shopping, New Orleans Square shows it off as a fine spot to spend a few relaxing hours.

The New Orleans Square attractions described below are listed as you encounter them when strolling from east to west.

PIRATES OF THE CARIBBEAN: The last attraction that Walt Disney worked on extensively himself, this 13-minute boat trip through a series of sets portraying a pirate raid on a Caribbean village offers one of Disneyland's best adventures. It attracts so many guests throughout the day that waits sometimes exceed an hour when the park is busy. If you're visiting during a peak period, stop here soon after opening (or just before closing). The experience is well worth rising early. Beginning with a short cruise through a bayou where will-o'-the-wisps glow just above the grasses and fireflies twinkle nearby while stars spangle the twilight-blue sky overhead, the attention to detail nearly boggles the mind. There are flowerpots that explode and mend themselves—and an Audio-Animatronic cast of 64 human figures and 55 animals: drunken pigs whose legs actually twitch in their soporific contentment, chickens so realistic that even a farmer might at first mistake them for the real thing, and a piccolo-playing pirate whose fingers move and cheeks puff as he toots out his little ditty. The keen-eyed will note the hairs on the leg of one swashbuckler perched atop a bridge overhead. The attraction's theme song, "Yo-Ho, Yo-Ho—a Pirate's Life for Me," manages to transform what is actually a picture of some fairly savage buccaneering into a good time for all. A must—again and again.

HAUNTED MANSION: In a British radio interview, Walt Disney once explained how sorry he felt for those homeless ghosts whose hauntable mansions had fallen to the wrecker's ball. Feeling that they sorely needed a home, he offered this Haunted Mansion. It's unquestionably one of the park's top attractions. From its stately portico to the exit corridor, special effect is piled upon special effect to create an eerie, but not quite terrifying, mood. Judicious applications of paint and expert lighting heighten the shadows that play ghoulishly on the walls outside, and maintenance crews foreswear the dusting and vacuuming that keep the other attractions looking so spiffy.

The jumble of trunks and chairs and dress forms and other assorted knickknacks in the attic are always appropriately dirty. (Additional dust is purchased from a West Coast firm by the five-pound bagful, and is distributed by a device that looks something like a grass seeder. Extra cobwebs, which come in liquid form, are strung under the supervision of set-design experts who have more than once had occasion to rebuke the custodial workers for being too conscientious about their cleaning.)

The eerie music and the slightly spooky tones of the Ghost Host often set small children to whimpering as soon as their parents carry them through the door, and some members of the crews who work in the mansion at night find their nerves so taut they start at sudden noises. Nonetheless, any adult who expects to get the fright of his or her life may be in for a bit of a disappointment. What makes the seven-minute attraction so special is the attention to, and abundance of, details—so many that it's next to impossible to take them all in during the first, or even the second, time around. In the Portrait Chamber (the room full of fearsome-looking gargoyles that adjoins the chandeliered and lace curtain-adorned foyer), it's fun to speculate on whether the ceiling moves up or the room goes down; it's one way here and the opposite way at the mansion's Walt Disney World counterpart.

Once in your Doom Buggy, look for the raven that appears again and again as you go through the house, the bats' eyes on the wallpaper, the TOMB SWEET TOMB plaque, and the rattling suit of armor in the Corridor of Doors. Then there are the dead plants and flowers and broken glass in the Conservatory, where a hand reaches out of a half-open casket, the terrified cemetery watchman (and his mangy mutt) in the Graveyard, the ghostly teapot that pours ghostly tea, the ectoplasmic king and queen on the teeter-totter, the bicycle-riding spirits, the transparent musicians, and the headless knight and his supernatural Brunhilde. Nice stuff all.

The mansion was constructed in 1963, based on studies of houses around Baltimore, and the attraction itself opened in 1969. "Grim Grinning Ghosts," composed especially for the Haunted Mansion, is the name of the music. The voice of the Ghost Host belongs to veteran radio actor Paul Frees.

Frontierland

With Big Thunder Mountain punctuating the skyline to the north and the Rivers of America lapping at its shore, rural Frontierland telescopes the lands that the pioneers knew as they pushed westward. It highlights such rough wilderness outposts as Forts Pitt and Defiance, shows off life on the Mississippi as Tom Sawyer might have known it, confronts the dangers of unexpected attacks, and marvels at the dense forests that early settlers took for granted. Hosts and hostesses wear denim, long skirts, and other period togs; security hosts dress like cavalrymen. Shops, restaurants, and attractions are walled in with unpainted barn siding, stone, or adobe. The sights here are just about as pleasant as they come at Disneyland. And that's especially true in the afternoon, when the riverboat *Mark Twain*—looking a bit like an oversize wedding cake with its elaborate wooden lacework trim—pulls majestically away from its dock for a cruise along the clay-bottomed Rivers of America.

Be sure to note the landscaping. Near the *Mark Twain* dock, the bougainvillea "tree" is actually the skeleton of an Australian tea tree (*Leptospermum laevigatum*) entwined with branches of real bougainvillea nearby. In front of *River Belle Terrace* there's an immense old rubber tree. A gift of a major oil company, it had a good-size fuel-carrying pipe embedded in its root system. When it was transplanted, the oil company had to shut down operation temporarily and lay a new pipe section around the roots so the Disney gardeners could cut the old pipe and move the tree—which to this day grows around that section of pipe.

The following Frontierland attractions are discussed in the order in which visitors come upon them while moving westward from the Central Plaza gateway toward Big Thunder Mountain.

FRONTIERLAND SHOOTIN' ARCADE: This shooting gallery is completely electronic. The 18 rifles fire infrared beams which, if they strike the red reactive targets, trigger humorous results. The arcade is set in an 1850s town in the Southwest Territory. Gun positions overlook Boothill, a town complete with bank, jail, hotel, and stables. Hit the jail target and the cell door opens, freeing the prisoner; a strike at the "Boothill" sign causes it to read FOR SALE; zero in on the mine entrance and an ore cart races out one side and back in the other. The toughest target is the moving shovel which, when struck, causes a skeleton to pop out of a grave. **Note:** Disneyland Passports do *not* include use of the arcade. The cost is 50 cents for 15 shots.

GOLDEN HORSESHOE STAGE: A half-hour show at the *Golden Horseshoe Saloon* stars Miss Lily Langtree; three vivacious and savvy young women in search of stardom; Sam, the saloon's owner, bartender, and chief cook and bottle washer; and his three cowboys. Miss Lily is in love with Sam, but won't admit it; and Sam is wild about Lily. She belts out a few fine songs, and her troupe of three shines brightest in the cancan number. There's a dance competition between Sam's boys and Lily's girls, and some amusing audience-participation sequences. Walt Disney had his own private box, the one just to the left of the stage. The hall itself, said to have been inspired by a *Golden Horseshoe Saloon* that once flourished in New York City, is lovely, with its polished floors, a long brass railing, and chandeliers.

There are usually five shows per day (except Tuesdays, Wednesdays, and Thursdays during the off-season), but performance times change throughout the year, so check on show times when you arrive at the park. Reservations are required, and they must be made in person on the day of the performance. Since they are accepted on a first-come, first-served basis only, it's important to present yourself at the hall to claim one shortly after park opening. If you don't have a reservation, you can queue up for cancellations by arriving at the door at least 45 minutes before show time. Chili and soft drinks are available here, making it a good spot for a snack.

BIG THUNDER MOUNTAIN RAILROAD: As roller coasters go, this one is relatively tame. It's short on the kinds of steep climbs and precipitous drops that put hearts in throats and make stomachs protest, but long on tight curves that provoke squeals of glee and delighted laughs. The big deal on this ride is not the speed, however, or the thrills, but the scenery along the way—a pitch-black bat cave, giant stalactites and stalagmites, a waterfall, a canyon inhabited by coyotes, a natural-arch bridge that affords fine views over the Big Thunder landscape, mine walls ready to cave in, and the quaint mining town.

The show is almost the equal of New Orleans Square's Pirates of the Caribbean, though you might think it's even better because it starts in the queue area. There, in the aforementioned community—which boasts two hotels, a newspaper, and a dance hall, in addition to its saloon and general store—life goes on usually in full view. If you listen closely, you'll hear a local barmaid flirting with a miner to the accompaniment of such songs as "Red River Valley" and "Listen to the Mockingbird." As you proceed toward the loading area, the walls on either side are made of about a hundred tons of real gold ore from Rosamond, California—brownish-colored stone that sold for around $80 a ton when the attraction was built, and purplish rocks that cost $120 a ton. The Silver Queen Mine (in the same former mining center) also yielded a real, ten-foot-tall stamp mill designated BIG THUNDER MINE 1880—rare because most are about twice the size. At the time it was spotted by the Disney scouts, it was owned by four partners, each of whom had to be contacted before the sale could go through. In the loading area, there's a single-bore compressor engine that really works, from Tonopah, Nevada. Elsewhere around the attraction, there's a scattering of corrugated tin, most of it found on the roofs of mining shacks in the Southwest. The steam engine that sits just below the town was used in the 1978 Disney feature film, *Hot Lead, Cold Feet.* The Pat Burke identified on one of the packing crates helped scour the swap meets, abandoned mines, and even museums in Colorado, Minnesota, Nevada, and Wyoming, where the thousands of dollars worth of authentic mining equipment in the queue area (and the attraction itself) was located.

As for the mountain itself, it is entirely

TIPS ON TIMING

This is a very popular ride, so try to visit first thing in the morning, during a parade, or just before park closing, when the lines are shorter. For the best of both worlds, ride twice—once by day, when you can see the scenery much better, and again after dark, when there's the added pleasure of hurtling through the cool night.

Disney-made, composed of steel and cement by the ton and of paint by the thousands of gallons—about 3,000 to 4,000 gallons. It was built by a crew of diversely skilled rock makers, who layered cement and paint, threw stones on the product, kicked dirt at it, and banged on it with sticks and picks. Inspired by Utah's Bryce Canyon and named in reference to an old Indian legend about a certain sacred mountain in Wyoming that would thunder whenever white men took out its gold, the mountain required seven years of planning, two of them spent on actual construction, and cost some $16 million—almost as much as all of Disneyland in 1955.

Incidentally, while the ride itself is similar in many respects to the one offered at Walt Disney World's Big Thunder Mountain Railroad, there are several small differences both inside and out. In Walt Disney World's Magic Kingdom, for instance, you won't find the wonderfully scenic queue area that prefaces the ride here. But the Florida mountain is much larger, rising to a height of 197 feet, in keeping with the larger scale of that park. Also, instead of the handsome little mining town that greets passengers at the end of Disneyland's trip, WDW's Big Thunder Mountain Railroad riders have a flooded mining town full of real-looking chickens, donkeys, a rainmaker, and a sinking saloon, midway through the trip.

Note: Pregnant women and guests who suffer from heart conditions, motion sickness, weak backs, and other limitations should not ride. Children must be at least three years old and at least 40 inches tall to board. Children under seven must be accompanied by an adult.

BIG THUNDER RANCH: A recreation of a late 1880s working horse ranch wouldn't be complete without a ranch house, harness shop, pasture area, and petting barnyard. The pasture area showcases the award-winning Disney draft horses, Lipizzaners, and miniature horses. Also, in the spring there are calves and baby goats.

***MARK TWAIN* STEAMBOAT:** One of the original Disneyland attractions and the first paddle wheeler built in the United States in half a century, this five-eighths-scale vessel, circumnavigates Tom Sawyer Island. It passes by *River Belle Terrace*, the *Royal Street Veranda*, the docks for the Tom Sawyer Island Rafts, and piney Critter Country, and takes in a waterfall and an abandoned railroad track (which old Disneyland hands will remember as part of the Mine Train Thru Nature's Wonderland attraction, superseded by Big Thunder Mountain), plus moose, elk, a burning cabin, and lovely dense woods full of the alders, cottonwoods, maples, and willows that might have been found along the Missouri frontier more than a century ago.

The ducks are real; the other animals come to Disneyland thanks in part to the efforts of Bob Mattey, who also helped design the creatures that haunt the jungle rivers in Adventureland. The hull of the paddle wheeler was built at Todd Shipyards in San Pedro, the superstructure at Walt Disney Studios. Constructed in sections and then dismantled, it was shipped over the freeways in pieces and then reassembled at Disneyland.

All in all, the 14-minute ride provides a pleasant respite from the crowds on a busy day. And if you manage to get one of the few chairs in the bow, the *Mark Twain* also offers a golden opportunity to put your feet up.

Flags on the *Mark Twain* dock: It's always fun to pick out the eight flags that fly above this Frontierland landing. The John Cabot Flag, the first flown over the American mainland as the *Constant* brought settlers to Jamestown in 1607 and the *Mayflower* transported by the Pilgrims to Plymouth 13 years later, bears the red cross of St. George (an *X*) on a white field. The King's Colors Flag, the one that flew over the Colonies for more than a century, superimposes England's red cross of St. George on Scotland's white cross of St. Andrew (a plus sign) on a blue background.

The Continental Flag, carried at the Battle of Bunker Hill, is red with a green pine tree on a white field in the upper corner. The Pine Tree Flag, carried by the American navy when it amounted to a mere six ships, bears a green pine tree and the words AN APPEAL TO HEAVEN in black on a white field. The Grand Union Flag, which General Washington raised at Cambridge in 1776, has 13 stripes and, in the upper corner, the red cross of St. George and the white cross of St. Andrew on a blue

field. The Betsy Ross Flag, adopted by the Continental Congress in 1777, has the same 13 red and white stripes, but in the upper corner, representing the new constellation of states rising in the sky, a circle of 13 stars shines on a blue field. The Star-Spangled Banner, the flag that inspired the words of the national anthem, has 15 stars and 15 stripes. And, finally, there's Old Glory with its 13 red and white stripes and 24 stars. Adopted in 1818, it was named in 1831 by a young Salem, Massachusetts, sea captain.

SAILING SHIP *COLUMBIA*: Though operating only when the *Mark Twain* is not in service (and then providing a 16½-minute ride), this full-scale replica of the ten-gun, three-masted "Gem of the Ocean," the first American craft to circumnavigate the globe, is an imposing sight towering majestically over the treetops at Fowler's Harbor, opposite the Haunted Mansion, where she is usually moored. The original ship, a 212-ton merchant vessel registered as the *Columbia Rediviva*, was constructed in Plymouth, Massachusetts, in 1787, at a cost of $50,000. Her maiden voyage, which began on September 30, 1787, took her around Cape Horn and into Nootka Sound, just off the coast of what is now Vancouver, British Columbia.

On this trip, her first captain, later dismissed, cheated the ship's owners, tried to shortchange Nootka Indians from Oregon to Alaska in the fur trade, and, before sailing for China, mounted armed raiding parties to slip ashore at night and steal Indian furs to trade later for china, teak chests, spices, and tea. During her second voyage, made under the command of Captain Robert Gray, the Columbia River was discovered and became the vessel's namesake; her owners' names are still attached to many small harbors and coves along the river's shores. When the *Columbia* sailed into the river, natives turned out by the hundreds to gaze at her in wonder, as Gray reported in his log. Under other captains, the *Columbia* made other fur-trading trips before she eventually disappeared "somewhere in the Orient" without a trace. (Some legends say

that a crew member took her over and made her a pirate ship.) The only picture of the ship is a steel engraving in the Massachusetts Historical Society's *Voyages of the Columbia*, and it was this document, supplemented by research in the Library of Congress and in ports along the Massachusetts coast, that inspired the design for Disneyland's ship. Some of it was built in a dry dock adjoining the Rivers of America, and completed in a yard representative of an 18th-century New England shipyard, using, in part, antique tools of the period.

Measuring 110 feet from stem to stern, 83 feet 6 inches along the deck, with an 84-foot main mast, she was the first ship of her kind to be built in more than a century and had cost about $300,000 by the time of her dedication on June 14, 1958. She has a steel hull, a deck planked with Douglas fir, and stays, shrouds, and ratlines made of steel-wire rope wrapped with Manila. During an eight-week renovation in 1984, the ship was completely rerigged and redecked. The work crew was the same one that had built the *Columbia* 29 years before. Since most of the work was done during Disneyland's operating hours, crew members wore sailor costumes so as not to take away from the special ambience at Frontierland.

Below Decks: This maritime museum, on view whenever the *Columbia* is operating, illustrates the way sailors lived on the original vessel during its later voyages, as reported in the ship's log and in letters between the owners and the captain. Emile Kuri, once chief art director for Walt Disney Studios and Walt Disney's personal interior decorator, was in charge of set decoration. (This attraction operates only during busy periods.)

TOM SAWYER ISLAND: The landfall that the *Mark Twain*, the *Columbia*, and Davy Crockett's Explorer Canoes circle as they ply the Rivers of America was once the highest point in Disneyland. This is the archetypal treehouse, right down to the spyglasses and peepholes that let visitors see out over the treetops to the *Mark Twain* dock across the river. The treehouse is only one of the wonders on this island planted with sweet gums and southern red cedars, Carolina cherry, sycamores, live oak, honeysuckle, and blackberry bushes. There's the Suspension Bridge, which heaves and bounces wildly enough to make a weak stomach churn, and the floating Barrel Bridge, where it's nearly impossible to maintain a stride more decorous than a lurch. Near the Suspension Bridge, there's a small hill studded with log steps up which kids like to scramble.

And then there's Castle Rock Ridge, a fantastic group of boulders that includes the mightily spinning Merry-Go-Round Rock; the aptly named Teeter-Totter Rock; and inside the Ridge, the spacious Pirate's Den and the smaller Castle Dungeon, full of niches and

cul-de-sacs just the right size for a six-year-old, but so narrow and low-ceilinged in places that grown-ups who don't bend double or turn sideways risk getting stuck, just like Pooh Bear. Even cooler, darker, and spookier than either of these, though, is the labyrinthine Injun Joe's Cave, one of the best spots on the island. At the landfall's southernmost extremity, not far from its entrance, there's the perpetually creaking Old Mill.

At the island's opposite end is Fort Wilderness, where air rifles (free) make lots of noise but emit no bullets, and statues of a buckskin-clad Davy Crockett and George Russel that look for all the world like Fess Parker and Buddy Ebsen, who acted the parts of those historical figures on the old "Disneyland" show. The flag that flutters above the fort is the same 15-star, 15-stripe model that inspired Francis Scott Key at Fort McHenry in 1814.

Small signs point to all of these landmarks on the island. Even though the footpaths are decidedly well trodden, the time spent on Tom Sawyer Island always seems like an adventure and may well offer some of the happiest moments at Disneyland.

Be sure to see all the wonderful details: leather thongs that bind the split rails together to fence the landing for the rafts to Tom Sawyer Island; the wooden packing cases on the landings that punctuate the pathway along the east side of the island; and the trash bins, here designed to look like oversize logs. The names on the graves near Fort Wilderness are, for the most part, fictitious.

On the island, there are two sets of rest rooms—one set in Fort Wilderness, the other on the southeast corner near Injun Joe's Cave, opposite the mainland's *Mark Twain* dock. Snacks are available at the *Fort Wilderness Canteen*. **Note:** The island closes at dusk. Check at the dock for excursion times.

Critter Country

Crocodile Mercantile and the Indian Trading Post has become The Briar Patch. (Actually, the old Trading Post was one of the last remnants of 1950s Frontierland, way back when this section of the park was an Indian Village, complete with tepees and a ceremonial dance circle.)

Critter Country is still one of the most pleasant corners of Disneyland, bordering lush shady forests full of Aleppo, Canary Island, Monterey, and Italian stone pines, coast redwood, locusts, white birch, and evergreen elms.

Attractions are described according to their east-to-west locations.

SPLASH MOUNTAIN: Disneyland's mountain range of thrill rides—Matterhorn Mountain, Space Mountain, and Big Thunder Mountain—has another peak, Splash Mountain.

Unlike the preceding attractions, however, in which passengers ride roller-coaster style cars down tubular steel tracks, Splash Mountain, as its name implies, takes visitors on a 9¼-minute waterborne journey through backwoods swamps and bayous, down waterfalls and, finally, over the top of a steep spillway, hurtling them from the peak of the mountain to a briar-laced pond five stories below.

Splash Mountain is based on the animated sequences in Walt Disney's 1946 film *Song of the South*. The principal characters from the movie—Brer Rabbit, Brer Fox, and Brer Bear—appear in the attraction through Audio-Animatronics technology. In fact, Splash Mountain's stars and supporting cast of 103 performers constitute the largest group of Audio-Animatronics characters ever assembled in a single Disneyland attraction.

Comparisons to the Pirates of the Caribbean are particularly apt, as Splash Mountain was consciously designed as a "How do we top this?" response to the long-running popularity of the pirate adventure. The Disney Imagineers used such time-proven elements as a watery drop into a fantasy world, humorous characters, and a scrupulously detailed show in an entirely new way.

Splash Mountain's designers not only borrowed the attraction's characters and color-saturated settings from *Song of the South*, they also included quite a bit of the film's Academy Award-winning music. As a matter of fact, the song in the attraction's finale, "Zip-A-Dee-Doo-Dah," has become something of a Disney anthem over the years.

Splash Mountain breaks new ground in a number of ways. In addition to setting a record for total animated characters, it also boasts one of the world's tallest and sharpest flume drops (52½ feet at a 47-degree angle),

Regular visitors to Disneyland will notice transformations, both large and small, in the park's northwestern territory. In 1972, this land debuted as Bear Country, the backwoods home of the perennially popular Country Bear Playhouse. During 1989, the bears were joined by foxes, frogs, geese, rabbits, crocodiles, and a fair number of the other critters who make up the Audio-Animatronics cast of Splash Mountain. To make their neighbors feel welcome, the bears (and a handful of Disney Imagineers) rechristened the area Critter Country.

A quick walk through the premises will make it readily apparent how quickly everyone has adapted. Observant guests will spot scaled-down houses, lairs, and nests tucked into hillsides and along the river. Some of the neighborhood shops have new proprietors— the former Wilderness Outpost is now and it is the fastest ride ever operated at Disneyland. If you're interested in getting wet, try to sit up front. Seats in the back provide a smaller splash.

One other twist makes Splash Mountain unique in the annals of flumedom: After hurtling down Chickapin Hill, the seven-passenger log boats hit the pond below with a giant splash—and then promptly sink underwater (or seem to) with only a trace of bubbles left in their wake.

A point for Disney trivia buffs: The voice of Brer Bear is performed by Nick Stewart, the same actor who spoke the part in *Song of the South* when it was released in 1946.

Note: You must be at least 40 inches tall and three years old to ride Splash Mountain.

DAVY CROCKETT'S EXPLORER CANOES: Of all the boats that circle the Rivers of America, these 35-foot fiberglass crafts—replacements for the wooden originals were made by Maine's Old Town Canoe Company—may offer the most fun, at least for the stalwart. They're real canoes, and they're not on tracks. Though the helmsman and the sternsman are always strong enough to do the work, the guests' contributions also matter when it comes to completing the 2,400-foot trip.

Note: This attraction operates only on selected days, and it closes at dusk. Check at the landing for excursion times.

COUNTRY BEAR PLAYHOUSE: A handful of blasé travelers do manage to sit through this 16-minute country-and-western hoedown without cracking a smile, but they're few and far between, because this is surely another one of the park's best attractions. Ostensibly dreamed up by one Ursus H. Bear at the end of an especially good winter's nap, it is pre-

sented, with remarkably believable results, by an assortment of nearly 20 Audio-Animatronics bruins—among them Henry, the sporty, seven-foot-tall master of ceremonies; the big-bodied pianist, Gomer; the Five Bear Rugs (Zeke on banjo, Zeb on fiddle, Ted on white lightnin' jug, Fred on mouth harp, and Tennessee picking the guitarlike one-string "phang"); and the ample Trixie, lamenting her lost love after being jilted at an ant-plagued picnic. Dressed in a yellow slicker, rain bonnet, and red galoshes, Teddi Barra floats down from the ceiling crooning "Singing in the Rain." Bubbles, Bunny, and Beulah, in sweet harmony, sing "Wish They All Could Be California Bears." The cast is completed by Wendell, the "over-*bear*-ing *bear*-itone"; Liver Lips McGrowl; and last but not least, the show-stopping Big Al, one of the few Audio-Animatronics figures in the park with a following great enough to create a demand for his image on postcards and stuffed animals.

The same cast members show up in several other parts of the park, and it's interesting—but usually next to impossible—to see whether you can recognize them from one persona to the next.

TEDDI BARRA'S SWINGIN' ARCADE: This entertainment center, named for one of the big stars of the Country Bear Playhouse, is no ordinary arcade. Marksmen test their accuracy on empty honey pots, and Big Al, also from Country Bear Playhouse, challenges golfers. The basketball game features the stars of Walt Disney's 1946 film, *Song of the South*.

Fantasyland

Walt Disney called this a timeless land of enchantment, and his successors term it the happiest land of all. It is the sort of European village that provides the background for all the best fairy tales—on a day that the circus has come to town. The village lanes twist between houses done in half-timbers, brick, stone, and stucco, often embellished by brightly colored folk paintings. Weathered beams peek from below roofs of slate or shingles, and the rooflines lurch and lean this way and that as turrets and towers above poke at the heavens. The skyline, dominated by the peak of the Matterhorn, fairly bristles with chimneys and weather vanes in more shapes and styles than any single architect could possibly imagine. At the center of it all, as if brought to town by a traveling carnival, is the King Arthur Carrousel.

When Walt Disney originally created Snow White's Scary Adventures, Mr. Toad's Wild Ride, and Peter Pan's Flight, the blacklight and glow-in-the-dark paints he used (which became so popular during the psychedelic 1960s) were great novelties. But in recent decades the palette of available hues and the spectrum of special effects techniques have taken quantum leaps forward, and Fantasyland's major adventures have become the prime beneficiaries of these remarkable technological advances. Fiber optics, rear projection, holography, and other advanced special effects techniques (developed in the course of the construction of Epcot at Walt Disney World and Tokyo Disneyland) have been put to good use. As a result, Fantasyland is now a visual treat for all.

Parents of young children should be aware that some of Fantasyland's attractions take place in the dark. These include Peter Pan's Flight, Mr. Toad's Wild Ride, Alice in Wonderland, Matterhorn Bobsleds, Snow White's

Scary Adventures, and Pinocchio's Daring Journey. Attractions are described here as you come upon them when moving roughly counterclockwise from Sleeping Beauty Castle.

SLEEPING BEAUTY CASTLE: Rising above the treetops at the end of Main Street, it seems like something you've just imagined, especially on warm summer nights, when fireworks explode about the battlements like Tinkerbell's pixie dust. Closer inspection, however, shows the building to be real enough. A composite of various medieval European castles, primarily in the French and Bavarian styles, Sleeping Beauty Castle is constructed of concrete with towers that rise to a height of some 77 feet above the moat. And the whole thing looks even larger because of the use of forced perspective. In a real castle, blocks of stone near the top appear smaller than those at the bottom simply because they really are farther away. By artificially decreasing the dimensions of Sleeping Beauty Castle's uppermost blocks, the structure is made to appear much taller.

The drawbridge functions just like a real one, too. It was lowered when the park first opened, in 1955. The swans that inhabit the moat surrounding the castle are as real as most people think; they were obtained in exchange for 300 homing pigeons in a "trade" with Walt Disney World. The vegetation around the water's edge is juniper—planted there because it's one of the few green plants that the big birds will not eat. The two graceful trees to the right of the drawbridge (on the way into Fantasyland) are not weeping willow, as you might first guess, but willow leaf pit-

tosporum (*Pittosporum phillyraeoides*), which bear hundreds of tiny yellow flowers in spring, and melaleuca (*Melaleuca nesophila*), bedecked with fragile lavender flowers for several weeks in early summer.

SNOW WHITE GROTTO: Tucked away off Matterhorn Way, at the eastern end of the moat around Sleeping Beauty Castle, this is one of those quiet corners of the park easily overlooked by visitors. There's a wishing well (the coins go to charity); and then every so often Adriana Caselotti, the original voice of Snow White, can be heard singing the lovely

Larry Morey/Frank Churchill melody "I'm Wishing," from the Oscar-winning 1937 film based on the Grimm Brothers' fairy tale. While she sings, jets of water rise and fall in the waterfall-fountain just on the other side of the walkway, and a quartet of small fish rise up from the bottom of the pool at the base of the cascade to swim around in little circles.

You might well think that this grotto has been here since the very beginning of the park's history. Not true: The Seven Dwarfs and the Snow White figure, all of them sculpted from blocks of pure white marble, arrived at Walt Disney's studios one day in packing crates—an anonymous gift postmarked from Italy. Surmising that the carving may have been executed by a class of art students and based on some Seven Dwarfs hand soaps recently licensed at that time, Walt Disney made a place for them. An art director was not as delighted with the idea as Walt seemed to be, mainly because the Snow White figure was the same height as the dwarfs—an error no Disney carver would ever have made. By elevating her to the top of the fountain, however, designers made sure that Snow White's diminutive size would go almost unnoticed. Ironically, when plans were being laid for Tokyo Disneyland, the Japanese sponsors insisted that *their* Snow White Grotto be identical to this one.

PETER PAN'S FLIGHT: This attraction (based on the play by the Scottish writer Sir James M. Barrie about the boy who wouldn't grow up, by way of Walt Disney's 1953 animated feature), a little over two minutes long, is the most unabashedly beautiful one. The special effects soar to celestial heights as the pirate ships carry travelers through the clouds and into a sky full of infinite numbers of tiny fiber-optic stars. The water ripples and gleams softly in the moonlight. The lava on the sides of the volcano glows with almost the intensity of the real thing. And then the ship seems to pass *through* a waterfall—and back into reality, an unloading area that is all the more jarring after the magic of the trip through Never Land.

Disneyland trivia lovers will be interested to learn that of the approximately 350 miles of fiber optics used throughout Fantasyland, the majority appears in this attraction, and the twinkling London layout is an enlarged model of an authentic map of the city.

MR. TOAD'S WILD RIDE: Based on the 1949 Disney film *The Adventures of Ichabod and Mr. Toad*—which was partly inspired by Kenneth Grahame's classic novel *The Wind in the Willows*—this zany attraction, housed in an English manor bristling with ornate chimneys that really smoke, takes guests on a wild ride with the eccentric but lovable Mr. Toad. He loves automobiles but is about as inept a driver as you would expect a toad to be.

During his peregrinations he crashes through the fireplace in his library, scattering the embers; bursts through a wall full of windows; careens through the countryside; charges headlong into a warehouse full of TNT, which blows up; lurches through the streets of London and (still in his car) rams into, and out of, an evocative pub; goes to court and is soundly berated for his tomfoolery by a local judge; nearly collides head-on with a railroad train; and eventually, as if in expiation of his sins, ends up in a fiery inferno that features some of Fantasyland's best special effects. (The place even *feels* hot.)

The whole journey takes place so quickly (it's over in two minutes) that passengers are apt to overlook some of the details that make the settings so enchanting. Take the ornaments on the exterior of the building—vines interspersed with pictures of little toads. Or the Toad Hall shield emblazoned with the words *Toadi Acceleratio Semper Absurda*, which translates roughly as "speeding with Toad is always absurd." Or the titles of the books in the library at the start of the journey—*Anderson's Froggy Tales*, *Famous Paintings by Van Toad*, *Frogeon Psychology*, *Frogs I Have Loved*. In Toad Hall, as you burst through the leaded-glass window, the observant will note a tiny shadow of Mickey Mouse near the center, close to the sill. In Winky's Pub, the label on one of the liquor bottles reads: "Walt Disney's Distilled Spirits of

London." Nearby, above the bar, guests who have already visited Critter Country will recognize the head of Melvin the Moose from the Country Bear Playhouse. The slip of paper tacked to the wall next to the dart board announces a marriage and a celebratory "wild party" (which really did take place when one of the principal sign painters tied the knot during the course of work on the show). The shadow of Sherlock Holmes (complete with pipe and cape) can be seen in the window on the second story. Then there are the lovely sets, where stars glitter like diamonds in a dark-blue moonlit sky, and lights twinkle in windows along dark city streets. The ride vehicles are all named after friends of Mr. Toad, and the music comes straight from the film.

ALICE IN WONDERLAND: Characters and scenes from the motion picture are brought to life for this tale of Alice's crazy chase after the White Rabbit. Traveling in oversize caterpillars, visitors fall down the rabbit hole—and embark upon a bizarre adventure in that strange world known as Wonderland. It is populated by Tweedledum and Tweedledee, a garden full of singing roses, the Cheshire Cat, the Queen of Hearts and her playing-card soldiers, the White Rabbit, and more. At the end of the nearly four-minute-long ride, the explosion of the giant "un-birthday" cake provides a suitably exciting climax.

MAD TEA PARTY: The sequence in Walt Disney's 1951 production of Lewis Carroll's *Alice in Wonderland* in which the Mad Hatter hosts a tea party for his un-birthday is the theme for this attraction—a group of oversize pastel teacups that whirl wildly on a spinning platform. (Be sure to let a reasonable interval pass after eating before you embark on this mad whirl.) A bright festive look, with colorful Japanese lanterns that hang above the tea table, is part of the design. This was the park's original thrill ride back in 1955; it lasts

1½ minutes, so if the line is long, you might choose to return later. Don't miss the shrubs outside that spell A–L–I–C–E.

MATTERHORN BOBSLEDS: Like the more sophisticated Space Mountain and Big Thunder Mountain Railroad attractions, this ride has to be counted among Disneyland's most thrilling. The Matterhorn bobsleds were quite a novelty when they were dedicated in 1959 (by Richard Nixon, who was then Vice President) because of the block system dispatch, unique at that time, which allowed more than one car to be in action at once, and because of the cylinder-rail track and urethane wheels, which have since become quite commonplace on modern roller coasters.

The real allure of the 2½-minute ride is that along with the speed goes a show. You take a long climb into the cold, black innards of the mountain and make a speeding, twisting, and turning descent through a cloud of fog and past giant icicles and ice crystals—the wind howling about you all the while—toward a brief encounter with the awesome Abominable Snowman (a sort of albino version of King Kong) and a splashdown in an alpine lake. The speed of the downhill flight away from the creature seems even greater than it really is, since much of the journey takes place inside tunnels.

The designers carefully studied photographs of the real peak when developing the designs, so the mountain itself is a pretty good reproduction of the real one, which Walt saw when traveling through Europe. It even faces in the proper direction. The mountain's hooked peak is a bit more bent than that of the original in Switzerland, and this Matterhorn is one-hundredth the size of the real McCoy. Like the Sleeping Beauty Castle, it uses forced perspective to make the summit look even loftier than the approximately 147 feet it actually is.

Even the trees and the shrubs get into the act. The ones at the timberline—that is, 65 to 75 feet from the base of the mountain—are far smaller than those at the bottom. In fact, these Atlas and deodar cedar, European white birch, and Chinese tallow trees are among the most interesting aspects of the attraction. Growing in cement pockets whose small size retards root growth and plant growth above ground, they're watered by a gardener who must walk the attraction's bobsled track to reach them.

Note: Pregnant women, children under the age of three, and guests who suffer from weak backs, heart conditions, motion sickness, and other physical limitations should not take the ride.

IT'S A SMALL WORLD: The background music for this attraction—"It's a Small World," written by Richard M. and Robert B. Sherman (the Academy Award–winning composers of the music for *Mary Poppins*, among other Disney scores)—is almost maddeningly cheerful

and singsong. Children and senior citizens love it, and the more sophisticated among the in-betweeners wish they could expunge it from their consciousness after disembarking from the boats that carry them through the 12-minute attraction. It does seem to become more lovable as you know it better, however, much like the show itself. While not necessarily the most sophisticated, it certainly is splendid, from the gloriously towered-and-turreted multi-colored facade to the troops of stylized Audio-Animatronics dolls, representing all the world's children, on view along the way.

In all, there are 297 children representing some 100 regions, plus 256 toys native to those areas—a real pageant. The pastel facade, which is embellished with stylized representations of the Eiffel Tower, the Leaning Tower of Pisa, Big Ben, the Taj Mahal, and other world landmarks, is equally splendid—and the fantastic mechanized clock outside, whose loud ticktock can be heard from most parts of Fantasyland, is frosting on the cake.

The parade of toys and jesters and the whirring of gears and springs that marks every quarter hour alone warrant a trip to the attraction's spacious plaza on the edge of Fantasyland. Just as fascinating are the topiary figures—an assemblage of living olive, podocarpus, eugenia, and dodonea plants grown over chicken-wire frames and pruned into the shapes of giraffes, a llama, unicorns, elephants, seals, lions, and other animals to form a balletic troupe almost as whimsical as the attraction itself.

STORYBOOK LAND CANAL BOATS: This seven-minute cruise past miniature scenes from classic Disney animated films is not one of Disneyland's major attractions (such as Pirates of the Caribbean or Big Thunder Mountain Railroad), yet few who take the trip deny that the journey is one of the loveliest on the property, chock-full of delightful details and wonderful little scenes. Even after several trips, there are still new sights to see. For the church near the beginning of the trip, Walt

insisted on having imported stained glass. "The day we start cutting the detail," he declared, "is the day we won't have a Disneyland." And so it goes, from the home of the Three Little Pigs to the Old English Village of Alice in Wonderland (where the White Rabbit boasts his very own mailbox) to the London park that Peter Pan, Tinkerbell, and Wendy, John, and Michael Darling flew over on their way to Never Land. You'll drift past Agrabah and the marketplace where Aladdin met Princess Jasmine, go through the Cave of Wonders and see the magic lamp, then pass by the Seven Dwarfs' home and mine, and Cinderella's castle.

Ken Anderson, one of the art directors intimately involved with the project, tells of his anguish when he learned that union laborers (and not skilled craftsmen from the Walt Disney Studios) would be building the mountain at the base of the delicately pink castle there. The clock at the top of the castle reads midnight, and the turrets are covered in gold leaf. Anderson himself applied the first coat and, not being experienced in the technique, initially watched a good deal of the precious tissue-paper-like substance blow away.

Near the end of the cruise are the three mills from the film *The Old Mill*, Geppetto's village, Prince Eric and Ariel's Castle, and King Titan's castle. Because funds were short when the attraction was being developed (just after Disneyland opened), expensive Japanese bonsai trees were out of the question. But at Van Dam State Park, one scout turned up a handful of stunted, suitably small-scale redwoods growing on a cliffside. A bit more hunting unearthed a few more of these dwarf trees nearby on a piece of private property whose owners were willing to sell.

DUMBO, THE FLYING ELEPHANT: When President Harry Truman came to Disneyland in 1957, he and his wife visited almost every attraction in the park except this one—"a Republican symbol," he proclaimed. A more plausible explanation is that it has always been something of a kiddie ride, a less-than-two-minute experience especially loved by youngsters in the two-through-seven age group (and their parents, who happily go along to watch their kids' smiles). The ride is a showpiece of the area, and this mechanical marvel, full of filigreed metalwork and cogs and gears and pulleys galore, can hold even the most blasé grown-up's attention. The pipes that spew water out of the base are plated with brass—not only for the show value of their gleaming brightness, but also for ease of maintenance. The music is supplied by a vintage band organ housed in a small, ornate structure nearby. The baroque wooden casing is a recent Disney design. The topiary elephants, similar to those in front of It's A Small World, were moved here from Walt Disney World in Orlando, Florida. Dumbo was the flying elephant character in the 1941 film about a baby elephant who discovers, after drinking from a bucketful of champagne, that his inordinately large ears, which have previously been such a source of embarrassment, can actually help him to fly. Timothy Mouse, who becomes Dumbo's manager after the flying elephant is hired as a star (by the same circus folk who once scoffed at him), stands in command at the center of the attraction.

CASEY JR. CIRCUS TRAIN: One of the key sequences in Walt Disney's 1941 film *Dumbo*, in which the engine named Casey Jr. pulls a circus train up a steep hill, is the inspiration for this attraction—a 3½-minute train trip that circles Storybook Land. The fact is, the Canal Boats are better for viewing the landscaping and the details there, but it's hard to resist the charm of a ride inside one of those wild-animal-cage cars—the kind that always show up in circus films. Each train has two of them—plus a real caboose. Children seem to love this ride. (Listen as the engine chugs "I think I can" and then "I thought I could" as it negotiates the hill.) The tree next to the Casey Jr. railroad station is a Chinese weeping elm.

SNOW WHITE'S SCARY ADVENTURES: Even this attraction's facade, with its sober plantings, somber shingled roof, and castellated towers, suggests that the adventure within includes many of the same frightening moments found in the Oscar-winning 1937 film of the Grimm Brothers' fairy tale on which it was based. Look above the castle door and you might see the evil Queen pulling apart red velvet curtains and peeking out through her small-paned Gothic window. Ornamental stone ravens perch on carved stone skulls atop a stone tower, and the base of the twisted pillars supporting the half-timbered section of this foreboding structure is composed of hearts pierced through with a sword. Inside, the visitor's route snakes through the Queen's cobweb-draped dungeon, inhabited by ghostly voices.

With all this preparation, you might well expect an attraction even scarier than the Haunted Mansion. It isn't, though the tale of Snow White as it unfolds in the course of this brief (less than two minute) ride in small cars named after the Seven Dwarfs includes several fairly menacing scenes. There's one in which the Queen changes into a scraggly haired, wart-nosed old hag right before your eyes, for instance, and another in which this wicked green-eyed crone turns and offers a poisoned apple to you. The cars travel through another skeleton-scattered dungeon, pass the workshop where the Queen labors over a steaming caldron of poisoned apples, and then venture into the Frightening Forest, where mists swirl around floating logs that look like crocodiles, and smoke-wreathed, moss-draped trees point talonlike branches at unwary travelers as if to snatch them away from the relative safety of the small vehicles. The visit to the jewel mines, where the Seven Dwarfs labor during the day-

WHO'S WHO?

In the cottage scene at the beginning of Snow White's Scary Adventure, that's Grumpy playing the organ, Sleepy on fiddle, Bashful on the guitar, Happy on the accordion, Doc on the mandolin, and Dopey, who has climbed up on the shoulders of Sneezy.

time, is more beautiful than scary, full of masses of glow-in-the-dark topaz, emeralds, rubies, and sapphires.

Happily, it all ends in true storybook fashion: As the evil Queen attempts to roll a stone down the side of a mountain to crush the dwarfs below, she tumbles over the edge of a cliff and dies, leaving Snow White, her handsome prince, and the Seven Dwarfs to live happily ever after, as portrayed in the mural near the exit.

Curious visitors will be gratified to know that the bizarre calligraphy in the Queen's recipe book in the caldron scene reads "Poison Apple Antidote." In the "magic mirror, on the wall" scene, the floor on which the Queen stands is actually painted wood (the fact that it looks exactly like stone even when examined very closely is a tribute to the skill of the painters who worked here). The music comes from rare recordings used to create the film's original sound track.

PINOCCHIO'S DARING JOURNEY: This addition to the roster of Fantasyland attractions, based on Walt Disney's 1940 animated feature, is a sort of small, three-minute morality play, with Jiminy Cricket, conscience personified, as host and guide. Pinocchio, the creation of the toy maker Geppetto, goes to Pleasure Island, a land of popcorn and candy-cane Ferris wheels where a happy green worm lives in a fire-engine-red candy apple, to find the right way to live. But almost imperceptibly, vehicles move to the seamy world of Tobacco Road. Here the Mona Lisa wears a mustache, the candy is broken or half-eaten, and the brightly colored Pleasure Island hues are supplanted by drab, dirty shades of brown and gray. This is the home of the Rough House and its perpetual free-for-all, and the poolroom where little boys turn into donkeys and the coachman sells them to the salt mines. Pinocchio escapes that fate, nearly misses being gobbled up by Monstro the Whale, and ends up back at home in the care of Geppetto—to live happily ever after.

It's worth noting that the poolroom scene in which Lampwick turns into a donkey was the first in which Disney designers used holograms at Disneyland. The tableau at the end, in which the dazzling Blue Fairy turns into a cloud of sparkles right before your eyes—and then disappears, leaving only a pile of pixie dust on the floor—is accomplished partly by fiber optics. The tree out in front, an *Acer oblongun* found in a Claremont, California, nursery, is a sort of aberrant maple tree that Disney landscape gardeners attest is unique in the world. Atop the turreted ride building, be sure to note the attractive weather vanes. These represent Monstro the Whale, a school of fish, and a stork, a bird that is supposed to bring good luck in the part of eastern Europe that provided the inspiration for the onion-shaped dome that tops one of the turrets.

KING ARTHUR CARROUSEL: Guests can see this graceful and colorful park landmark as they stroll toward the Sleeping Beauty Castle passageway into Fantasyland. One of the few attractions in the park that is an original rather than a Disney adaptation, the carousel boasts 18 rows of 4 elaborately carved horses each—72 in all, no two alike (plus 13 spares). According to Bruce Bushman, one of the early park planners (whose name adorns a window on Main Street), the main unit of the carousel, an 1875 Dentzel model, was purchased in Canada, but at the time it wasn't a carousel at all—it had a whole menagerie of giraffes, lions, and other creatures, plus some sleighs, in addition to its handful of horses, and not everything moved. But Walt wanted all the animals to move, and he wanted them all to be horses, so he sent his scouts out to search for the prancing

steeds that grace the big turntable today. Neglected for most of the first half of the century, they're now as pampered as the live Belgian horses on Main Street, cared for by an expert painter whose responsibility it is to keep them looking as sleek and shiny as they must have been when they were carved in Germany over a century ago. At the rate of about 40 painting hours per horse, it takes about two years to get to them all—and then the cycle starts again—always using the original color scheme. The same care goes into keeping the 182 brass poles on the carousel turntable shiny. The man in charge of the job spends six hours at it every night.

Incidentally, the shields on the lances that support the big overhead canopy are those of the Knights of the Round Table, and because there were more shields needed than authentic designs, the crests of the various families involved in the park in the early days are included as well. Atop the carousel's main face, note the nine hand-painted panels bearing scenes from the film *Sleeping Beauty*.

Mickey's Toontown

Disneyland legend tells us that when Mickey Mouse burst onto the movie scene in 1928 in the first sound cartoon *Steamboat Willie*, his success was so great that his schedule demanded that he practically live at the Disney Studios. Thirty cartoons later, in the early 1930s, he had a chance to take a breather, and he established a quiet residence in a "Toon Only" city south of Hollywood.

Over the years, many of Mickey's cartoon friends flocked to this enclave, making Mickey's Toontown (as the area quickly became known) a popular hideaway for Hollywood's Toon stars—both past and present. Minnie lives here, as do Pluto, Goofy, Chip 'n' Dale, Roger Rabbit, and Gadget. Donald Duck, whose permanent residence is at Duckburg, U.S.A. (at Walt Disney World) docked his boat, the *Miss Daisy*, here on Toon Lake.

As Mickey's career blossomed, he opened his own home movie studio in the barn behind his house. That way he could continue to work on his own projects in addition to his work at the Disney Studios.

During the early 1950s, Mickey's dear friend Walt Disney became the first human to set foot in Mickey's Toontown. As Walt and Mickey sat on Mickey's front porch, Walt discussed his new idea for a theme park that would appeal to "youngsters of all ages." Mickey suggested that Walt build his dream Disneyland adjacent to the secret entrance to Toontown.

And so when Disneyland opened to the public in 1955, little did anyone realize that

when they were riding It's A Small World, they were right next door to Mickey's Toontown.

In 1990, Mickey and his friends decided to allow non-Toons to visit their neighborhood and their homes. In preparation for the grand opening, all of Toontown was given a new coat of ink and paint.

The opening of Mickey's Toontown in January 1993 marked the first new "land" to debut at the Magic Kingdom in 20 years. Bear (now Critter) Country opened in 1972.

Legend aside, the construction of Toontown was a constant challenge. There are no straight lines in Toontown. Conventional buildings served as the framework and then wire and lath skins were sculpted over them by hand to create the airy look. The effort was to create a living, breathing, three-dimensional cartoon environment—a cartoon world where everything is twisted and turned and falling over.

Guests enter this land under the Toontown Train Depot of the Disneyland Railroad. A population counter runs wild showing numbers, fruits, and question marks, and once inside the gates, you've entered a whole new world. Mickey's Toontown is a complete character community with a downtown area including a commercial center and an industrial zone, a suburban neighborhood, and rural areas where Disney characters work and play. The houses here actually look like their owners.

Visitors can interact with just about everything in Toontown including manhole covers, the public mailbox, and the police emergency phone. Everything is meant to be touched, pushed, and sometimes even jumped on, making this a perfect place for younger children. Adults will relish the attention to detail and the assortment of jokes and gags designed with them in mind.

Each of the Toontown neighborhoods is described in detail below, as are the three actual "attractions" in Toontown—Gadget's Go Coaster, Jolly Trolly, and Roger Rabbit's Car Toon Spin. There are two shops and three fast-food eateries in Mickey's Toontown. The shops are described in the Magic Kingdom shopping section later in this chapter and the eateries are described in the *Good Meals, Great Times* chapter.

Downtown Toontown

In Toontown's "business" zone, at the **Cab Co.**, skid marks lead to smashed pillars and an animated Toontown taxi teeters off the second-floor balcony. Here visitors will find **Roger Rabbit's Car Toon Spin.** This chaotic attraction offers a rollicking ride that combines the technology of the Mad Tea Party teacups and the tracks of Fantasyland attractions such as Mr. Toad's Wild Ride to create a fast-paced journey with Benny the Cab and Roger Rabbit. The dizzying ride takes guests through the back alleys of the Toon underworld made famous in *Who Framed Roger Rabbit?* The mission of each car is to save Jessica Rabbit from the evil weasels while avoiding the Toon's dreaded weakness, the Dip.

Roger Rabbit's Fountain, outside the Cab Co., is worth a look, too. The statue of Roger is suspended in midair and floats on a column of water erupting from a broken fire hydrant that Roger has seemingly crashed into. Notice that Roger is still holding the steering wheel from the cab he was driving. Surrounding the hydrant, four floating cab tires conceal fish spouting water into the air in arcs.

Be sure to stroll slowly by the manhole covers here where you might hear such questions as "How's the weather up there?" Also stop and lift the receiver of the police phone outside the Power House where you may hear "You have reached the Toontown Emergency Phone Line. If an anvil has been dropped on your foot, please dial One now. If your eyes have bugged out, dial Two. If you've been hit by a ton of bricks, dial Three. Have a nice day." The mailbox offers such comments as "Close the door, I'm trying to get some sleep down here" or "Thanks, I needed a little oxygen down here."

Around the corner from the Cab Co., **The Glass Factory** sports a shattered second-story glass window. Guests who ring the doorbell are greeted by the sound of breaking glass. The sign outside the **GAG Warehouse** states that rib-ticklers, rip-snorters, slap-

sticks, and wisecracks are stored there. Outside the building are an assortment of crates that when opened send forth sound effects such as fog horns and car noises. The **Safe Company** can be found easily by looking for the crashed safe wedged into the sidewalk out front. The **Power House** is home to light bulbs, industrial smokestacks, coils, and miscellaneous gizmos that electrify visitors.

A Toontown favorite, the **Fireworks Factory** features a plunger outside its door that when pressed sets off an explosive response. Good thing the **Toontown Fire Department** (Company #101), with a bug-eyed fire truck outside and the requisite dalmatian looking out the window, is right next door. At the **Camera Shop**, ringing the bell causes the window in the door to flash like a camera. The **Dog Pound** has huge rubber bars where guests can pose for pictures and at **Horace Horsecollar's Gymnasium,** barbells have just crashed through the window and landed on the ground outside.

Toontown Square

The "civic center" of Toontown, located between the downtown area and the residential section, is where visitors find **City Hall**. It is from this building and through the gazebo that fronts it that Toon residents emerge to greet their guests, entertain them with their antics, and provide many a photo opportunity. Toontown visitors can tell when a character is about to arrive because the colorful "Clockenspiel" high above City Hall comes to life as mallets ring bells, gloved Toon hands pull whistles, and figures of Roger Rabbit and Mickey Mouse pop out of cannons, blowing shiny horns that, in turn, produce bouquets of flowers.

The Square also is home to the **3rd Little Piggy Bank**, the **Courthouse**, the **Depart-**

ment of **Street Repair**, the **Library**, the **Department of Ink & Paint**, the **Toontown Skool**, and the **Planning Commission** (with its unplanned sign). Be sure to take note of the second stories of these buildings. Above the Library, for example, is Laugh-O-Gram Films, Inc., W. E. Disney Directing Animator. On the second floor of the Courthouse, the window advertises Scrooge McDuck, Investment Counselor.

Toontown's three eateries are located in this area. *Clarabelle's Frozen Yogurt*, *Pluto's Dog House*, and *Daisy's Diner* are described in the *Good Meals, Great Times* chapter.

On the way to Mickey's neighborhood, visitors pass **Goofy's Gas**, where a sign that touts an additive that "Makes Your Car Backfire and Sputta, Just the Way a Toon Car Oughta!" Animated fish blow bubbles inside the tanks. Other signs proclaim "Unlicensed Mechanic on Duty" and "Car Won't Backfire? It Will When We're Done With It!" The gas station houses the restroom facilities and public telephones for Toontown guests.

Mickey's Neighborhood

The centerpiece of the residential area is **Mickey's Fountain**. A statue of the world's most famous mouse stands in the center of the pool surrounded by realistic sculptures of musical instruments. The homes in this neighborhood sit at the base of the 40-foot-tall Toon Hills—complete with the Toontown version of the Hollywood sign. The houses are described here as a guest would encounter them traveling in a counterclockwise direction from Mickey's Fountain.

Minnie's House is a lavender and pink creation with a heart theme. The windows are heart-shaped as are the welcome mat and the weather vane. The mailbox out front is in the shape of Minnie's face. Once inside, guests can see Minnie's living room with its chintz sofa and magazines on the coffee table—*Cosmousepolitan* and *Mademouselle* are her favorites. On the answering machine are messages from Goofy and Mickey. Guests also

have the opportunity to create new fashions for Minnie on an interactive computer in her dressing room.

In Minnie's kitchen, a cake in the oven rises when the knob is turned, spoons clatter and pots and pans clank out a melody when the stove is turned on, and the dishwasher churns when the button is pushed. The Cheesemore refrigerator is stocked with an assortment of cheese products including Cheese Chip Ice Cream, Cheeseatsup, Cheesonaise, and Golly Cheeze Whiz. The shopping list tacked on the outside of the fridge gives a clue to Minnie's favorite cheeses, including Not So Gouda. Check out the diet cookies on the kitchen table.

Heading out the kitchen door into the backyard, Minnie's wishing well offers guests some parting thoughts. "Wishes make the world go around," "Always keep a wish in your heart," and "Wishes make everyone happy," are among the messages.

The path from Minnie's backyard leads right to the front door of **Mickey's House**. The welcoming yellow-and-red clapboard house with the huge green door and green shutters is home to the Toon who started it all. The mailbox out front has Mickey's face on it and the welcome mat is in the shape of his head with ears.

Inside, there is a protective gate on the staircase with a cutout of Pluto in the middle. Among the items on Mickey's "Things to Do" list are mousercise and call Minnie. There is a player piano and a curio cabinet with some wonderful memorabilia in his living room. Pluto's bed is here, complete with a huge bone and a half-eaten shoe. In the laundry

room, the washing machine is running and Mickey's glove and Minnie's dress can be eyed through the door. The stock of laundry supplies includes Toonox Bleach, Toonwy Fabric Hardener, and Toonite (for delicates). On another shelf are Mouse 'n' Glo and Formula 408½.

From the laundry room, guests pass through the greenhouse and into Mickey's backyard. Here Pluto's doghouse can be seen and in the garden, carrot tops disappear underground only to be replaced by the head of a Toon gopher who appears quite enchanted with his tricks.

Moving along to **Mickey's Movie Barn**, the first stop is the Prop Dept. where costumes and props from some of Mickey's most famous cartoons are stored. Donald's Painting Dept. where a "Duck at Work" sign is posted, and Goofy's Music Machine are on the way to the Screening Room where clips from remakes in progress such as *Steamboat Willie*, *The Band Concert*, *Thru the Mirror*, and *The Sorcerer's Apprentice* are being projected by a bumbling Goofy.

Mickey is usually hard at work on one of these films and guests have a chance to enter a soundstage in small groups for a photo and autograph session with the star.

Coming out of Mickey's house, Toontown visitors can head for the **Chip 'n' Dale Tree Slide and Acorn Crawl**. The traditional "ball crawl" is recreated here with brown and yellow acorns. Kids who are at least three years old and no taller than 48 inches can park their shoes in cubbies provided and get mired in the Acorn Crawl. Then they (and adults too) can go for a climb up a tree and take a bumpy slide back down.

Working your way around Toontown in a counterclockwise direction, the next stop is **Gadget's Go Coaster**. Thick red steel tracks give the impression of a very tame ride but the actual minute-long trip has quite a few thrills right up to the final turn into the station. The coaster is constructed with an assortment of Gadget's gadgets. For the uninitiated, Gadget is the brilliant inventor from the TV cartoon "Chip 'n' Dale's Rescue Rangers." The tracks are supported by giant toy blocks and the train is made up of hollowed-out acorns. Bridges are made of oversize combs, pencils, paper clips, and rubber bands, and the entire trip is visible from the queue area, which snakes under part of the coaster. The ride lasts less than a minute, so if the line is very long, it's best to save this trip for later in the day.

Note: Guests must be at least three years old to ride Gadget's Go Coaster, and children under seven must be accompanied by an adult. The trip is not advised for pregnant women.

Donald Duck's boat, the ***Miss Daisy***, is permanently docked in Toon Lake, adjacent to the Go Coaster. This is another house where the younger set has the advantage. Parents can sit

in a shaded seating area near a pretty waterfall while their kids explore this houseboat that looks very much like its owner. Guests may recognize Donald's eyes in the large portholes of the pilot house, his jaunty blue sailor's cap in the cabin roof, and his face in the shape of the hull. Kids can climb a rope ladder or a spiral staircase up to the pilot house of the ship. Would-be sailors can steer the wheel that turns the compass or toot the boat's whistle. A spiral slide brings visitors back to the lower deck through the boiler room.

The next just-for-kids attraction is **Goofy's Bounce House** located right next door to the *Miss Daisy*. Goofy's garden boasts an odd variety of delights including stalks of popcorn, spinning flowers, very watery watermelons, jack-o'-lanterns, and squashed squash. Kids who are at least three years old and no taller than 52

inches park their shoes in cubbies and head inside the inflated abode where they can literally bounce off the walls, the furniture, and even the fireplace. The windows are made of netting so parents can get a good view and some nice photos. Observant visitors will notice that Goofy's house also resembles its owner, right up to the green hat on top. Next to Goofy's Bounce House, **Toon Park** is a toddler's play area with a soft-surface environment and seating so that parents can watch comfortably.

Transportation around Toontown is provided by the **Jolly Trolley** which winds and weaves its way on figure-eight rails to and from each end of Toontown. A large gold wind-up key on top of the engine turns as the trolley runs.

Tomorrowland

Walt Disney cherished great hope for the future. "Tomorrow," he said in 1955, offers "new frontiers in science, adventure, and ideals: the atomic age . . . the challenge of outer space . . . and the hope for a peaceful and unified world." To this vision he dedicated Tomorrowland, "a vista into a world of wondrous ideas signifying man's achievements, a step into the future, with predictions of constructive things to come." Certainly, in terms of today's big-budget sci-fi films, Tomorrowland doesn't look much like the contemporary fantasy view of the years to come. Instead it represents a more accessible tomorrow, one that is truly within our grasp. So while there are attractions focused on space travel, there are others that offer more realistic options for tomorrow's transportation.

Tomorrowland entertainment is not futuristic but contemporary: Groups perform rock music at *Tomorrowland Terrace.* There's also the Starcade nearby, full of the hottest video games around. Movement is everywhere: The Rocket Jets whirl and bob high above the small cars of the PeopleMover, and submarines circle through the Disneyland sea while miniature motorcars *vroom* and sputter along the scaled-down highways of the Tomorrowland Autopia and sleek monorails glide from their station toward the *Disney-land Hotel.* Meanwhile, just to remind everyone where it all began, the traditional trains of the Disneyland Railroad chug into the Tomorrowland depot, a bit of the past visiting the possible future. It could only happen in Disneyland.

Be sure to note Tomorrowland's landscaping, which was not easy to develop. The designers decided to use familiar materials available in contemporary landscape design. Many trees and bushes have been pruned into geometric shapes; note the poodle-cut ligustrums around the train station. Other plants were picked for their slightly exotic natural configurations. But there's warmth in Tomorrowland, too: The flower beds at the entrance are the setting for the park's greatest show of annuals—more than 5,000 plants for each season. The results of these efforts make for a comfortable, inviting sort of place.

The following attractions are described as you come upon them when moving in a counterclockwise direction from the entrance to Tomorrowland.

STAR TOURS: One of the most spectacular attractions at Disneyland was inspired by George Lucas's *Star Wars* film trilogy. It offers guests the chance to board Star-Speeders, which are actually the same type of flight simulators that are regularly employed by the military and commercial airlines in the training of pilots. Synchronizing a stunning film with the virtually limitless motion of the simulator allows guests to truly feel what they see. Seatbelts are required.

Visitors enter an area where the famed *Star Wars* characters R2D2 and C3PO are working for a galactic travel agency. They spend their time in a bustling hangar area servicing the Star Tours fleet of spacecraft. Riders board the 40-passenger craft for what is intended to be a leisurely trip to the Moon of

Endor, but which quickly develops into a harrowing flight into deep space, including encounters with giant ice crystals and laser-blasting fighters. The flight is out of control from the start, as the rookie pilot proves that Murphy's Law applies to the entire universe. The sensations are extraordinary and the technology quite advanced. The voice of the spacecraft's captain belongs to Paul Reubens (Pee-Wee Herman).

Note: Passengers must be free of back problems, heart conditions, motion sickness, and other physical limitations to ride. Pregnant women and children under three are not permitted to board. Children under seven must be accompanied by an adult. The least bumpy seats are near the center of the compartment; for thrills, sit in the back.

STARCADE: This two-level games arcade (adjoining Space Mountain) is by all accounts the best in Orange County—if not in all of California. There are about 200 games—though which ones are on hand at any given time may vary. There are always a few for traditionalists and a couple that were custom-made for Disneyland to allow more than one player to participate at a time. Most of the rest are whatever happens to be hottest at the moment—and there's someone on the Disney staff to keep an eye on the games field to make sure that no state-of-the-art machine is omitted. A notable addition is the R360, a turbulent 360-degree pilot game. All the machines take from 25¢ to $4. There are $1 and $5 change machines, as well as a cashier, on the premises.

SPACE MOUNTAIN: Without a doubt one of the best attractions in the park, and certainly one of the most popular, Space Mountain also must rank among the best roller coasters in existence. Its greatness derives not so much from the fact that it will leave your stomach behind as from the fact that most of the trip shoots through pitch blackness with stars whizzing by on all sides. It's an experience so splendid and magical that it can be enjoyed many times without any disappointment. It's not a rocket journey, really: The 12-passenger "rockets" are similar to those boarded by many a roller-coaster buff, with two-abreast seating, and the ride's route is traveled at the relatively moderate speed of about 30 miles per hour. But between the stars and the Cosmic Vapor Curtain and the Solar Energizer and the glowing nebula, the attraction boasts such beauty that it's not hard to understand why Southern Californians queued up for as long as two hours to experience it when it first opened. (Though the situation isn't nearly so bad nowadays, it still behooves a queue-hater to make a beeline for the mountain immediately upon arriving in the park.)

Such a marvel doesn't develop overnight. Walt Disney had the idea for the attraction early in the park's history—long before the technology to operate it had been developed. The original sketch for the many-spired white cone, not all that different from the present structure, was drawn in 1964. Subsequently, workers representing about 150 different crafts and specialties put almost a million hours into the design and construction of this bit of man-made mountain magic. It took nearly two years to construct, and the whole thing is sunk 17 feet into the ground—so as not to dwarf Sleeping Beauty Castle or the Matterhorn.

Those who don't normally enjoy roller coasters should be sure to ride the People-Mover instead, since it offers a look at the scenic wonders inside the mountain. Those who decide they might want a still closer look should line up with the brave at the base of the Speedramp. The ride lasts three thrilling minutes.

Note: Pregnant women, children who are under three, and guests who suffer from weak backs, heart conditions, motion sickness, and other physical limitations should not ride. Children under seven must be accompanied by an adult; you must be at least 40 inches tall to ride.

COLD FEET?

If your courage fails you, there are three "chicken exits" in the queue area of Splash Mountain en route to the loading dock—one just past the entrance to the building, another farther along by the turnstiles, and the last at the loading area. Parents can wait with their kids up to this exit and then rendezvous with them when the ride is over.

CAPTAIN EO: This 17-minute 3-D musical fantasy stars Michael Jackson as the captain of a spaceship. His band of characters include Hooter, Fuzzball, and The Geek. Their mission: to transform the dismal planet ruled by the Evil Queen (played by Academy Award-winner Angelica Huston) into a happy place through the magic of music and dance. Jackson wrote and performs two original

songs: "We Are Here to Change the World" and "Another Part of Me." The Magic Eye Theater has been redesigned and outfitted with state-of-the-art audio and video equipment, as well as the wherewithal to provide a dazzling group of special effects.

DISNEYLAND RAILROAD: The old-fashioned trains that circle the park in 19 minutes can be boarded in Tomorrowland, as well as in the Frontierland station (in New Orleans Square), in Toontown (this serves as the stop for adjacent Fantasyland), and on Main Street. Though the latter usually boasts the fastest-moving queue, those who want to ride only long enough to view the Primeval World and Grand Canyon dioramas that constitute the scenery between the Tomorrowland and Main Street stations may want to board here.

TOMORROWLAND AUTOPIA: Anyone who contends with the Southern California freeways every day may find it difficult to get excited about queuing up to steer these small, streamlined sports cars around an equally pint-size highway. But youngsters absolutely adore the trip and can spend hours driving these Mark VII-model, ten-foot-long, 1,100-pound vehicles along the twisting roadways here. To someone used to steering nothing more powerful than a bicycle, the top speed—seven miles an hour—comes as a big thrill.

Engines are one cylinder, four cycle, air cooled, and made of cast iron, generating seven horsepower each. **Note:** You must be at least 52 inches tall to drive alone, and at least one year old to be a passenger.

SUBMARINE VOYAGE: The scenery in this eight-minute ride is compelling enough to keep you engrossed from the plunge at the start of the journey through the Graveyard of Lost Ships, the trip under the North Pole, to Atlantis, and on to your rendezvous with a sea serpent. Most of the sights en route approximate those associated with the sea now and down through the ages: Giant clams, weighing 500 pounds or more, really do inhabit coral environments of the East Indies and Australia. There actually was a submarine trip under the North Pole—made in 1958 by the U.S.S. *Nautilus*. Giant squids can be found in waters deeper than 600 feet; they do grow to lengths of 50 feet and more. Mermaids have figured in the folklore of the sea for centuries, and Atlantis was described in Ignatius Donnely's *Atlantis, the Antediluvian World* in 1882, while marine monsters have appeared regularly in world literature since the earliest years of Chinese history. The lagoon holds about six million gallons of water, and is said to be 25 times as clean as drinking water, since any bit of grease or dirt would distort viewing of the underwater "show."

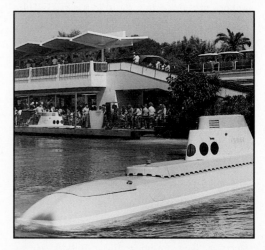

DISNEYLAND MONORAIL SYSTEM: America's first daily operating monorail system was a novelty when it was introduced in 1959. A decade later it was replaced with four sleek Mark V, five-car trains, and it's always a thrill to see them gliding through the park. The 2½-mile-long "highway in the sky" adds immeasurably to Tomorrowland's aura of urban futurism, and it provides a nine-minute round-trip through the edge of Tomorrowland across the street to the *Disneyland Hotel* and back again to Tomorrowland. Straddling its concrete beamway, the train has rubber tires to move it along, plus braking wheels atop the beam and guiding and stabilizing wheels on either side.

PEOPLEMOVER: Disneyland's PeopleMover, 38 zippy white cars with a rainbow stripe, takes guests on a 12-minute tour of many of Tomorrowland's attractions. The cars meander through the preview area of Star Tours and then go into Space Mountain (just long enough to entice those who plan to go on and to help the indecisive make up their minds). You'll see the spires of It's A Small World from a distance, and view the Matterhorn close-up. The ride can be bumpy and you can't always hear the accompanying narrative; the outdoor segments usually are more appealing than the indoor parts. The PeopleMover's cars are motorless; the track itself contains electric motors that keep things moving along.

ROCKET JETS: This is a thrill ride, pure and simple—though it does add considerable visual interest to Tomorrowland as viewed from the Central Plaza. A good choice for anyone who loved Space Mountain, but doesn't want to get in line all over again. Especially popular with kids (who must be at least 1 year old to ride), it last 1½ minutes.

WORLD PREMIERE CIRCLE-VISION: Motion pictures created for Walt Disney World's Epcot in Florida provided a testing ground for this type of film technique. *Wonders of China*, an Epcot creation that surrounds viewers with spectacular footage from that country, is presented from park opening to 1:30 P.M. The Disney group, by the way, was the first Western crew to film some sites in China. From 3 P.M. to park closing, *American Journeys* literally surrounds the viewer with breathtaking scenery—Rocky Mountain meadows, the Mississippi River, and New York City's Park Avenue—while telling a visual story of America's heritage.

Shops in the Magic Kingdom

Until you really get to know Disneyland, you might not expect that anyone would visit just to go shopping. But among Southern Californians, Disneyland is a favorite spot in which to consume conspicuously. Employees find Christmas and birthday presents here, and it's not unusual for local residents to make a special trip to the park to purchase an item they may have noticed during a previous visit.

It's easy to see why Disneyland is such a popular shopping site. Mickey Mouse key chains, mugs, T-shirts, hats, and other such souvenirs are all found here in abundance, but there also are many other enticing treasures.

Antiques and silver-plated tea sets, egg-beaters and cookbooks, mock pirate hats and muskets, 14-karat-gold charms, and filigreed costume jewelry are among the available goods. Shops stock merchandise to complement the themes of the various lands. And so, in Adventureland, there are jewelry and leather accessories, wood carvings, and *Aladdin*, *Lion King*, and *Pocahontas* merchandise, as well as rain forest novelties. In New Orleans Square, you'll find perfume and antiques, silver, and specialty cookware. In Frontierland, leather belts and hats, Native American crafts, and Western clothing are the main items. In Fantasyland, there are sweets aplenty, toys, and European handicrafts. In Tomorrowland, Disney character merchandise is the big deal, but so are futuristic-looking lamps and clocks. Nearly every store offers a broad selection, from the inexpensive to the quite costly.

Consequently, there's no need to spend a fortune to acquire mementos from Disneyland. Budget watchers should be aware of the vast temptation to buy on impulse and plan expenditures carefully in advance.

MAIN STREET

NEWSSTAND: Located outside the main gate, this is a good spot to pick up a last-minute souvenir on your way out—but be prepared for crowds.

SOUVENIR STANDS: Located on both sides of the Disneyland Railroad depot in Town Square, these kiosks sell film and Disney-related books, postcards, stuffed animals, key chains, children's sunglasses, and the like. The selection is not as wide as elsewhere, but that can be an advantage if you have a good idea of what you want.

West Side of the Street

EMPORIUM: The wares in this sprawling establishment at the Town Square end of Main Street are by no means as old-fashioned as the mansard-roofed, tin-ceilinged, velvet-curtained setting might suggest. Sunglasses and jewelry, china figurines and music boxes, T-shirts and sweatshirts, folding umbrellas and nylon totes, and character hats make up the bulk of the stock. There's a little bit of everything, and the variety of the selections is likely to please. China figurines come in all kinds and sizes: Mickey Mouse appears as sorcerer, cyclist, policeman, doctor, baseball player, tennis player, jogger, and golfer; even Donald and Minnie are seen in an assortment of roles. Goofy, Pluto, Daisy, Lady, Tramp, the Dalmatians, Alice, the Cheshire Cat, the White Rabbit, the Mad Hatter, Dumbo, Peter Pan, Tinkerbell, Mary Poppins, and other familiar Disney figures also crowd the shelves. There are more than three dozen cash registers, and at the

end of the operating day they're all mobbed. As you're queuing up to pay for your purchases, it's easy to understand why the store accounts for better than 25 percent of all Disneyland merchandising sales annually. For maximum enjoyment, by the way, visit the Emporium in the morning, when Disneylanders have the most time to show off their wares. Also, be sure to note the detailed window displays, usually related to the latest Walt Disney Company film release.

CARRIAGE PLACE CLOTHING CO.: This shop, an extension of the Emporium, sells a variety of Disney apparel and accessories for children and adults. This is where you can find one of the best selections of children's character clothing anywhere.

STORYBOOK STORE: Children's books are the stock in trade in this section of the Emporium building. Coloring books and children's classics—in the standard versions, as well as the Disney editions—are all available: *Heidi*, *Black Beauty*, *Treasure Island*, *Charlotte's Web*, and *The Adventures of Tom Sawyer* are among the most popular. Golden Books, compact discs, dolls, and games are in stock.

NEW CENTURY TIMEPIECES AND JEWELRY SHOP: Timepieces in all shapes and sizes are displayed in polished wood cases at this store across from the *Carnation Ice Cream Parlor*. There are Mickey Mouse alarm clocks and Donald Duck clocks, plus Mickey Mouse watches and original-art watches where your favorite character is hand-drawn to create a personalized timepiece expressly for you. There also are clocks for the kitchen and the living room, clocks with and without chimes, clocks for travel, and clocks meant to roost on a bedside table. The pins, earrings, necklaces, pendants, and rings available here are more delicate and more feminine looking than those sold in most of the other Disneyland shops. Among the choice offerings are 14-karat-gold charms of Tinkerbell, Donald Duck, and Minnie Mouse.

CANDY PALACE: An old-fashioned pageant in pink and white, this shop is alluring at any time of day, but never more than when the candy makers are at work in a glass-walled kitchen confecting candy canes, chocolate-covered strawberries, fudge, and other temptations for a sweet tooth. Their aromatic scents perfume the air on this part of Main Street (greatly abetted by a strong fan). The sweets produced are for sale on the premises, along with a bounty of chocolates, peanut brittle, almond rocky road, caramel pecan rolls, divinity, hard candies, licorice, and more.

East Side of the Street

DISNEY SHOWCASE: Merchandise from the latest Disney movie releases and from the popular Disney afternoon cartoons is featured at this spot across the street from the Emporium.

MAD HATTER SHOP: This hat shop sells bowlers, top hats, and frilly bonnets that beg for an Easter parade, Mickey Mouse ears in black and various colors, and a good assortment of other toppers to protect tender skin from the sun.

MAGIC SHOP: Some years ago when a film star came to Disneyland, she tired of being hounded for her autograph, so she bought herself a pair of long, false eyelashes, a pirate's hat, and a special sword that looked as if it pierced her head. People kept on stopping her, but not because they recognized her—they just wanted to know where she had

bought her crazy hat. The array of possible disguises for sale in this boutique, the surviving member of a pair of magic shops that graced Disneyland for years, is wonderful indeed. With adequate funds and the aid of some realistic-looking latex masks, you can transform yourself into Frankenstein's monster or a gorilla, a grandfather or a ghoul, a skeleton or Darth Vader. Smaller budgets only may allow for a pair of bloodshot eyes, or a box of clown makeup. But because this is a magic shop, there also are plenty of tricks and books about tricks. Store personnel will occasionally demonstrate the magic tricks they sell.

GREAT AMERICAN PASTIMES: It's located next to the Magic Shop, and sports enthusiasts will love the trading cards, team hats, and pins. Even the most avid baseball or football fan will find that special collectible in this Main Street shop.

MARKET HOUSE: This Disney version of an old-fashioned general store sells pickles, nuts, preserves, malted milk balls, candy sticks, spice drops, rock candy, and other staples of daily life in years gone by. But this is one case in which the setting really outshines the merchandise. At the entrance, for instance, there are a half-dozen captain's chairs surrounding a real antique potbellied stove and an honest-to-goodness checkerboard where the competitive among the footsore actually do strike up games. Scattered around the warm, paneled premises are a few old-fashioned telephones. You can listen in on a typical turn-of-the-century conversation in which a mother expounds to her daughter on fried-onion poultices as a cure for the common cold, newfangled union suits, hauling water and cutting wood, eligible bachelors, the use of sliced cucumbers to perk up a complexion, and the exorbitant price of steak—all of 11¢ a pound! In the southeast corner of the store, there's a small room with seasonal merchandise, and a line of cooking utensils emblazoned with Mickey Mouse's image. And on the east wall of the store there is a handful of quaint old photographs and antique tools.

DISNEYANA SHOP: Collectors and the curious will find rare and unusual Disney merchandise including original "cels," short for celluloids, from Disney-animated classics (priced from around $250 for a single image unframed to about $6,000 for a set of four in a good case). Mickey and Minnie Christmas figurines and plates, limited-edition Disney commissioned bronze statues, Capodimonte sculptures, Mickey Mouse telephones, and similar items round out the selection.

DISNEY CLOTHIERS, LTD.: Disney-character merchandise has always been popular, as evidenced by the number of T-shirts, Mickey Mouse ears, wristwatches, and sweatshirts sold each year. This shop caters to fashion-conscious shoppers with a love for Disney gear. There is a vast array of men's, women's, and children's clothing and accessories, all of which incorporate Disney characters in some way. There are men's golf shirts with a small Mickey Mouse embroidered on the pocket, women's oversize nightshirts with Mickey or Minnie Mouse, and satin-look jackets with Mickey (as the Sorcerer's Apprentice in *Fantasia*) embroidered on the back. Hats, ties, and exercise clothing round out the selections.

MAIN STREET PHOTO SUPPLY CO.: If your film gets stuck or you can't get it loaded in the first place, or if you encounter other minor mechanical problems, the folks who work here will try to help you out. If not, they can rent you a Kodak 35mm or instant camera, or sell you a new one from the gleaming cases full of popular models from Kodak, Canon, Olympus, Pentax, and other well-known makers. The selection of film is the best in the park. The shop is presented by Kodak.

CRYSTAL ARTS: Gleaming glasses and pitchers, mugs and trays, and other mementos can be engraved and monogrammed while you wait, or you can purchase them unornamented. There is a similar shop with a similar name in New Orleans Square. Both are presented by Arribas Brothers.

SILHOUETTE STUDIO: Working at the rate of about 60 seconds per portrait, Disneyland's silhouette artists are a wonder to watch. They have endless patience, terrific senses of humor, and wonderful showmanship that makes queuing for a turn almost as much fun as receiving the final product. Horses, cats, dogs, and loved ones (scissored according to a careful description) have all been portrayed. The art form itself, made almost obsolete by the invention of the camera, was developed in the mid-18th century by a French finance minister, Etienne de Silhouette.

CHINA CLOSET: This bastion of breakable things offers the usual assortment of Disney character figurines, but they make up only a very small percentage of the merchandise. Teacups and teapots come in dozens of colors and styles. Canisters and soap dishes, jars and lamps, and sugar bowls and creamers in colored glass fill the shelves, along with accent pieces from Royal Doulton, statuettes from the Spanish company Lladro, Hummels, intriguing Norman Rockwell plates, and Fitz & Floyd giftware. Blessedly, the aisles are wide enough so that there's little danger of knocking anything over.

CAREFREE CORNER: A wide selection of greeting cards, plus ribbons and wrapping paper, party supplies, pens, postcards, and postage stamps. A large assortment of stuffed animals also is available.

NEW ORLEANS SQUARE

Shops are described as you encounter them when moving from east to west through this area of the park.

ONE OF A KIND SHOP: A must. This popular and eminently browsable corner of New Orleans Square once sold props from Disney movies. Nowadays, antiques and reproductions are the stock in trade, but the selection is as intriguing as ever. The recent manufactures are mainly replicas of ephemera of a century ago. Expect to find such temptations as jewelry, antique-style clothing, dolls, chandeliers, inlaid boxes, paintings, some furniture reproductions, paperweights, china cups and porcelain decorative pieces, and unique patio items. The bridal veils and hand-made, custom-decorated hats for men and women are a big draw.

PIECES OF EIGHT: Wares with a pirate theme are purveyed at this shop near the exit from the Pirates of the Caribbean attraction. A quarter can get you a "noggin o' seamanly advice" from a scuzzy-looking redheaded, green-eyed Audio-Animatronics character named Fortune Red, who occupies a glass box atop the steps. For intermediate sums, there are pirate rings, T-shirts, ship's lanterns, stocking caps, and fake knives and swords in plastic and rubber.

CRISTAL D'ORLEANS: The marble floor and doorsteps make a beautiful setting for the transparent trinkets and glasses glittering atop mirrors in this small Royal Street boutique. Glasses and chandeliers, decanters and ashtrays, pitchers and paperweights are typical treasures here. It's presented by Arribas Brothers.

LE BAT EN ROUGE: If Dracula had a day job, it would be here, in the world of decorative bats and leering gargoyles. The shop also sells jewelry, picture frames, and candles—all with an element of mystery or the grotesque. It's great fun.

LE GOURMET: Anyone who enjoys puttering around in the kitchen will relish this store, which is chockablock with interesting cookware. The selection of cookie cutters is purely and simply fabulous: They come, for instance, not in one Mickey Mouse shape but three—a head and two full body shapes. Soup tureens, butter dishes, dippers and Delftware, scrub

On your way out, take a look at the bronze plaque adorning the wall above the drinking fountain outside. It was discovered by members of the prop department while on a buying trip to New Orleans. The fountain, not part of the original plan, was added just to show it off to best advantage.

THE DISNEY GALLERY: Located above the entrance to the Pirates of the Caribbean, in several rooms originally designed as an apartment for Walt Disney, this gallery displays original drawings and designs for Disneyland, as well as artwork from Disney Art Editions, featuring classic Disney animation. Changing exhibits feature the works of Disney Imagineers, long stored in vast archives. Selected pieces of artwork have been reproduced in limited editions and are for sale.

L'MASCARDE D'ORLEANS: The excitement of Mardi Gras is recreated here with dazzling displays of harlequin dolls, masks, jester and princess hats, other festive apparel, handbags, and glittery, sequined jewelry. The merchandise features the traditional Mardi Gras colors: purple, green, and gold.

brushes and rolling pins, linen towels and napkin rings, cheese slicers, soufflé dishes, wooden bowls in a regular menagerie of shapes, pretty chandeliers for the kitchen, copper pots that will last a lifetime, tea kettles and corkscrews, and even artichoke cookers—all are on display, some in pretty antique chests, which also are for sale. There's an excellent selection of first class cookbooks, too. The store also is the headquarters for all Mickey gourmet products, including Mickey Mouse pasta, sauces, and seasonings.

MLLE. ANTOINETTE'S PARFUMERIE: If prizes were to be given for the most beautiful of Disneyland's shops, this tiny, fragrant corner of New Orleans Square would get the blue ribbon. Doorsteps are lovely marble mosaics, cabinets have doors made of glass, and lighting is from an antique chandelier that Walt Disney himself brought from Louisiana just for this purpose. The floor is decoratively tiled and the woodwork a soothing pink overglazed with silver leaf. In addition, there are eight reverse-painted mirrored panels around the shop, shining marvels—believed to be the largest of their type ever created—exemplifying a Chinese art that was popular in Europe from the 14th century to the beginning of the 19th. Painting the butterflies, bluebirds, garlands, and bouquets meant executing the detail work first, then the background—just the opposite of the technique used when putting oils on canvas—then silvering the entire piece. The effect is unabashedly pretty, perfect for displaying the shop's wares—potpourri, scented soaps, atomizers, body and bath oils, lotions, Venetian muds, and bath salts. Perfumes can be blended to order using eight different basic oils, small paddle-shaped blotters, graduated cylinders, and long, glass funnels. The formula you choose is recorded with thousands of others in a large black notebook, so you can reorder.

CANDY CART: Sweets always have been an important part of New Orleans life, and New Orleans Square has its own purveyor of confections—licorice, hard candies, gumdrops, and such—stationed prominently outside *Café Orleans*, near the entrance to Royal Street.

FRONTIERLAND

Shops are described in the order in which they are encountered moving from east to west through the land.

WESTWARD HO TRADING COMPANY: Hitch up your wagon and come on in, where you'll find an assortment of dolls, toys, decorative and gift items, jewelry, and clothing—all with a country theme.

FRONTIERLAND CANDY SHOP: A variety of mouth-watering treats, from delicious, old-fashioned saltwater taffy to tempting candy bars.

THE SPIRIT OF POCAHONTAS: Located to the left as you enter Frontierland from the Central Plaza, this shop with log walls and a wooden sidewalk out front carries all kinds of *Pocahontas* paraphernalia—in fact, you can think of it as one-stop shopping where Pocahontas is concerned—themed apparel for adults and children, stationery, decorative items, stuffed animals, and toys. Non-themed items include turquoise jewelry, Native American toys and pottery, Kachina dolls, and beautifully crafted webs called dream catchers. A figure of Grandmother Willow stands in the middle of the store, reminding those who enter to let their heart be their guide.

FRONTIERLAND SOUVENIR SHOP: Next door to The Spirit of Pocahontas shop, it sells standard Disneyland gift items and memorabilia, including stuffed animals, character souvenirs, autograph books, stationery, T-shirts, and, especially for the kids, coonskin caps and Frontierland Mickey cowboy hats.

BONANZA OUTFITTERS: Mosey in and try on the wildest western apparel this side of the Mississippi. Custom-designed jackets, western shirts, boots, and fancy pants are

just a few of the duds that can be found in this Frontierland shop. Once you've acquired the cowboy or cowgirl clothes, you can top off the outfit with a western-style hat. Western jewelry and accessories, and everything else you need to round out a western look, also are available here.

CRITTER COUNTRY

Shops are described in the order in which you come upon them while you're strolling toward Critter Country.

BRIAR PATCH: Located right at the base of the Splash Mountain briar patch, this little dwelling specializes in Winnie the Pooh. There are decorative items, honey, books, and apparel. The grass on the roof is real, seeded with a variety known as creeping red fescue. The grass is hand mowed around the carrots, which grow right through the roof and can be seen from inside the shop.

CROCODILE MERCANTILE: This lace-curtained, log-walled, woodsy-looking emporium is the Disneyland source for collectible bears. Buyers comb the Appalachian countryside and other rural quarters for many of the wares: carvings, tote bags that would be perfect for carrying diapers, bear pencils, country-themed decorative items for the home, along with a whole assortment of dolls, including some in pigtails and sailor outfits. Among the more unusual items on display are the pins and cufflinks and other jewelry made of Black Hills gold, which, because of the copper and zinc mixed into the metal, has sections tinged with green and pink. Toy rifles, Big Al dolls and mugs and cookie jars, and Splash Mountain T-shirts, sweatshirts, and key chains also are available. The store is a good place to buy film, too.

ADVENTURELAND

Shops are described in the order in which they are encountered while strolling from east to west through the land.

ADVENTURELAND BAZAAR: Except for the fact that bargaining is impossible, this small marketplace is well named. There are goods from most of the exotic corners of the world: from India, assorted brass-crafted jewelry and leather accessories; from Africa, wooden zebras and giraffes and other carvings; and there is a selection of rain-forest-inspired clothing. This also is the best location for souvenirs themed to the popular *Aladdin* and *Lion King* characters.

SOUTH SEA TRADERS: Adjacent to the Adventureland Bazaar, this is the place to browse for men's and women's casual wear. The store features colorful contemporary designs, along with a wide selection of tropical hats. A basic straw model can be decorated to guests' specifications, with beads, ribbons, and/or feathers.

TROPICAL IMPORTS: Opposite the Adventureland Bazaar, an island of its own near the entrance to the Jungle Cruise, this emporium is nearly irresistible to young kids. The reason: Rubber snakes and iguanas are part of the stock in trade. The squeamish will, of course, be more interested in the seashells and other souvenir items. There also is a large selection of stuffed "jungle" animals, including a five-foot-tall gorilla. Film is available here as well.

INDIANA JONES ADVENTURE OUTPOST: This outfitter can supply the most daring expeditions with all manner of souvenirs, T-shirts, hats, and jackets, not to mention artifacts brought back by the legendary archeologist Indiana Jones from the Temple of the Golden Eye.

FANTASYLAND

Shops are listed in the order in which a visitor would encounter them while moving in a clockwise fashion through Fantasyland.

CASTLE HERALDRY SHOPPE: At this tiny shop in Sleeping Beauty Castle, you can trace your family name through centuries and continents and have a history of it printed up (a great gift idea for the geneologically minded). Or choose from hand-painted marble or bronze shields, coat-of-arms certificates, rings, T-shirts, and hats emblazoned with your family crest.

TINKER BELL TOY SHOPPE: This wonderland installed at the western end of Sleeping Beauty Castle is Disneyland's main stop for serious toy shopping. Youngsters who have some vacation money burning a hole in their pockets will go for the inexpensive souvenirs. Fond grandparents will relish the children's fantasy costumes—red-and-white polka-dotted Minnie dresses and pale-blue pinafored Alice in Wonderland dresses, as well as Snow White and Pocahontas outfits for little girls, and Peter Pan and Aladdin costumes for little boys. Books, tapes, paint-by-number sets, games, and the like complete the offerings. The selection of dolls is particularly good, and includes fairy-tale figures, Madame Alexander, and other limited-edition collectible dolls. Longtime Disneyland fans may recognize the two cannons sitting atop the poop deck at the far end of the store as the weapons from the pirate ship that occupied a prominent place in Fantasyland before its renovation.

CASTLE CHRISTMAS SHOPPE: If anything can make thoughts turn to the yule season in the heart of Southern California in July, it will be this slate-floored, beam-ceilinged establishment in Sleeping Beauty Castle. Decked out in red and green, with Christmas music playing year-round, this holiday boutique offers all manner of Christmas souvenirs, Mouse-themed and otherwise, that should prove well-nigh irresistible to even budget-conscious guests—trinkets like Santa Clauses and wooden soldiers, bells and drums and Christmas sleighs, plus trifles in velvet, dough, and china to decorate next year's tree or mantelpiece.

GEPPETTO'S TOYS AND GIFTS: Situated alongside Pinocchio's Daring Journey, this shop is a treasure trove of European-style gifts. Cuckoo clocks, some of which have movable figurines, fill a whole wall. You'll also find trolls from Norway, cowbells from Austria, and from Germany, character dolls,

101

nutcrackers, and "smokers," which are carved wooden figurines with a receptacle for an incense pellet and an outlet in the mouth for the smoke to escape.

STROMBOLI'S WAGON: Located near the *Village Haus*, this stand offers everything from Disney plush toys to Mickey Mouse sunglasses. Other items available include character key chains, pens, buttons, and candy. The shop is named after the villain in *Pinocchio*.

IT'S A SMALL WORLD TOY SHOP: Just at the exit of It's A Small World, this shop stocks a wide assortment of Barbie dolls and accessories, Hot Wheels, and Disney-licensed Mattel toys, dolls, and games featuring the Disney characters.

SMALL WORLD GIFTS: Souvenirs predominate at this stand, near It's A Small World, but there also are plush characters, T-shirts, sweatshirts, hats, and candy.

CHARACTER CARROUSEL: Near the Matterhorn and It's A Small World plaza, this is a good spot to pick up a trinket or two and avoid the brouhaha of Main Street's Emporium or Tomorrowland's Star Trader. Children's sunglasses, postcards, decals, change purses, pens and pencils, key chains, and the like—all of them bearing likenesses of the Disney characters—are typical wares.

MAD HATTER: Always a great place for hats. There are traditional black bowlers, and fedoras in several colors, Mouse ears, cowboy

hats, feathered Tyrolean hats, gangster hats, and such. This establishment looks something like the dwelling inhabited by the famous rabbit from *Alice in Wonderland*. (The small door and window on the Mad Tea Party side are meant to be the entrance of the White Rabbit's house.) The thatching atop the whole structure is, by the way, non-flammable plastic. Imagine the spectacle of a crew of brawny construction workers clambering over the rooftop wielding a half-dozen hair dryers to provide the heat to mold the "straws" into the curved edge of the roof! The tree next to the side facing the King Arthur Carrousel is a cork oak (*Quercus suber*), whose bark provides the material for bulletin boards and the like.

DISNEY VILLAINS: This shop, tucked away in a quiet corner of the castle courtyard has a large assortment of merchandise displaying favorite villains from Disney's classic films including Malificent from *Sleeping Beauty*, Cruella DeVille from *101 Dalmatians*, and Ursula from *The Little Mermaid*. One of Disneyland's least obvious pleasures is offered by the wicked witch who occupies a glass-walled cage in the center of this shop. She has a bulbous nose, huge round yellow eyes, and a black mouth, and she looks so altogether frightening that little children cling to their parents, especially when, every so often, she moves. Her chains clank, and she begs you to

let her out, promising to show you how to fly and to turn water into gasoline if you do—and then threatening you if you don't. She was originally part of a display in the windows of Walt Disney World's Emporium. The crew of Imagineers who created her decided to animate her at the last minute and added the audio only hours before shipping her to California. So successful is this creation that occasionally it is difficult to concentrate on the shop's wares.

MICKEY'S TOONTOWN

GAG FACTORY: A Laugh-O-Meter outside this shop gives some indication of the wares to be found inside. Smirk, giggle, chuckle, laugh, guffaw, bellow, and roar are the options available. Hand buzzers, slippery banana peels, and all the other gags Toons need in their daily work and play are available here, as are many costumes, Disney-character merchandise, clothing, and videotapes.

TOONTOWN FIVE & DIME: Situated in the same building as the Gag Factory, this shop stocks a variety of magic tricks plus an array of Toontown memorabilia including T-shirts, sweatshirts, pens, pencils, hats, and more.

TOMORROWLAND

Shops here are listed counterclockwise from Tomorrowland's Central Plaza entrance.

STAR TRADER: One of the best places in the park for Disney-themed items, it offers T-shirts and sweatshirts galore, pens and rulers, tennis balls and shoehorns, back scratchers, jewelry, mugs, figurines, lollipops, key chains, watches, pewter charms, and more—all emblazoned with the names and likenesses of one or more of the Disney characters. Stuffed animals are here by the hundreds, including oversize Roger Rabbits, Plutos, and Dumbos for $250 to $350 each, which can be ordered when not in stock, and can usually be mailed to guest's homes. In addition, because this is Tomorrowland, there's naturally a good selection of space-age items.

PREMIERE SHOP: Found next to World Premiere Circle-Vision, this shop specializes in Anaheim Mighty Ducks hockey team merchandise, as well as other sports-themed gifts including T-shirts, hats, mugs, and keychains with professional team logos. You can also purchase "Team Mickey" and "Goofy about Sports" items here.

HATMOSPHERE: Adjacent to the Autopia, this emporium stocks hats in all styles—hats made of tweed, felt, and terry cloth; hats with bills and hats with ears; as well as pirate hats, sailor hats, and hats in a dozen other styles. Names can be embroidered on most for free. Get your ears here.

Entertainment

Together with Walt Disney World, Disneyland books more entertainment than any other organization in the world. While no two years provide quite the same mix of shows, what follows is typical of the variety that you can expect. Check your entertainment schedule for current offerings.

Performers & Live Shows

A bevy of musicians strolls, marches, croons, and plucks its way through the Magic Kingdom every day. They perform so frequently that you don't have to try very hard to find them.

Main Street

DAPPER DANS: The official greeters of Main Street, this classic singing quartet performs the standards in perfect four-part harmony. They may be found strolling on the sidewalk or pedaling along on their bicycle built for four. Five days a week during the summer and holidays.

DISNEYLAND BAND: Disneyland's own signature group is as versatile as can be. They'll be performing in the Central Plaza at the end of Main Street, but if you miss them there you can catch them at any number of other locations. Check at City Hall for a schedule. Their repertoire is mainly turn-of-the-century band music, but they can play just about anything.

COKE CORNER PIANIST: Someone is almost always on hand to tickle the ivories on the snow-white upright at this centrally located soda-and-hot dogs restaurant. Daily.

DISNEYLAND BIG SWING BAND: Performing in the *Carnation Plaza Gardens*, this group recreates great sounds from the swing era. Grand entertainment for dancers and listeners alike. Saturday evenings only.

Adventureland

AMAZON BASIN JUNGLE OUTREACH PROGRAM: This wacky troupe of misadventurers usually can be found near the entrance to the Indiana Jones Adventure, entertaining those waiting to explore the Temple of the Forbidden Eye with their improvisational comedy skills. Four days a week during the summer.

FIRST SWING DIVISION BRASS: In the tradition of the big bands, this nattily attired eight-piece band fills the air with the sound of swing from atop the Jungle Cruise boathouse. Four days a week.

LOST ARKYOLOGISTS: This lively five-piece group leads you on a happy musical journey as you wend your way through the Indiana Jones Adventure queue. Four days a week.

TRINIDAD TROPICAL STEEL DRUM BAND: Enjoy the delightful calypso rhythms of this colorful group. They perform near the entrance to the Jungle Cruise.

New Orleans Square

BRASS BROTHERS: They look like the Blues Brothers, complete with black suits and sunglasses, but the eight members of this brass ensemble play jazz and Dixieland music in the *French Market*. Afternoons daily.

ROYAL STREET BACHELORS: Their style is early traditional New Orleans Dixieland, a flat four-beat sound influenced by the old funeral marches once commonly heard in the Storyville section of the Crescent City. The Bachelors perform near the One of a Kind shop.

SIDE STREET STRUTTERS: A six-member Dixieland jazz group performs at the *French Market*. Weekends only.

Frontierland

BILLY HILL & THE HILL BILLIES: A four-piece bluegrass ensemble featuring fiddle, bass, and mandolin players entertains in the *Casa Mexicana* restaurant and also strolls through Critter Country.

GOLDEN HORSESHOE STAGE: This lively musical show usually is staged five days a week, and performance times change throughout the year. The routine is funny and well worth your while, so reserve a place as soon as possible after you arrive in the park. For more in-depth information, see page 74. Reservations are required.

FANTASMIC!

Without a doubt, this is the best Disney extravaganza yet. A spectacular 22-minute mix of magic, music, live performers, and sensational special effects lights up the Rivers of America nightly on weekends, holidays, and throughout the summer season. In an unprecedented display of pyrotechnics, lasers, fog, fiber optics, and giant props, 51 performers put on an unforgettable show.

This is a tale of good versus evil and it's up to Mickey to overcome a vast array of villains. He first appears at the tip of Tom Sawyer Island and he uses his imagination to make comets shoot across the sky while the river waters dance. The scene is created through a carefully choreographed combination of effects: A live Mickey appears in a cone of specially programmed lights, and pyrotechnics appear to shoot from his fingers.

Topping it all off is the spectacular technology used in Fantasmic! As Mickey works his magic, a specially prepared film sequence appears, seemingly in mid-air above the river. This effect is achieved by projecting 70mm film onto three giant mist screens, each one 30-feet tall by 50-feet wide. Adding to the overall impact, the screens are transparent so that live performers behind and in front of them appear to be interacting with the filmed images.

There is a scene in which Monstro the Whale from *Pinocchio* makes waves in the real water of the Rivers of America. In a "Pink Elephants on Parade" scene, the animated pachyderms from *Dumbo* interact with live performers in flexible, glow-in-the-dark elephant costumes.

These illusions build toward a breathtaking confrontation of good and evil, in which Disney villains attempt to disrupt Mickey's fantasy. Fearsome creatures all have their chance—a 20-foot-tall Ursula the Sea Witch from *The Little Mermaid*, an animated Chernabog demon, and finally the evil Maleficent, who turns into a 45-foot-tall, fire-breathing dragon from *Sleeping Beauty*.

The villains turn Mickey's dreams into nightmares and he must overcome them with his own powers of goodness, plus a little help from his friends. The *Columbia* sailing ship parades through the show with the swashbuckling cast of *Peter Pan* on board and the *Mark Twain* riverboat brings along a host of favorite Disney characters.

The best viewing spots are in front of the *French Market* restaurant or Pirates of the Caribbean (or the balcony of The Disney Gallery, but its reservations-only dessert buffet costs $30). You can get a take-out picnic from *La Petite Patisserie* or a snack from the *Stage Door Café*.

Note: Fantasmic! is shown twice nightly during busy seasons. The later show is always less crowded. Parents of young children should be aware that some of the effects are quite realistic and may be too intense for small kids.

FANTASY IN THE SKY

Even the rare diehards who put fire-works displays in a class with other people's home movies find few bones to pick with Fantasy in the Sky, the spectacular fireworks show presented nightly in summer, on selected nights in May, on New Year's Eve, and on other special occasions. At about 9:30 P.M. each evening during these times, Tinkerbell waves her magic wand to start the spectacular fireworks, which are accompanied by a medley of Disney tunes and traditional patriotic favorites. More than 250 rockets are used each evening for this extravaganza. One shell is fired every couple of seconds, right in time to the music. The rockets, Roman candles, saxons, shells, and stars that make up the show come from all around the world. The ones from England look as if they have been poured from a pitcher, with color concentrated at the center. The Japanese and Chinese shells create the symmetrical star bursts. The fireworks are set off at a site off the Disneyland property and are programmed to light up the sky when they *seem* to be just over the castle.

Critter Country

FARLEY THE FIDDLER: He strolls the area near Splash Mountain, delighting guests with a blend of country and bluegrass fiddling.

Fantasyland

THE SPIRIT OF POCAHONTAS STAGE SHOW: At the Fantasyland Theater, this is a story of love and nature. In a mystical forest setting, the storyteller, Werowance, invites the audience to join the tribe in celebrating the tale of Pocahontas, who appears out of mist from a pool of water. In her search for her destiny, she asks Grandmother Willow, an ancient spirit who inhabits a tree (and whose face magically appears and disappears in its trunk), for advice. Grandmother Willow encourages her to listen to the spirits of the earth, the water, and the sky. On her path, Pocahontas meets and falls in love with the English adventurer, John Smith, who magically appears from a ball of flames. Their love grows naturally, but the clash of cultures between the tribespeople and the English is inevitable. The stirring finale is filled with special effects, including swirling leaves that envelope the lovers and shower the audience. The 28-minute show features 17 performers, traditional costumes and colors, and songs from the acclaimed Disney film. Check your entertainment schedules for times.

SWORD IN THE STONE CEREMONY: Children are appointed king or queen of the realm by pulling the magical sword, Excalibur, from the stone in front of King Arthur Carrousel. Merlin the Magician presides over this ceremony five days a week.

Mickey's Toontown

SAX QUINTET: The members of this group toot away on soprano, alto, tenor, baritone, and bass saxes. They originally came in as extras for a big party in the park, but were so popular that they were invited to stay on. Mickey's Toontown is their primary playing ground; you might see them in the Central Plaza, at the fire station, or at Carefree Corner. They also have been known to play along Matterhorn Way. Their repertoire includes everything from the *William Tell Overture* to Glenn Miller tunes, plus an occasional country-and-western favorite. Weekends.

TOONTONES: This wildly attired group—representing Toontown's Public Works—takes part in a colorful ceremony performed several times each day with the characters.

Tomorrowland

MAGIC KINGDOM CORPS: In the tradition of some of the finest drum and bugle corps, this band dazzles with precision drills.

TRANSTAR: A futuristic, two-member electronic band performs intergalactic versions of Top-40 tunes. Performances are held near the *Space Place* restaurant.

VOYAGER and DISCOVERY: High-energy rock and Top 40 tunes are the staples of these contemporary groups, who perform at the stage at *Tomorrowland Terrace*. Daily.

Parades

No Main Street is really complete without a parade, and Disneyland has always had plenty. The usual route is between Town Square and It's A Small World. The direction varies somewhat from time to time, as does the route, so it's wise to inquire at City Hall on your way into the park. The Lion King Celebration Parade, based on the hit film, brings the majesty and rhythms of Africa to Main Street, with more than 75 performers, all representing animals.

On summer evenings, Disneyland features the Main Street Electrical Parade, a splendiferous spectacle of lights—500,000 in all—arranged on floats to depict various scenes from classic Walt Disney motion pictures. At Christmas, a unit features toy soldiers out of a scene from *Babes in Toyland*, with Santa Claus himself bringing up the rear.

Where to watch: Of all the spots along the route, the single best vantage point is the center of the platform of the Disneyland Railroad's Main Street depot. The second-best viewing point is from the curb on either side of Main Street. There's more space here, as there is on either side of the plaza leading to It's A Small World, whose multi-colored pastel facade provides a whimsical only-in-Disneyland backdrop. The terrace, outside the *Plaza Inn*, is pleasant, though the seating is more limited. In any case, it's important to arrive about an hour beforehand to claim your piece of curb. If you hate crowds, Main Street isn't for you, and any other location in the park will do better. Better still, time your visit to catch the later parade on nights when there is more than one (see "Suggested Disneyland Itineraries" at the end of this chapter).

Dancing

Between the parades, the fireworks, the fireflies twinkling in the trees of the Central Plaza, there's scarcely a more romantic place in the world than Disneyland on a summer evening. An unsung pleasure that tops off the experience is dancing. You can do it to big band sounds in *Carnation Plaza Gardens* and to contemporary music on the dance floor at *Tomorrowland Terrace*. On your way into the park, be sure to inquire about where (and when) to shake a leg.

Where to See the Characters

It's Disneyland policy that there will always be plenty of Disney characters roaming visibly through the park. They put in appearances daily at shows at *Carnation Plaza Gardens* on Main Street and at the *Tomorrowland Terrace*. You may even find them keeping company with one of the musical groups during a performance. For pictures, your best bets are in Town Square, in front of The Walt Disney Story, and at the Central Plaza. And be sure to visit Mickey's Toontown where Mickey, Minnie, Donald, Goofy, Roger Rabbit, and some of their other Toon friends live.

Holiday Celebrations & Special Events

Except for Christmas, New Year's Eve, and Easter, Disneyland does not celebrate specific holidays in a major way. Yet there are plenty of special events all year-round. Some of these simply offer a bit more in the way of live entertainment during regular park operating hours. For others, the park is only open to those who purchase special admission tickets. The number of tickets available is restricted so visitors will enjoy a higher-quality experience, and the level of live talent on hand tends to be better.

Since Disneyland's plans do change, it is a wise idea to call the park's Guest Relations office (999-4565) for up-to-date information on any specific event in which you may be interested.

For more detailed information about seasonal goings-on in the park, see our discussion of when to visit in *Getting Ready to Go*.

NEW YEAR'S EVE: This big, end-of-the-year bash is one of the best of Disneyland's annual affairs. Hats and noisemakers are handed out at the main gate, top-name talent entertains, and fireworks go off at midnight over Sleeping Beauty Castle and other areas.

EASTER: Always a popular time to visit. The park remains open late during the week before and the week after Easter.

SUMMER PREVIEW WEEKENDS: During the spring, the Main Street Electrical Parade makes its yearly debut, running every weekend until the summer season. Then it is presented nightly until Labor Day weekend.

SUMMER SEASON: Scheduled from mid-June through early September, this is Disneyland's busiest season, and with good reason. The park is open daily from 8 A.M. to 1 A.M. The Lion King Celebration Parade takes place two times daily; the Main Street Electrical Parade is featured twice nightly; Fantasy in the Sky fireworks are presented every night at 9:30 P.M.; and Fantasmic! is shown three times each night. The greatest names in big band music are scheduled to perform nightly at Main Street's *Carnation Plaza Gardens* stage, and nearly every attraction in the park is operating (as opposed to the off-season, when refurbishments often take place).

FOURTH OF JULY: One of the busiest days of the year—and one to avoid if you don't like crowds—this patriotic day also features a bigger-than-usual fireworks display.

THANKSGIVING WEEKEND: Extended hours, musical entertainment, and the first installment of Mickey's Very Merry Christmas Parade (on Thanksgiving Day) are the highlights.

CHRISTMAS: If there's a single time of year when Disneyland looks its prettiest, it may well be at Yuletide. Main Street is decked to the nines with traditional red-and-greenery, including hundreds of poinsettias and a huge white fir (trucked in from Northern California) flecked with tiny Styrofoam beads, decorated with some 4,000 lights and ornaments, and surrounded by oversize Christmas packages. Carolers straight out of Dickens stroll along Main Street, and on two nights at the beginning of the holiday season there's a special ceremony that features a candlelight procession from Sleeping Beauty Castle to the train station, and Christmas music by a thousand-voice choir, backed by appropriate instruments, and a reading of a holiday story by a well-known actor. The "Hallelujah Chorus" from Handel's *Messiah* supplies the rousing finale.

Also during the season, the Very Merry Christmas Parade, a Disney Yuletide favorite, is featured. Live music and hundreds of performers bring to life many Christmas traditions of the past. Christmas activities, when all the holiday decorations are in place, begin on Thanksgiving Day.

Note: The week *before* Christmas is one of the best times of the year to visit the park. The crowds are relatively small and the entertainment usually abundant. In contrast, the day *after* Christmas is usually a madhouse: Perhaps all that holiday togetherness makes Southern Californians fidgety and motivates them to come to the park in droves. Once they get there, the queues are enormous, and the seasonal chill in the air can make the waiting unpleasant. If you plan to visit at this time of year, be sure to bring warm clothing.

109

Special Tips

When purchasing tickets you will be given a guidebook to the park. Keep it as a reference.

• Study a map of Disneyland before you arrive so you understand the layout and have some idea of what you want to see and do.

• Check the entertainment schedules available at City Hall and Bank of Main Street.

• Give yourself plenty of time to take it all in—don't try to do too much in a single stretch.

• If you hate crowds, avoid the park in summer, at Christmastime, and on weekends throughout the year. If you do visit on a weekend, try for Sunday rather than Saturday, and remember that Sunday night is one of the least crowded times in the park; ditto for Sunday morning. If you visit in summer, try to arrive during the last two weeks of June, the last week in August, or the first week in September. If you're not really eager to see the fireworks, the first half of June also is fine.

At the end of the year, visit the week following the Thanksgiving holiday through Christmas Day. The park is pleasant then, beautifully decorated, and not too crowded. Avoid the week between Christmas and New Year's Day, when it is usually mobbed. Year-round, Tuesdays, Wednesdays, and Thursdays are the least crowded days to visit. For the most satisfying experience in Disneyland, study our suggestions about when to go in *Getting Ready to Go* before you make your travel plans.

• Measure your child before your visit so you'll know ahead of time which attractions he or she is too short to ride. This will avoid intense disappointment later.

• Wear your most comfortable shoes. Blisters are the most common malady reported to Central First Aid. (Note that no bare feet are permitted inside the park.)

• Break up your time in the park (unless you only have one day). Arrive early, see the major attractions until things seem to be getting congested, return to your hotel for a swim and a nap, and then return to the park in the evening. Remember to have your hand stamped and keep your Passport to re-enter later in the day.

• Reserve your place at the Golden Horseshoe Stage immediately after arriving in the park. It's a good place to get off your feet (and to get away from the crowds during later showings).

• Have your lunch before 11 A.M. or after 2 P.M., and your dinner before 5 P.M. or after 8 P.M., to avoid lines. Note that the *Hungry Bear* restaurant in Critter Country usually slows down before other eating spots on busy days.

• Wait times are updated every hour or so and padded by ten minutes. If the board says there's a 30-minute wait for a certain attraction, figure on 20.

• Avoid Space Mountain, Splash Mountain, the Matterhorn, and Star Tours immediately after meals. Weak stomachs—and strong ones—have been known to revolt.

• Roller coaster haters should view the inside of Space Mountain from the People-Mover and think twice before skipping the rocket ride. It's simply too pretty to miss. Non-riding parents should note, however, that they can queue with their offspring until they reach the loading area, where they will find the last of three "chicken exits."

• At mealtime, look at all the lines before stepping into the nearest (and usually longest) one. The lines on the left are often shorter.

• At busy times and on busy days, use the Big Thunder Trail to get between the east and west sides of the park.

• Remember that lines for riding the Disneyland Railroad move most quickly at the Main Street station.

• Ride the major attractions—the Indiana Jones Adventure, Pirates of the Caribbean, Space Mountain, Star Tours, Big Thunder Mountain Railroad, the Jungle Cruise, the Haunted Mansion, the Matterhorn, and Splash Mountain—early in the day or during parades. In the busy afternoon hours, go to the smaller attractions where the lines are comparatively shorter; the *Mark Twain* Steamboat is a good choice. This also is a fine time for shopping, for enjoying outdoor musical performances, and for a show at the Golden Horseshoe Stage.

• Avoid shopping at times when everybody else does—that is, in late afternoon and at the end of the park's operating hours. Shops are a good place to escape the midday heat.

Tops at The Magic Kingdom

Everybody has his or her favorites, but these consistently receive the highest ratings:

Adventureland: Indiana Jones Adventure, Jungle Cruise

Critter Country: Splash Mountain

New Orleans Square: Haunted Mansion, Pirates of the Caribbean

Frontierland: Big Thunder Mountain Railroad

Fantasyland: The Matterhorn, It's A Small World, Pinocchio's Daring Journey, Snow White's Scary Adventures, Peter Pan's Flight

Tomorrowland: Space Mountain, World Premiere Circle-Vision, Star Tours

Mickey's Toontown: Toontown Square, Mickey's Neighborhood, Roger Rabbit's Cartoon Spin

What to Do When It's Packed

At busy times on busy days, visit the following less-crowded attractions:

Main Street: The Walt Disney Story featuring "Great Moments with Mr. Lincoln," Main Street Cinema, Penny Arcade, Disneyland Railroad

Adventureland: Enchanted Tiki Room, Swiss Family Treehouse

Critter Country: Country Bear Playhouse, Big Thunder Ranch

Frontierland: *Mark Twain, Columbia*

Fantasyland: It's A Small World

Tomorrowland: Starcade, PeopleMover

● Soak up some Disney lore at the current exhibition at The Disney Gallery, near the entrance to Pirates of the Caribbean in New Orleans Square.

● Rent a camera at the Main Street Photo Supply Co. and take pictures around the park.

● Go shopping for souvenirs, then store your purchases in lockers on Main Street.

● Enjoy one of the park's many musical groups, or if you've made reservations, a show at the Golden Horseshoe Stage.

● Head for Snow White's Grotto, in Fantasyland, and make a wish in the wishing well for the crowds to disappear.

● Hop on the monorail (but get your hand stamped first) and go over to the *Disneyland Hotel* and explore the shops and grounds, then return to the park later in the day.

WHERE TO FIND THE RESTROOMS

Restrooms always rate a high priority. Happily, there are plenty. Here's where to find them:

MAIN STREET
● In Town Square behind the Bank of Main Street, just through the entrance tunnel to your right as you walk through the main gate
● Adjacent to Disneyland City Hall
● Just south of the *Carnation Ice Cream Parlor*, behind that restaurant's outdoor eating area
● In the *Plaza Inn* restaurant
● In the Central Plaza, behind the seating area in *Carnation Plaza Gardens*

ADVENTURELAND
● Adjoining the Adventureland Bazaar
● Just inside the Enchanted Tiki Room

NEW ORLEANS SQUARE
● Between the *Mint Julep Bar* and L'Mascarade d'Orleans

FRONTIERLAND
● On Tom Sawyer Island: one inside Fort Wilderness, the other at the entrance of Injun Joe's Cave
● At Big Thunder Ranch behind *Big Thunder Barbecue*

CRITTER COUNTRY
● Below the *Hungry Bear* restaurant

FANTASYLAND
● Just off Matterhorn Way
● Next to *Village Haus* restaurant
● Inside the Fantasyland Theater, next to *Meeko's* snack stand

MICKEY'S TOONTOWN
● Behind Goofy's Gas

TOMORROWLAND
● At the exit to Space Mountain
● Next to Hatmosphere
● On the Tomorrowland side of the *Plaza Inn* restaurant

SUGGESTED DISNEYLAND ITINERARIES

THE MAGIC KINGDOM

| DURING BUSY SEASONS, AND SATURDAYS AND SUNDAYS YEAR-ROUND, WHEN THE PARK IS OPEN LATE | THE REST OF THE YEAR |

ONE-DAY VISIT
There's so much to see that it's impossible to do it all. But you can get the flavor of the Magic Kingdom if you plan your visit carefully.

DURING BUSY SEASONS, AND SATURDAYS AND SUNDAYS YEAR-ROUND, WHEN THE PARK IS OPEN LATE

- Arrive in the parking lot half an hour before park openiing. On entering, take a round-trip on the Disneyland Railroad to get the lay of the Land.
- Make a dinner reservation at the Blue Bayou at Reservations Services beside Great Moments with Mr. Lincoln, then window-shop your way down Main Street;. grab a bite to eat at the Carnation Ice Cream Parlor or the Blue Ribbon Bakery.
- Go to Space Mountain and Star Tours in Tomorrowland.
- Check out the Matterhorn and Peter Pan's Flight in Fantasyland.
- Glide through It's A Small World.
  LUNCH: At one or more of the fast-food eateries in Toontown. Then explore Mickey's neighborhood, including his house.
- Visit Splash Mountain in Critter Country and the Indiana Jones Adventure in Adventureland.
- Grab a snack at the Bengal Barbecue in Adventureland.
- Catch the second afternoon Lion King Celebration parade (times are in your schedule).
  DINNER: At the *Blue Bayou* in New Orleans Square.
- Check the time for Fantasmic! (or the Main Street Electrical Parade) and snag a good viewing spot about an hour early.*
- Watch Fantasy in the Sky fireworks.
- Visit Big Thunder Mountain in Frontierland and the Haunted Mansion and Pirates of the Caribbean in New Orleans Square before park closing.*
- Do some shopping along Main Street on your way out.

* **Note:** If there are no children in your party, or if they are older, it is better to reorder the evening's activities so that you visit Big Thunder Mountain, the Haunted Mansion, and Pirates of the Caribbean during the early showing of the Main Street Electrical Parade, then take in Fantasmic! , follow it with a snack, and watch the second showing of the parade.

THE REST OF THE YEAR

- Arrive in the parking lot just before park opening.
- Stroll down Main Street, stopping at Reservations Services beside Great Moments with Mister Lincoln to book lunch.
- Visit Space Mountain and Star Tours in Tomorrowland.
- Indulge in enchantment in It's A Small World.
- Explore Mickey's Toontown.
- Take the Disneyland Railroad to Frontierland and visit Big Thunder Mountain.
  LUNCH: At the *Blue Bayou* in New Orleans Square.
- Experience Pirates of the Caribbean and the Haunted Mansion in New Orleans Square.
- Test the waters at Splash Mountain in Critter Country.
- Brave the Indiana Jones Adventure in Adventureland.
- See The Spirit of Pocahontas Stage Show at the Fantasyland Theater.
- Grab a snack at the *Carnation Ice Cream Parlor* on Main Street and then do a little shopping.
- Visit Fantasyland and see the Matterhorn and Peter Pan's Flight.
  DINNER: If time allows, at the *Plaza Inn* on Main Street.

TWO-DAY VISIT
This length of stay lets you see more than just the highlights.

FIRST DAY
- Same as above.

SECOND DAY
- Arrive in the parking lot a half-hour before park opening.
- Enjoy a character breakfast at the *Plaza Inn* on Main Street.
- See The Spirit of Pocahontas Stage Show at the Fantasyland Theater.
- Browse the Main Street shops.
- Visit the Swiss Family Treehouse and go on the Jungle Cruise in Adventureland.
  LUNCH: At the *Carnation Ice Cream Parlor* on Main Street.
- Ride the *Mark Twain* Steamboat or Davy Crockett's Explorer Canoes, then head over to Tom Sawyer Island.
- Take in Fantasyland attractions you missed on your first day.
- Return to your hotel for a swim (but get your hand stamped so that you can come back later).
  DINNER: At your hotel; or return to the park and dine at *Café Orleans* or the *French Market* at New Orleans Square.
- In the park, enjoy the Main Street Electrical Parade (or Fantasmic!), followed by Fantasy in the Sky fireworks.
- Listen to live jazz, blues, and Dixieland music at the *French Market* in New Orleans Square.
- On your way out of the park, drop by the Main Street Cinema and the Penny Arcade.

FIRST DAY
- Same as above.

SECOND DAY
- Arrive a half-hour before park opening.
- Have breakfast at the *Carnation Ice Cream Parlor* on Main Street.
- Visit the Jungle Cruise and Swiss Family Treehouse in Adventureland.
- Ride the *Mark Twain* Steamboat or Davy Crockett's Explorer Canoes, then go to Tom Sawyer Island.
  LUNCH: At the *River Belle Terrace* in Frontierland.
- See The Lion King Celebration parade.
- Take in any Fantasyland attractions that are open, plus those in other lands you may have missed.
  DINNER: At *Café Orleans* or the *French Market*.
- On your way out of the park, stop at the Main Street Cinema and the Penny Arcade.

THREE-DAY VISIT
This length of stay allows for a really in-depth look.

FIRST AND SECOND DAYS
- Same as above.

THIRD DAY
- Spend the day revisiting your favorite attractions, exploring the shops, and taking in the live entertainment.

FIRST AND SECOND DAYS
- Same as above.

THIRD DAY
- Follow program for the third day of a three-day visit as outlined at left.

GOOD MEALS, GREAT TIMES

While you're enjoying the Louisiana fare at the *Blue Bayou* restaurant in Disneyland's New Orleans Square, soak up the show all around you. It's part of the experience of dining at Disneyland, where there's always more to a meal than just food.

In Anaheim, which in the past has been noted more for its fast-food establishments than for haute cuisine, there nevertheless are some emerging first class restaurants. If you venture farther afield—into other areas of Orange County and Los Angeles, for example—you can indulge in some memorable dining.

This chapter is divided into two main sections, the first devoted to eating at Disneyland, the second to eating in Anaheim and environs, with additional information on nightlife. The Disneyland section is arranged by "land" and then according to type of restaurant—full service, buffeteria, (Disney's word for cafeteria), and fast-food and snack facilities, then within price category. Off-property restaurants are classified by location—first those in the Anaheim hotels and elsewhere in Anaheim proper, then in the rest of Orange County, and then in Los Angeles.

In the following restaurant descriptions, the letters that conclude each paragraph refer to the meals offered there: breakfast (B), lunch (L), dinner (D), or snacks (S).

Unless otherwise noted, all phone numbers are in the 714 area code.

First-time visitors to Disneyland expect to find little more than hamburgers and hot dogs, french fries, and fizzy soft drinks on the park's menus, so they're usually surprised to find Disneyland's food so varied. Waiters and waitresses serve platters of pita-bread sandwiches stuffed with chicken and avocado at the *Carnation Ice Cream Parlor*. Tacos, New Orleans-style fritters, massive fruit salads topped with kiwi in season, New York-cut steaks, and chicken dishes with exotic sauces are no less unexpected. And health-conscious eaters who enter the park resigned to misery will be thrilled to find salads and other low-calorie fare at fast-food establishments, as well as unsweetened fruit juices, frozen-juice bars, and fresh fruit at snack wagons located throughout the park.

Cash, traveler's checks, or personal checks (imprinted with a guest's name and address, drawn on a U.S. bank, and accompanied by proper identification—a valid driver's license and a major credit card such as American Express, Carte Blanche, Diners Club, MasterCard, or Visa) can be used as payment at all Disneyland sit-down and fast-food restaurants, as well as buffeterias. American Express, Visa, and MasterCard credit cards also may be used to pay for food at these places. Only cash is accepted at the ice cream, popcorn, and snack carts in the park.

In the following descriptions, restaurants and eateries have been designated expensive (lunches over $20, dinners over $35), moderate (lunches from $10 to $20, dinners from $10 to $30), or inexpensive (lunches and dinners under $10). These prices are for an average meal for two adults, not including drinks, taxes, or tip. **Note:** An asterisk after the meal designation letter means that the meal is served only during Disneyland's busy seasons (see *Getting Ready to Go*).

Main Street

FULL SERVICE

CARNATION ICE CREAM PARLOR: On the west side of Main Street, this bright red-and-white establishment is at its best in springtime, when the floral planters that surround its outdoor garden are ablaze with scarlet tulips. But it's an exceptionally pleasant place at any other time of year, too, and if you're in the mood for a California-style sandwich or salad, it's well worth a detour. At breakfast, Danish pastry, Mickey Mouse-shaped waffles, cereal, or eggs with bacon, sausage, or ham and fried potatoes are the offerings. For lunch and dinner, there are hamburgers, sandwiches made with ham and cheese, chicken breast with honey-mustard sauce, or avocado and turkey. The two main selections on the menu that are not a salad or a sandwich are marinated chicken breast and grilled New York steak, both of which are served with a baked potato and soup or salad. Portions are ample. A children's menu is available.

Since this is, after all, first and foremost an ice cream parlor, select from a variety of fancy sundaes and don't overlook the Golden West Freeze, which resembles a milkshake and is made with orange sherbet (an excellent variation, much favored by cast members (Disney terminology for park staffers) in the know, is made with half sherbet, half vanilla ice cream).

Children's specialties are available. Note that Fantasia ice cream—made with burgundy cherry, pistachio, and banana—was developed by Carnation specially for Disneyland. On the hottest days, you may want to eat indoors, the better to admire the long, polished-wood fountain and the frosted crystal light fixtures. When you crave the sun, a seat on the terrace warrants the wait. Tables nearest Main Street are the most pleasant. Moderate. B, L, D, S.

BUFFETERIAS

PLAZA INN: Facing the *Plaza Pavilion* across the Hub, this was one of the restaurants that made Walt Disney proudest, with good reason. Tufted velvet upholstery, gleaming mirrors, and a fine, ornate floral carpet elevate this cafeteria well above similar eateries. The draperies are a lovely shade of coral, and the silk-satin valances are trimmed with custom-made fringes, rosettes, and borders. Two of the ceilings are stained glass, framed by elaborate, painted moldings. Sconces made of Parisian bronze and Baccarat crystal are mounted on the walls, and two-dozen basket chandeliers, also of crystal and bronze, hang from the ceiling. There's even a 200-year-old French chandelier, found in an antiques shop, that's hung from the ceiling on a chain that allows the fixture to be raised and lowered for cleanings. (Plain old ammonia and water are used, and the process takes 3 1/2 hours.) The four-shelf French cabinet, elaborately inlaid with fruit woods and trimmed in bronze ormolu, is just as old, and the ornaments that embellish it (and the rest of the establishment) are antique as well. Among the few decorative objects here that are not true antiques are the two ornate coffee urns behind the counter. The setting is so lovely that the food—spaghetti with meat sauce, pot roast, rotisserie chicken, and a daily fresh fish dish—pales a bit by comparison. There are seasonal variations in the menu also, and when the park opens before 10 A.M. (see hours of operation in the *Magic Kingdom* chapter), a character breakfast is held here. Children's portions are available. Moderate. B*, L, D, S.

PLAZA PAVILION: Facing the *Plaza Inn* across the Hub, this much less ornate establishment offers open-air dining during the summer and holiday seasons. For lunch and dinner, the menu's varied selections include fried chicken, baked rosemary chicken, spaghetti, barbecued ribs, soups, and several salads, including pasta, fresh fruit, and chicken breast. Children can select chicken strips or a small portion of spaghetti. Moderate. B*, L*, D*, S*.

FAST FOOD & SNACKS

COCA-COLA REFRESHMENT CORNER: *Coke Corner*, as this lively establishment at the northern end of Main Street (opposite Carefree Corner) is commonly called, is presided over by a talented ragtime pianist who tickles the ivories from park opening until the end of the day, while visitors nibble hot dogs, brownies, chips, soft drinks, milk, cookies, juice, hot chocolate, coffee, and, when the weather is cool, chili and beans. Inexpensive. L, D, S.

CARNATION PLAZA GARDENS: West of the Sleeping Beauty Castle, this place has red-and-white striped awnings and a pol-

ished terrazzo dance floor, and is one of the most festive and invitong spots in the park. The small stage is the setting for character shows in the afternoons, and for band concerts (with dancing) on summer evenings—usually from about 7 P.M. until park closing. When the mirrored ball sends stars shooting all around, it's hard not to feel transported back a half century in time. Vanilla, strawberry, chocolate, chocolate chip, Fantasia, and orange sherbet in sugar cones are available, along with cheeseburgers, french fries, and lemonade. L, D, S.

MAIN STREET CONE SHOP: Between the Disney Clothiers and *Market House*, this window-service ice cream shop serves a limited selection of Carnation ice cream flavors, including vanilla, chocolate, strawberry, orange sherbet, and a flavor of the day. Ice cream sundaes (with two scoops of the flavor of your choice) are served in a waffle cone and covered with hot fudge, strawberry, or caramel toppings, plus real whipped cream and a cherry. One-scoop junior sundaes, root beer floats served in souvenir mugs, and soft drinks also are available. Tables with umbrellas provide a pleasant and shady resting spot. It's presented by the Carnation Company. Inexpensive. S.

MARKET HOUSE: South of the *Carnation Ice Cream Parlor*, this quaint turn-of-the-century market offers a generous selection of fancy cookies, tangy dill pickles plucked right from a barrel, dried fruit, and various candies. Hot coffee and ice-cold apple cider also are available. Inexpensive. S.

BLUE RIBBON BAKERY AND YOGURT SHOP: Fresh-baked cookies, muffins, and pastries are tempting treats at this snack spot north of *Carnation Plaza Gardens*. Low-fat and nonfat frozen yogurt also are offered

with a variety of toppings, including candy, nuts, cookies, fruit, and hot and cold syrups. Inexpensive. S.

MAIN STREET FRUIT CART: Tucked in between the Disney Clothiers and *Market House* this old-fashioned fruit cart is stocked with premium, seasonal whole fruit, juices, bottled water, and soft drinks. Cappuccino also is served. Inexpensive. S.

LITTLE RED WAGON: Between the Main Street Photo Supply Co. and the *Plaza Inn*, it's representative of the delivery trucks of the early 1900s, with ornate chipped and gilded glass panels. Guests can enjoy hand-dipped corn dogs, available nowhere else in the park. Soft drinks and coffee also are served. Inexpensive. L*, D*, S*.

Adventureland

FULL SERVICE

ALADDIN'S OASIS: In the spot formerly occupied by the *Tahitian Terrace* and near the Enchanted Tiki Room, it may not serve as many as 1001 Arabian bites, but it does offer a varied menu with some health-conscious choices. Dinner fare includes vegetable shish kebab (the Alad-ternative), saffron noodles and shrimp in garlic cream sauce, grilled chicken breast with couscous and fresh vegetables; tabbouleh salad, a fresh-fruit plate; lemon-and-herb marinated chicken, grilled sirloin, and fish of the day. The desserts are as tempting in name as in reality, among them Make a Wish (a chocolate lamp filled with chocolate mousse), The Magic Carpet Ride

(chocolate cake), The Three Wishes (assorted baklava), and Lamp Lite (fresh strawberries served with crème anglais). It's open only during the summer. Reservations can be made at the restaurant. Moderate to expensive. D*.

FAST FOOD & SNACKS

BENGAL BARBECUE: Near the entrance to the Jungle Cruise, it serves skewered chicken, beef, and vegetables; fresh fruit with a raspberry yogurt dip; and fresh vegetables with a dill dip. Inexpensive. L, D, S.

TIKI JUICE BAR: Located at the entrance to the Enchanted Tiki Room, this stand sells fresh Hawaiian pineapple spears and pineapple juice. Hot coffee and soft-serve frozen pineapple dessert also are offered. It's presented by Dole. Inexpensive. S.

Critter Country

FAST FOOD & SNACKS

HARBOUR GALLEY: This Critter Country restaurant is tucked into the shanties that line the docking area for the *Columbia* and the *Mark Twain*. Cajun and seafood specialties, clam chowder served in a carved-out loaf of bread, and deep-fried catfish nuggets fill a seafaring appetite. Inexpensive to moderate. L, D.

HUNGRY BEAR: At the bottom of the bridge to Critter Country on the right, this is an immense place, yet when you sit on the ground-level veranda, with the Rivers of America lapping so close to your feet that you could cool your toes on a hot day, the activity of the rest of the park seems miles away. Ducks dive for occasional tidbits, canoeists in Davy Crockett's Explorer Canoes paddle by, the *Mark Twain* towers above you as it steams downriver, and the air rifles in Tom Sawyer Island's Fort Wilderness (just opposite) are tap-tap-tapping away. There's commotion all around, but you're strangely (and quite pleasantly) removed from it all. Better yet, during busy periods, the restaurant's crowds begin to build up a little later in the day than they do at more centrally located establishments, and they also thin out a little earlier. The menu includes hamburgers, cheeseburgers, grilled chicken-breast sandwiches, french fries, freshly made cold sandwiches and seasonal salads, and an array of sweets. Inexpensive to moderate. L, D, S.

BRER BAR: You'll find it alongside Teddi Barra's Swingin' Arcade, and if a hot dog or sandwich will do, drop by this lace-curtained, paisley-wallpapered establishment. But even if you prefer something more substantial elsewhere, stop in for a look at the polished-wood bar, which almost looks as though it's a mile long thanks to an ingenious arrangement of

mirrors. Hot Mickey Mouse pretzels, chips, cookies, ice cream snacks, and soft drinks all are available along with coffee, cappuccino, and espresso. There are small tables set up on the board sidewalk outdoors, by the waterfall at the exit to Country Bear Playhouse—an altogether lovely, sweet-smelling, fern-decked corner of the park. Be sure to look at the three figures above the bar—Melvin the Moose, Buff the Buffalo, and Max the Stag, the Audio-Animatronics heads that preside over the Country Bear Playhouse next door. Inexpensive. L, D, S.

CRITTER COUNTRY FRUIT CART: Located on the riverside just across from Splash Mountain, this peddler's cart is full of seasonal fresh fruit, muffins, raisins, dill pickles, juices, bottled water, and cookies. Inexpensive. S.

New Orleans Square

FULL SERVICE

BLUE BAYOU: This popular dining spot on Royal Street offers food in a Louisiana bayou setting. For lunch, choose from Monte Cristo sandwiches, Cajun shrimp, chicken entrées with a Southern spin, specialty salads, and clam chowder. For dinner, consider fresh salmon, sautéed prawns with a light rosemary cream sauce, and a combination seafood salad with lobster, crab, salmon, and shrimp. Prime rib is served at lunch and dinner. If you're a chocolate lover, be sure to save room for dessert. A children's menu is available.

The lure here, it should be noted, is as much the atmosphere as the menu. Occupying a terrace alongside the bayou, near the departure point for Pirates of the Caribbean, the restaurant has lighting that makes it appear perpetually moonlit. Fireflies twinkle above the bayou grasses, and stars shine through Spanish moss draped languidly over the big, old live oaks, against a sky that manages to be bright blue and dark at the same time. Careful listeners will hear bullfrogs calling and crickets chirping, and off in the distance an old settler rocks away on the porch of a tumbledown shack, apparently watching over the boats full of sightseers heading off into the bayou and their Disney adventure among the Pirates of

the Caribbean. Busiest periods are from noon to 2 P.M. and again from 5 P.M. or 5:30 P.M. until 8 P.M. or 9 P.M. Pick up a box of Blue Bayou Mints on your way out. Expensive. L, D.

BUFFETERIAS

CAFE ORLEANS: Visitors can dine inside on small, round, oak-topped tables, or outside under blue-green umbrellas on a terrace that offers a splendid view of the gristmill on Tom Sawyer Island, and of the *Columbia*, the *Mark Twain*, and other craft plying Disneyland's main waterway. On the menu, there's the Croissant Mardi Gras (ham, turkey, Swiss cheese, lettuce, and tomato); Cajun-spiced chicken; Orleans Deli Classic (turkey, cold cuts, mozzarella cheese, tomato, bell pepper, and spiced cream cheese); and the Plantation Prime Rib (prime ribs, herb roll, jalapeño cream cheese, onions, lettuce, and tomato). For dinner, selected sandwiches are joined by beef bourguignonne, seafood Parisienne, and poulet de la maison (chicken breast sautéed in spicy marinara sauce, served over fettuccine). There's a small children's menu available. Dessert offerings include assorted pastries, pies, and cheesecake. Moderate. L, D, S.

FRENCH MARKET: Adjoining the Frontierland depot of the Disneyland Railroad and much more than New Orleans Square's largest food facility, this Esplanade Street cafeteria is a destination in its own right: On sunny days, it's relaxing just to sit on the open-air terrace and lunch on fettuccine, fried chicken, catfish with Cajun rice, roast-beef sandwiches, beef stew, several filling salads, or the house specialty, jambalaya. Pies and cakes fill the bill for dessert. The dinner menu is the same, and children's portions of fried chicken and fettuccine are available. Dixieland music is played on stage periodically throughout the

evening, where, in summer, the Royal Street Bachelors hold forth with such spirit that you could listen for toe-tapping hours and get your money's worth and more. If all you want is a snack, stop at the adjacent *Mint Julep Bar*. Moderate. L, D, S.

FAST FOOD & SNACKS

DISNEY GALLERY BALCONY: Near the entrance to Pirates of the Caribbean, it provides the best spot in the park to view Fantasmic! and enjoy assorted desserts and beverages at the same time. This constitutes a super splurge ($30 per person) and a memorable evening. There are only 15 seats. Make reservations at the gallery. Expensive. S.

MINT JULEP BAR: Across from the Frontierland train station, it serves fritters (large, hollow, spherical doughnuts), which are among Disneyland's tastiest tidbits. When the last grains of sugar are polished off, it's hard to fight the desire to go back for more. Order a fritter and some hot chocolate or a specialty coffee and head to one of the small round tables on the *French Market*'s terrace. The mint juleps taste like lemonade spiked with mint syrup, and the real lemonade is a better choice. A variety of sweets and ice cream novelties (including Mickey's ice cream sandwiches) round out the selections here. Inexpensive. B, S.

LA PETITE PATISSERIE: Located behind *Café Orleans*, this snack shop's assorted pastries tempt passersby. Chocolate, fruit, and whipped cream are just a few of the prime ingredients. Hot and cold beverages also are served. A take-out menu is available in the evening, prior to Fantasmic! performances. Inexpensive to moderate. B, S.

ROYAL STREET VERANDA: Located opposite the *Café Orleans* and next door to the entrance to Pirates of the Caribbean, this small snack stand is Disneyland's only other source for those delicious fritters. Hot chocolate, frozen bananas, ice cream bars, a fruit punch that goes by the name of Mardi Gras

Punch, soft drinks, and creamy clam chowder served in a carved-out loaf of bread complete the menu. Be sure to look at the wrought-iron balustrade above the *Royal Street Veranda*'s small patio. The initials at the center are those of Roy and Walt Disney, and the balcony itself belonged to an apartment that was being constructed for Walt before he died; it now houses The Disney Gallery. Inexpensive. B, S.

Frontierland

BUFFETERIAS

BIG THUNDER BARBECUE: Beside Big Thunder Ranch and housed in a barnlike building with a shingle roof, surrounded by pines and a split-rail fence, it specializes in beef and pork ribs, and chicken cooked slowly over hickory logs and served chuckwagon style. Bring your appetite: Each lunch platter comes with ranch-style beans, and coleslaw. Dinner plates also include corn-on-the-cob. There's only outdoor seating at picnic tables. Children's portions are available. Open only on weekends and during busy seasons. Moderate. L*, D*.

CASA MEXICANA: Near the Shootin' Arcade, this Frontierland landmark offers the kind of Mexican food most often found in the American Midwest, so real aficionados of authentically spiced south-of-the-border specialties will find this restaurant's version mild by comparison. But because this is California, a state where residents know their tacos, there is hot sauce on every table. The tables on the west end of the patio offer terrific views of the runaway mine trains of the Big Thunder Mountain Railroad as they race around those sandstone-colored buttes, and the ramadas overhead and the stucco walls around the patio make for a pleasant dining ambience. The restaurant doesn't feel like Mexico—but it doesn't seem much like downtown Anaheim either. Menu items include burritos, tacos, enchiladas, taco salad, rice, and refried beans prepared fresh on the premises, along with various other specialties. Moderate. L, D, S.

KIDS DINE FOR ONLY $2.99

A special set-price child's menu for lunch and dinner is featured at the following restaurants. Available for children ages 11 and under. This special offer is subject to change.

Main Street	*Plaza Pavilion*, Refreshment Corner, Carnation Plaza Gardens*
New Orlean's Square	*Café Orleans, French Market*
Critter Country	*Hungry Bear*
Frontierland	*Casa Mexicana, River Belle Terrace, Big Thunder Barbecue**
Fantasyland	*Village Haus, Meeko's*
Mickey's Toontown	*Daisy's Diner, Pluto's Dog House*

* Open selected weekends and busy seasons only.

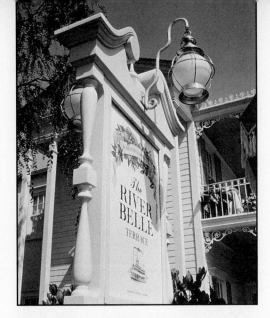

RIVER BELLE TERRACE: The terrace, near the entrance to Pirates of the Caribbean, offers one of the best views of the activity on the Rivers of America and of the passing throng, and the food is hearty and wholesome. Walt Disney himself used to breakfast here most Sunday mornings. The menu features scrambled eggs, potatoes, and bacon or sausage, as well as a fresh-fruit sampler. This is the only cafeteria in the park that serves breakfast cooked to order. A children's menu is available. Among the fare fixed specially for the younger set at breakfast, the prize goes to the Mickey Mouse pancakes—a large flapjack for the face, two silver-dollar-size pancakes for the ears, a curve of pineapple for the mouth, a maraschino cherry for the nose, and two blueberries for eyes. Later in the day, the restaurant offers vegetable stew in a carved-out loaf of bread, as well as fried chicken, and ham or turkey sandwiches—perfect for dinner prior to viewing Fantasmic! With its many mirrors, ornamental pillars, green terrazzo floor, and pale-pink walls, it's as delightful to eat inside this restaurant as it is to dine outside. A pleasure. Inexpensive to moderate. B, L, D, S.

FAST FOOD & SNACKS

STAGE DOOR CAFE: This small fast-food stand, adjoining the Golden Horseshoe Stage, serves grilled hamburgers and cheeseburgers, chicken-breast sandwiches, plus hot dogs, french fries, and cookies. When you're afflicted by a bad case of the eleventh-hour munchies, one that sweets from Main Street's Candy Palace simply can't satisfy, this is a place that usually stays open until about a half hour before park closing, so it can probably help you survive. Grab a seat at one of the café tables outside. L, D, S.

FORT WILDERNESS CANTEEN: Tucked away in a corner of Fort Wilderness on Tom Sawyer Island, this stand, which looks a bit like an old-fashioned store that might actually have been found in a 19th-century stockade, sells cookies, dill pickles, candies, nuts, ice-cream novelties, and apple juice, and an assortment of other thirst-quenching essentials such as Coke and lemonade. Inexpensive. S.

BIG THUNDER FRUIT & JUICE CART: This cart can provide the means to quench your thirst or refresh your palate. Parked at the entrance to Big Thunder Ranch, it's got soft drinks, apple juice, and premium fresh fruit. Inexpensive. S.

Fantasyland

FAST FOOD & SNACKS

VILLAGE HAUS: Located near Pinocchio's Daring Journey, this fast-food spot—a rather quaint creation with many gables, steep roofs, and wavy-glass windows—serves cheeseburgers, pizza, lasagna, salads, french fries, and cookies. A child's pizza also is available. Be sure to note the attractive murals, which are painted with such care that they do look almost like the tapestries they are supposed to represent. The fox that appears in many of them is Foulfellow, while his feline companion is named Gideon. The *Maytenus boaria* trees out in front were moved at a cost of nearly $10,000 each from the berm that rings the park. Inexpensive to moderate. L, D, S.

MEEKO'S: Located within the Fantasyland Theater complex, this snack stand is open during the theater's operating hours. Cheese or pepperoni pizza, 1/4-pound hot dogs, chips, candy, and frozen bananas are available. Inexpensive. L, S.

HAPPY BIRTHDAY, DISNEY-STYLE

A birthday party held at Disneyland's *Space Place*, in Tomorrowland, and thrown by your favorite Disney characters is a very special experience indeed. Besides lunch, there are cake, ice cream, birthday hats, balloons, and Disney party favors for everyone. The price is $19.95 per person. Call 520-5045 for reservations and information.

Goofy's Kitchen, at the *Disneyland Hotel*, also hosts themed birthday parties with characters in attendance. The price is $4 per guest plus the cost of the meal. Call 956-6401 for reservations and information.

Mickey's Toontown

FAST FOOD & SNACKS

PLUTO'S DOG HOUSE: On Toontown Square, it serves—you guessed it! Pluto's Dog House Special features an extra-long hot dog with chips, a large cookie, and a large soft drink. At the other end of the spectrum is the Tail Wagger kid's meal, with two Minnie hot dogs, chips, and a soft drink. There's also lemonade. Inexpensive to moderate. L, D, S.

CLARABELLE'S FROZEN YOGURT: Adjacent to *Pluto's Dog House*, it supplies "udderly" tasty chocolate and vanilla yogurt (swirls, too), along with toppings, cookies, and Mickey Mouse pretzels. Be sure to look at the second-floor window where 3 Nephews from Duckburg Catering has its offices. Inexpensive. L, S.

DAISY'S DINER: On the other side of *Pluto's Dog House*, it's got cheese and pepperoni pizza, hot and spicy chicken wings, and tossed salad. For those 11 years old and younger, there's Huey, Dewey, and Louie's kid's meal. Soft drinks, juice, and milk round out the menu. Inexpensive L, D, S.

Tomorrowland

FAST FOOD & SNACKS

LUNCHING PAD: Next to Rocket Jets, it has hot dogs, assorted frozen novelties, soft drinks, and popcorn. Inexpensive. L, D, S.

TOMORROWLAND TERRACE: Near the Premiere Shop and one of the largest dining facilities in Disneyland, this spot always seems crowded with visitors bearing small trays piled high with french fries, fried onion rings, charbroiled hamburgers, cheeseburgers, and salads. Fried chicken, tuna and turkey sandwiches, chicken strips, fruit, and cookies are among the other offerings. The *Tomorrowland Terrace* can handle approximately 3,000 people an hour when operating at full capacity—as it often does. Couple this activity with shows going on throughout the day (characters put inappearances) and rock music, and it's easy to understand why this eatery sometimes appears frenetic. The dance floor near the stage can get crowded on summer nights. A child's meal is available. It's presented by the Coca-Cola Company. Inexpensive. B, L, D, S.

DISNEYLAND RESTAURANTS WITH ATMOSPHERE

Most of the food served in Disneyland would hardly send a true gastronome into paroxysms of ecstasy. But the Disney talent for designing a dining spot that oozes atmosphere is another matter entirely, and the best here are the equal of many, enhanced by food prices as reasonable as one can find anywhere.

Main Street: *Coke Corner* when the pianist is performing, and *Carnation Plaza Gardens* during concerts and for dancing on summer evenings.

Adventureland: *Aladdin's Oasis*, for exotic decor and a sampling of flavorful Middle Eastern foods.

Critter Country: *Hungry Bear* restaurant, for its superb feeling of being right in the heart of it all, yet curiously removed.

New Orleans Square: The *Blue Bayou* restaurant, for its perpetual moonlight, its Spanish-moss-draped oaks, its stars, and its fireflies; the *French Market* when the Royal Street Bachelors and any of the park's talented Dixieland musicians are entertaining.

Frontierland: The *Big Thunder Barbecue*, for its outdoor setting (picnic tables under towering pines) and its chuck-wagon style.

Fantasyland: The *Village Haus* restaurant, for its picture-perfect views.

Anaheim & Environs

Some of the best restaurants in Anaheim are found in the hotels closest to Disneyland. There are, however, a number of other establishments in the area offering a surprisingly diverse range of culinary choices. The food runs the gamut from basic hamburgers and fries to seafood, Mexican specialties, and some respectable French dishes. Our recommendations for dining both in the hotels and elsewhere in and around Anaheim follow.

To provide some sense of what food will cost, we've designated restaurants as expensive (lunches over $20, dinners over $40), moderate (lunches from $10 to $20, dinners from $20 to $40), and inexpensive (lunches under $10, dinners under $20). These prices are for an average meal for two adults, not including drinks, taxes, or tips. Remember, however, that menus and prices can change. Major credit cards include American Express, Visa, MasterCard, and Diners Club.

In the Hotels

ANAHEIM CONESTOGA: Early western is the idea here, pardner. Telephone: 535-0300.

Chaparral Café: This is a pleasant hotel coffee shop. The high-back chairs are oak and look antique. And though the menu isn't especially imaginative, it does offer a wide selection that includes hearty sandwiches, various salads, and Mexican foods. Among the hot entrées are chicken-fried steak, fried chicken, and beef teriyaki. There are several items for light eaters, and some especially for kids—like a good, old-fashioned peanut butter and jelly sandwich. Wine, beer, and cocktails also are available. Ext. 616. Major credit cards. Moderate. B, L, D.

Original Cattleman's Wharf: In a building adjacent to the *Conestoga* at 1160 West Ball Road. Modern and angular design on the outside, eclectic inside. The five themed dining rooms each have an individual, elaborate design plan (from a simple garden to a formal dining room). The food—steaks, chicken, seafood, prime rib—is surprisingly good given the emphasis placed on decor. A lavish Sunday brunch is served. There is live entertainment Fridays and Saturdays in the lounge. And on summer nights, the fireworks at Disneyland are visible from the observation tower. Reservations recommended. 535-1622. Major credit cards. Moderate. D, Sunday brunch.

ANAHEIM HILTON: A casual, "Casablanca-style" café, a sushi bar, as well as two other specialty restaurants round out the Hilton's dining spots. Telephone: 750-4321.

Café Oasis: A café designed to create the atmosphere of a safari. A soup and salad buffet is featured at lunchtime. Relax with espresso or cappuccino and enjoy pastries and cakes baked fresh daily in the hotel's kitchens. Ext. 4412. Major credit cards. Moderate. B, L, D.

Pavia: Known for fresh seafood showcased in Italian specialties (scampi and a good fish soup) and for homemade pastas. The restaurant has Roman arches, cut-crystal windows, and marble floors, and it features live entertainment. Reservations suggested. Ext. 4419. Major credit cards. Expensive. D.

Hasting's Grill: An elegant yet casual grill featuring continental cuisine. Reservations suggested. Ext. 4422. Major credit cards. Expensive. D.

Sushi Bar: Seafood (delivered fresh daily) is prepared as you watch by a master sushi chef. Ext. 3905. Major credit cards. Moderate. D.

ANAHEIM MARRIOTT: One of Orange County's best restaurants is located here. Telephone: 750-8000.

JW's: The hotel's signature restaurant is named for the late J. Willard Marriott, Sr. This fine establishment's menu changes three or four times a year, but tasty appetizers have included glazed fresh baby artichokes with Parmesan cheese, escargot, and lobster and white-bean soup. Entrées have included delicious steaks, lobster, wild boar, Muscovy duck, and bouillabaisse. There is a comprehensive wine list. Reservations recommended. Ext. 102. Major credit cards. Expensive. D.

Alice's American Grille: Just off the hotel's lobby, this new eatery offers everything from baby back ribs to Cajun pasta, as well as a delicious breakfast buffet and a special menu for children 13 and under. Beer and wine are available, along with mixed drinks. Ext. 117. Major credit cards. Moderate. B, L, D, daily breakfast buffet.

DISNEYLAND HOTEL: Some of the restaurants have fine views of the hotel's appealing marina. Telephone: 778-6600.

Monorail Café: This 1950s-style eatery offers a varied breakfast menu; if you haven't had Mickey Mouse pancakes elsewhere, by all means try them here. The speedy waitresses bring coffee right away. For lunch and dinner, expect standard coffee-shop fare—salads, sandwiches, soups, and burgers. Near the curbside stop for the tram, this is a good place for a quick meal or an early-bird breakfast before heading into the park. Ext. 6401. Major credit cards. Moderate. B, L, D.

Goofy's Kitchen: This country-style dining room features immensely popular Disney character breakfasts and dinners, and offers personal encounters with Minnie Mouse, Goofy, and other Disney friends. Service here is buffet style, so fill your plates with Mickey Mouse-shaped waffles, scrambled eggs, bacon, potatoes, juice, cereal, and fruit at breakfast. For dinner, options include carved ham, prime ribs, mashed potatoes, corn-on-the-cob, chicken fingers, spaghetti, and salad. Open daily for breakfast year-round; open for dinner on weekends year-round and daily during the summer and holiday periods. Reservations suggested. Ext. 6755. Major credit cards. Moderate. B, D.

Granville's Steak House: An intimate, 104-seat restaurant that offers generous portions of steaks, prime ribs, fresh Maine lobster, swordfish, and poultry. A highlight is the Land and Sea Delight with both juicy prime ribs and fresh lobster. This is the hotel's top-of-the-line eatery, decorated with oak paneling, etched glass, and an all-American burgundy, white, and blue color scheme. Servers personally deliver a visual menu by bringing a serving cart tableside that's stocked with examples of selections. A private dining room that seats 18 people can be reserved. Reservations recommended. Ext. 6402 or dial direct 956-6402. Major credit cards. Expensive. D.

Stromboli's: Named after the villain in Pinocchio, it has open Mediterranean decor

with fountains, hanging plants, and a sidewalk-café area that runs along the hotel's marina. The emphasis is on favorite Italian dishes, and the ice cream is delicious. A children's menu is available. Ext. 6403. Major credit cards. Moderate. L, D.

Mazie's: In the Plaza Building, across from the swimming pool. This eatery is light and airy inside, and the tables outside provide the feeling of a sidewalk café. Its menu offers garnish-your-own burgers, hot dogs, and salads. Cravings for sweets can be satisfied with freshly baked cookies. Beer and wine are sold by the glass. Ext. 1570. Major credit cards. Moderate. L, D.

Shipyard Inn: On the wharf, overlooking the hotel's marina, it has a nautical look befitting what may be Anaheim's only waterside restaurant. You can get a peek at the Dancing Waters show at night. Fresh seafood specialties are the fare here, and there also is an oyster bar. A children's menu is available. The *California Wine Cellar*—a lounge that serves 100 award-winning California wines as well as desserts, grapes, bread, and cheese—is downstairs. Ext. 6404. Major credit cards. Moderate to expensive. D.

DOUBLETREE: The restaurants here have a very contemporary Southern California style. Telephone: 634-4500.

Napa Brasserie: A casual, café-style eatery, serving soups, salads, sandwiches, omelettes, burgers, and light pasta dishes. Prime ribs, swordfish, smoked breast of chicken, and filet mignon are among the dinner specialties. Major credit cards. Moderate. B, L, D.

City Club: This new restaurant features a variety of steak and seafood dishes, including prime rib and swordfish steak. Reservations recommended. Major credit cards. Moderate to expensive. D (except Sundays).

HYATT REGENCY ALICANTE: One of the restaurants here is located in the tallest atrium in the western United States. Telephone: 971-3000.

Café Alicante: Alfresco dining in a 17-story, glass-enclosed atrium, with flowering plants, palm trees, and fountains. A California-style menu is featured, including salads, sandwiches, seafood, and pasta specialties. Breakfast and lunch buffets and low-calorie items also are available. Ext. 6047. Major credit cards. Moderate. B, L.

Papa Geppetto's: The ambience is Mediterranean, with panoramic scenes of coastal Alicante, Spain. It serves family-style country Italian cuisine. The menu features a wide variety of pasta, veal, and nightly non-Italian specialties. Valet parking available. Ext. 6090. Major credit cards. Moderate. D.

PAN PACIFIC, ANAHEIM: Both restaurants here are located on the ground floor, and offer casual dining. Telephone: 999-0990.

Keyaki: Features authentic Japanese food, with the choice of private rooms with floor seating or a spot at the sushi bar. Reservations suggested. Ext. 5683. Major credit cards. Moderate. L, D.

Summertree: A California-bistro setting, with indoor/outdoor dining. Seafood (delivered fresh daily) and steaks are featured, along with a good selection of California wines. Ext. 5682. Major credit cards. Moderate to expensive. B, L, D.

QUALITY HOTEL AND CONFERENCE CENTER: Choose from a casual café or a restaurant. Telephone: 750-3131.

Tivoli Gardens: A small, attractive café, in a gardenlike setting. Soups, salads, sandwiches, and omelettes are among the menu selections. Ext. 3300. Major credit cards. Moderate. B, L.

Captain Greenhorn's: Nautical trimmings and a seafood and steak menu. Drinks are available from the adjoining lounge. Reservations are recommended for dinner. Ext. 3300. Major credit cards. Moderate. D.

SHERATON-ANAHEIM: The two restaurants here offer casual dining. Telephone: 778-1700.

Garden Court Bistro: Full breakfasts are served in the morning. Pasta, chicken, fish, and beef selections are the specialties at lunch and dinner. Ext. 3948. Major credit cards. Moderate. B, L, D.

Deli: This self-serve establishment features cereals and pastries for breakfast and a variety of sandwiches, salads, and soups for a quick lunch or dinner. Domestic wines by the glass, and domestic and imported beers also are available. Open 19 hours daily. Ext. 3834. Major credit cards. Inexpensive. B, L, D.

Around Anaheim

MR. STOX: A favorite with people who live in the area, not only for the food—swordfish, New York steaks, rack of lamb, fresh salmon—but for the wine list, which offers more than 900 selections of California, French, Italian, and German vintages. Also a good spot for a business lunch. They also are known for freshly baked breads and fine pastries. A nightly musical accompaniment to dinner is provided by a pianist. Valet parking. Reservations recommended. 1105 East Katella Ave.; 634-2994. Major credit cards. Expensive. L (Mondays through Fridays), D.

CHARLEY BROWN'S: Located near Anaheim Stadium, it's part of a chain best known for its beef specialties (particularly prime ribs), but the extensive menu offers much more, including several seafood, pasta, and chicken specialties. Full bar. Reservations recommended. 1751 South State College Blvd.; 634-2211. Major credit cards. Moderate to expensive. L (Mondays through Saturdays), D, Sunday brunch.

THEE WHITE HOUSE: The exterior of this turn-of-the-century mansion bears a resemblance to the President's residence. Inside, the menu is Northern Italian, and the food would please even a Presidential palate. Several veal dishes are noteworthy, in addition to scampi, duck, lobster, and rack of lamb. Reservations recommended. 887 South Anaheim Blvd.; 772-1381. Major credit cards. Moderate to expensive. L (Mondays through Fridays), D.

THE CATCH: Located directly across the street from Anaheim Stadium, this popular eatery is known for its fresh seafood. Also on the menu are some beef specialties, including prime ribs. Reservations recommended. 1929 South State College Blvd.; 634-1829. Major credit cards. Moderate to expensive. L (Mondays through Fridays), D.

BENIHANA OF TOKYO: This was the first *Benihana* on the West Coast to have a sushi bar. In the dining room, it's communal seating, with tables for eight. One of the main attractions is the show put on by the chefs, who prepare the food (hibachi steak, chicken, seafood, and vegetables) at the table/stove with a great flourish of knives and other utensils. There's a cocktail lounge. Reservations recommended; there can be a wait of 20 minutes or so from 6:30 P.M. to 9 P.M. 2100 East Ball Rd.; 774-4940. Major credit cards. Moderate. L, D.

EL TORITO'S: There are two of these popular eateries right in the area. If there's an occasion to celebrate, the waiters will gather with guitar and tambourines to salute it. The atmosphere is definitely lively. There's an extensive Mexican menu. Margaritas are a specialty. Reservations recommended. 2020 East Ball

Rd.; 956-4880; 1801 East Katella Ave.; 634-1888. Major credit cards. Moderate. L, D, Sunday brunch.

TIFFY'S: The menu is packed with homemade ice cream specialties, but there also are some good sandwiches, all sorts of egg combinations at breakfast, and some more ambitious dinner entrées than at similar restaurants in the area. 1060 West Katella Ave.; 635-1801. Major credit cards. Moderate. B, L, D.

TONY ROMA'S: This member of the national chain, located across the street from Disneyland, specializes in ribs served with plenty of tangy homemade barbecue sauce. Other typical dinner selections include New York-cut steaks, breast of chicken teriyaki, and swordfish. Full bar. Reservations not accepted. 1640 South Harbor Blvd.; 520-0200. Major credit cards. Moderate. L, D.

ACAPULCO: Small and pleasant, with hanging plants, the decor conveys the atmosphere of a courtyard in Old Mexico on a summer evening. A large menu features more than 100 items. Fajitas filled with shrimp, chicken, or beef are a specialty. There's a cocktail lounge that offers 15 flavors of margaritas. Reservations recommended. 1410 South Harbor Blvd.; 956-7380. Major credit cards. Inexpensive to moderate. L, D.

MARIE CALLENDER'S: Best known locally for its variety of dessert pies (30 in all), but the hamburgers are quite good here, too—the kind that ooze over your fingertips with every bite. There's a salad bar—try the spicy tomato dressing. Besides burgers and pies, there's also a complete menu of lunch and dinner selections. The location closest to Disneyland is at 540 North Euclid St.; 774-1832. Major credit cards. L, D. Inexpensive to moderate.

MILLIE'S COUNTRY KITCHEN: A *Birnbaum's Disneyland* reader liked this place so much for the food, value, and convenience that he took the time to write us about it. You can eat here all day long, starting early with a breakfast of cinnamon rolls or muffins (for which they're famous), eggs any style with potatoes or grits, omelettes, Belgian waffles, blueberry or multi-grain pancakes, french toast, or breakfast burritos. The lunch menu offers tortilla soup, fried zucchini, half a dozen burgers, and hot or cold sandwiches, served with fries or onion rings; cod fillet; a soup, salad, and cornbread combo; and hefty salads. Dinners (served from noon) include fried chicken, liver and onions, pot roast, meatloaf, steaks, and honey-glazed ham, all of which come with soup or salad, rice or vegetables, and cornbread and honey butter. You won't leave hungry, that's for sure. The restaurant is across the road from Disneyland. 1480 S. Harbor Blvd.; 535-6892. Major credit cards. Inexpensive to moderate. B, L, D.

RICHARD JONES PIT BBQ: This homey establishment is one of the few truly authentic Texas-style barbecues in Southern California. Meats are slowly cooked up to 16 hours in specially enclosed hickory-wood burning pits and are basted in secret sauces. The result is mouth-watering chicken, ribs, and Texas sausage, among many other delicacies. Platters include the Texas Sampler, which features pork spare ribs or baby-back ribs, Texas sausage, BBQ chicken, and beef brisket. Delectable sandwiches, including smoked prime rib and smoked sausage, also are a possibility. Lunch specials are featured daily, and children's dishes are available. 5781 Santa Ana Canyon Rd.; 998-5364. Major credit cards. Inexpensive to moderate. L, D.

SAL'S BIT OF ITALY: Eating at *Sal's* is like having a meal at home. You'll feel so comfortable in the surroundings that you'll be tempted to ask for an extra helping. Pizza, pasta, veal, chicken, and seafood are all on the menu. The lasagna and stuffed pizza are the specialties. 918 South Magnolia; 826-3590. MasterCard and Visa only. Inexpensive to moderate. L, D (closed Mondays).

FLAKEY JAKE'S: Located just down the block from Disneyland in a bright, gazebo-type setting, this fast-food eatery can provide a quick, but good meal at a great price. The menu includes pizza, burgers, sandwiches and salads, as well as a variety of desserts. There's also a breakfast buffet and a special children's menu, and special events are frequently held for the kids. 101 East Katella Ave.; 535-1446. MasterCard and Visa only. Inexpensive. B, L, D.

Noteworthy Orange County Restaurants

Some of the restaurants listed below are only a short distance from Anaheim; others are a bit farther afield. These are our recommendations for dining in the area.

ANTONELLO: Located in the South Coast Plaza Village, across the street from the major shopping mall and just a block from the Orange County Performing Arts Center and South Coast Repertory, this fine Northern Italian restaurant has a reputation for attentive service and excellent food. Calamari is one of the seafood specialties. Several veal dishes are noteworthy, and pasta is made fresh daily on the premises. The dessert pastries are quite delectable. Semi-formal dress. Valet parking available. Reservations recommended. 1611 Sunflower Ave. (South Coast Plaza Village), Santa Ana; 751-7153. Major credit cards. Expensive. L (Mondays through Fridays), D (except Sundays).

BELISLE'S: You can't miss this bright-pink building. The food is first rate, fresh, and of Brobdingnagian proportions. Nearly everything on the menu—including the mile-high pies (wondrous extravaganzas of whipped cream)—is available at all times. 12001 Harbor Blvd., Garden Grove; 750-6560. Master-Card and Visa only. Expensive. B, L, D.

BISTANGO: Modern art decorates the interior of this fashionable restaurant. The contemporary California/Italian cuisine is outstanding, and there's an excellent wine list. Among the enticing appetizers are confit of duck and Dungeness crab and corn crab cakes with roasted pepper sauce and baby greens. Entrées include a wide range of fish, veal, beef, chicken, and other specialties. Don't miss dessert. The three-chocolate parfait is rich and wonderful. Live music (usually light contemporary jazz) is featured nightly. Valet parking available. Reservations recommended. 19100 Von Karman Ave., Irvine; 752-5222. Major credit cards. Expensive. L, (Mondays through Fridays), D.

CELLAR: In the basement of a graceful old Spanish-style building hides one of the county's best restaurants, serving French and continental cuisine. Fresh ingredients are flown in from around the country and from as far away as New Zealand. There's an extensive and excellent wine list. Elegant dining for sure, and reservations are a must. Jackets recommended. 305 North Harbor Blvd., Fullerton; 525-5682. Major credit cards. Expensive. D (Tuesdays through Saturdays).

CHANTECLAIR: A French and continental menu is offered at this lovely restaurant in Irvine, about 12 miles southeast of Anaheim. Filet mignon is a specialty and all desserts and pastries are made on the premises. The strawberries Chanteclair, served with Grand Marnier and chocolate, are noteworthy. Jackets are recommended. Reservations required. 18912 MacArthur Blvd., Irvine; 752-8001. Major credit cards. Expensive. L (Mondays through Fridays), D, Sunday brunch in fall only.

DINING ROOM AT THE RITZ-CARLTON LAGUNA NIGUEL: Formal dining at one of Southern California's poshest resort hotels.

The service is outstanding, as is the food from Southern France and the Mediterranean, featuring beef, chicken, and seafood specialties. Jackets required. Valet parking. Reservations a must weekends, recommended weekdays. Ritz-Carlton Drive, Laguna Niguel; 240-2000. Major credit cards. Expensive. D.

FIVE CROWNS: Fashioned after *Ye Old Bell*, England's oldest pub on the Thames River. With heavy-leaded glass windows and cozy fireplaces, this is every inch the proper setting for meals of roast prime ribs of beef accompanied by creamed spinach and Yorkshire pudding, or roast duckling. Watney's beer is on tap, and the wine list is impressive. Reservations suggested. 3801 East Coast Highway, Corona Del Mar; 760-0331. Major credit cards. Expensive. D, Sunday brunch.

LA BRASSERIE: The charming country-style decor of this French café is warm and inviting. Traditional French and continental cuisine is served, and there's an excellent wine selection. Veal forestière (veal in a Madeira sauce with mushrooms) is a specialty. The dessert pastries are homemade. Reservations recommended. 202 South Main St., Orange; 978-6161. Major credit cards. Expensive. L (Mondays through Fridays), D (except Sundays).

NIEUPORT 17: Dine in the midst of a wonderful collection of aeronautical memorabilia. The food is continental, a good mix of fish and meats. Cocktails, imported and domestic wines, and entertainment. Reservations recommended. 13051 Newport Ave., Tustin; 731-5130. Major credit cards. Expensive. L (Mondays through Fridays), D.

SCOOPS, SOFT-SERVE, & OTHER SWEET TREATS

IN DISNEYLAND: The *Main Street Cone Shop* serves ice cream in sugar cones and sundaes in waffle cones. The *Carnation Ice Cream Parlor* features ice cream concoctions named for Disney attractions. *Carnation Plaza Gardens* offers a choice of cones or cups of ice cream, plus a hot-fudge brownie sundae or a strawberry sundae. The *Blue Ribbon Bakery and Yogurt Shop* features frozen lowfat and nonfat yogurt with a variety of toppings. Frozen yogurt also is available at *Clarabelle's Frozen Yogurt* in Toontown. The *Tiki Juice Bar* features soft-serve frozen pineapple dessert. *Brer Bar* has ice cream. The *Mint Julep Bar* and the *Royal Street Veranda* both have ice-cream novelties (order some fritters to go with them). The *Fort Wilderness Canteen* serves ice-cream goodies. *Meeko's* offers frozen bananas. The *Lunching Pad* has an assortment of frozen yummies.

IN THE HOTELS: Whether you like it in sugar or wafer cones, by the dish, smothered with gooey chocolate, or accompanied by strawberries, bananas, whipped cream, nuts, and chocolate chips, there is an ice cream place here to suit your fancy: *Stromboli's* and the *Wharf Galley* at the *Disneyland Hotel*, *Alice's American Grille* at the *Anaheim Marriott*, and the *Chaparral Café* at the *Anaheim Conestoga* hotel.

IN THE AREA: *Tiffy's* (1060 West Katella Ave.) and *Baskin-Robbins* (1646 West Katella Ave. and other locations) serve ice cream and sundaes. *Marie Callender's* (540 North Euclid St.) can satisfy with whipped cream pies.

KID STUFF

Almost every restaurant in the Magic Kingdom offers a children's menu. A bit rarer in the Anaheim area, they do exist.

EL TORITO'S: Children under 12 can order a hamburger or chicken strips with french fries; or enchiladas, quesadillas, tacos, or burritos with rice and beans (about $2.95). Adult entrées cost $6 to $10. 1801 East Katella Ave., Anaheim; 634-1888; 2020 East Ball Rd., Anaheim; 956-4880.

DENNY'S: At breakfast, child-size portions of pancakes and french toast are offered. Choices for lunch and dinner include hot dogs, grilled cheese sandwiches, hamburgers, and corn dogs. Children's (under 12) dinners cost about $2. Adult entrées cost $5 to $9.50. 1610 South Harbor Blvd.; Anaheim, 776-3300.

HANSA HOUSE SMORGASBORD: Children from ages 4 to 12 are charged 40¢ per year of age at breakfast (i.e., $4 for a 10-year-old), 45¢ per year at lunch, 60¢ at dinnertime, and 55¢ per year at Sunday brunch. For the same buffet selections, their parents pay $5.25 at breakfast, $6.25 at lunch, $9.95 at dinner, and $7.50 for Sunday brunch. Prices include dessert, but not a drink. 1840 South Harbor Blvd., Anaheim; 750-2411.

HOF'S HUT: Near the Crystal Cathedral and the City Shopping Center, this full-service, American-style restaurant has a fairly extensive children's menu at breakfast, lunch, and dinner. Cost of a child's (under 12) dinner, including dessert, is about $2.99. Adults can order steaks, seafood, ribs, a half-dozen kinds of burgers, and quiche for $5.50 to $11.25. 4050 West Chapman Ave., Orange; 634-8606.

MRS. KNOTT'S CHICKEN DINNER: Children's portions of the chicken dinner that made Mrs. Knott famous in the first place are smaller and less expensive than those their parents order. Cost is $9.95 for adults, $4.95 for youngsters under ten. 8039 Beach Blvd., Buena Park; 220-5080.

MARIE CALLENDER'S: Spaghetti, pizza, hamburgers, cheeseburgers, chicken tenders, and turkey or ham sandwiches cost $1.99 to $2.99, including a bakery treat and a drink for kids under 12. Adult entrées go for $6.95 to $10.95. 540 North Euclid St., Anaheim; 774-1832.

PAVILION: Located at the luxurious *Four Seasons* hotel in Newport Beach, the menu offers first class continental cooking with a contemporary California touch. Pepper-crusted lamb is a dinner specialty. There's an extensive wine list. Valet parking is available. Reservations recommended for lunch and dinner. 690 Newport Center Dr., Newport Beach; 759-0808, ext. 4338. Major credit cards. Expensive. B, L, D.

RITZ: Continental cuisine is the specialty at this restaurant across the street from Newport Center's Fashion Island mall. The wine selection is excellent, the service first-rate, and the decor reminiscent of a classic European dining room. Valet parking. Reservations recommended. Jackets recommended, but not required. 880 Newport Center Dr., Newport Beach; 720-1800. Major credit cards. Expensive. L (Mondays through Fridays), D.

ROYAL KHYBER: A bit of India comes to the beach. The menu here includes about 20 different curries, Chicken Tikka (diced chicken marinated in spices and herbs and cooked in a tandoori clay oven over charcoal), leavened bread stuffed with roast lamb, and rice mixed with lamb or chicken and nuts. Diners are served under a canopy. Full bar. Reservations recommended. 1000 Bristol St. North, Newport Beach; 752-5200. Major credit cards. Expensive. L (Mondays through Fridays), D, Sunday champagne brunch.

WATERCOLORS: Located at the *Dana Point Resort*. Dine in a restaurant where every table has a dramatic view of the Pacific Ocean.

127

The contemporary American menu is innovative, and the food is first rate. Maine lobster is a specialty. Casual dress. Valet parking. Reservations recommended for dinner. 25135 Park Lantern, Dana Point; 661-5000. Major credit cards. Moderate to expensive. B, L, D, Sunday brunch.

CRAB COOKER: Across the street from the Newport Beach pier, the *Crab Cooker* has an unceremonious atmosphere, complete with paper tablecloths, paper plates, and plastic cups. But the Manhattan clam chowder, mesquite-grilled fresh seafood, scallops, and crab legs are delicious. 2200 Newport Blvd., Newport Beach; 673-0100. No credit cards accepted. Moderate. L, D.

LOS ALAMITOS FISH COMPANY: One of the best values in Orange County, serving first-rate, fresh fish at surprisingly moderate prices. It is a very popular eating place, and since reservations are not accepted, there's usually a wait at peak dining hours. Desserts are quite good (try the moose pie). 11061 Los Alamitos Blvd. (at Katella), Los Alamitos; 310-594-4553. Major credit cards. Moderate. L, D.

PEPPERS: Decorated in a tropical motif, this eatery features grilled Pacific seafood and carefully prepared Mexican specialties. There is a bar that is very popular with locals. 12361 Chapman Ave., Garden Grove; 740-1333. Major credit cards. Moderate. L, D.

WOK INN: Specializing in Mandarin and Szechwan cuisines. The sesame beef is a particularly good choice. Full bar. 13053 Chapman Ave., Garden Grove; 750-3511. Major credit cards. Moderate. L, D.

ANGELO'S & VINCI'S RISTORANTE: The menu offers pizza, pasta, seafood, plus other Italian specialties. Part of the Old Market Place of 1912, the ceiling goes way up, and the Italian opera recordings in the background sound as full-throated as the originals in this cavernous room. In the summer, you can dine on the terrace. Reservations are required for groups of ten or more. 516 North Harbor Blvd., Fullerton; 879-4022. American Express, MasterCard and Visa. Inexpensive to moderate. L, D, Sunday brunch.

HARD ROCK CAFE—NEWPORT BEACH: Rock 'n' roll memorabilia decorate this member of the popular chain, where burgers, chicken, and milk shakes are staples on the menu. 451 Newport Center Dr., Newport Beach (at Fashion Island); 640-8844. Major credit cards. Inexpensive to moderate. L, D.

BACK BAY ROWING & RUNNING CLUB: The soups, salads, quiche, burgers, and sandwiches served here are all tasty. But the

EATING ETHNIC

Mexican food is certainly the ethnic favorite in Southern California, but you need not go far afield to satisfy other international preferences as well.

MEXICAN
- **Acapulco**—1410 South Harbor Blvd., Anaheim; 956-7380
- **Casa Mexicana**—Frontierland, Disneyland; 999-4565
- **El Torito's**—2020 East Ball Rd., Anaheim; 956-4880; 1801 East Katella Ave., Anaheim; 634-1888
- **Peppers**—12361 Chapman Ave., Garden Grove; 740-1333

CHINESE & JAPANESE
- **Benihana of Tokyo**—2100 East Ball Rd., Anaheim; 774-4940
- **Keyaki**—*Pan Pacific* hotel; 1717 South West St., Anaheim; 999-0990, ext. 5683
- **Wok Inn**—13053 Chapman Ave., Orange; 750-3511

INDIAN
- **Royal Khyber**—1000 Bristol St. North, Newport Beach; 752-5200

PIZZA & PASTA
- **Angelo's & Vinci's Ristorante**—516 North Harbor Blvd., Fullerton; 879-4022
- **Sal's Bit of Italy**—918 South Magnolia, Anaheim; 826-3590

real draw is the salad bar—regarded by many of the locals as the best in Orange County. It features myriad fresh fruits and vegetables, many varieties of lettuce, imaginative pasta and taco salads, unusually delectable potato salads, and much more. The house dressings are fresh and delicious (the honey and mustard dressing is particularly good). 3333 Bristol St. (South Coast Plaza), Costa Mesa; 641-0118. Major credit cards. Inexpensive. L, D.

BURRELL'S BARBEQUE & CAFE: Known for baby-back ribs, barbequed chicken, and a special macaroni and cheese dish made with American and mozzarella cheeses, this casual restaurant is the place to go when you feel like getting your hands dirty and your tummy full. 14980 Sand Canyon Ave., Irvine; 786-0451. Major credit cards. Inexpensive. B, L, D.

MRS. KNOTT'S CHICKEN DINNER: Started as a way to augment income from the family's berry farm during the Depression, this restaurant is now surrounded by a full-fledged amusement park (see *Anaheim*). The same good chicken dinner that Cordelia Knott initially served is still available here. The menu also includes home-made biscuits, mashed potatoes with gravy, salad, choice of desserts (try the famous boysenberry pie), and a beverage. 8039 Beach Blvd., Buena Park; 220-5080. Major credit cards. Inexpensive. B, L (Mondays through Saturdays), D (daily).

RUTABEGORZ: Think rutabagas and such. The focus here is on healthy dining, and enormous salads, tasty soups, and plenty of fresh, seasonal vegetables are featured—no fried foods. Desserts are made fresh daily, and the apple pie is particularly good. 211 North Pomona Ave., Fullerton; 738-9339. No credit cards accepted. Inexpensive. L, D (closed Sundays).

Los Angeles Restaurants

In spite of the overwhelming number of fine restaurants in Los Angeles, many of the more famous places reward the unsuspecting first-timer with lost reservations and tables beside the kitchen door. Confirm reservations on the day of your meal. Our choices follow, alphabetized within price range.

SPAGO: The unusual menu here is described by owner Wolfgang Puck as "California cuisine." The establishment is best known for its pizza with toppings of duck sausage, mozzarella, oregano, and tomato, or smoked lamb, eggplant, and roasted peppers. Entrées include chicken dishes, roasted baby lamb, and grilled fish. Reservations required (weeks ahead for weekends). 8795 Sunset Blvd.; 310-652-4025. Major credit cards, except American Express. Expensive. D.

DANTE: Old World Italian charm and superb service are the hallmarks of this quaint, intimate eatery in the heart of West Los Angeles. The pasta is first-rate, and house specialties include cioppino and other seafood dishes. 11917 Wilshire Blvd.; 310-479-3991. Major credit cards. Moderate to expensive. L, D.

MUSSO & FRANK GRILL: An American classic, it really is a grill, and it has been in Hollywood since 1919. True-blue American food. Breakfast is served starting at 11 A.M. Reservations recommended. 6667 Hollywood Blvd.; 213-467-7788. Major credit cards. Moderate to expensive. B, L, D (closed Sundays and Mondays).

CHEESECAKE FACTORY: More than 40 varieties of cheesecakes including fresh strawberry, white-chocolate raspberry truffle, and cookie dough options. Before dessert, choose from roughly 200 entrées on the

NIGHTLIFE

Anaheim/Orange County boasts plenty of after-dark entertainment. For information on dinner theaters in the area and the Orange County Performing Arts Center, see our *Anaheim* chapter.

NIGHTSPOTS: All the larger hotels have lounges offering soft jazz, piano, or guitar music. Some of the hotel lounges and other area nightspots offer even more. The **Neon Cactus**, at the *Disneyland Hotel*, has country decor but features classic rock 'n' roll with a live band Fridays through Sundays and a deejay the rest of the week. Appetizers and drinks are served. The *Anaheim Hilton* has an upbeat nightclub called **Pulse**, which offers dancing nightly to Top 40 music. **The Cowboy Boogie** (1721 South Manchester Ave., Anaheim; 956-1412) has country and western music nightly. Free western dance lessons are offered. **The Original Cattleman's Wharf** (adjacent to the *Conestoga* hotel at 1160 West Ball Rd., Anaheim; 535-1622) features a pianist and live band in the **Baron's Lounge** upstairs. **Mr. Stox** (1105 East Katella Ave., Anaheim; 634-2994) features piano music nightly. **Bill Medley's Music City** (18774 Brookhurst St., Fountain Valley; 963-2366) bears its owner's name; music and special events take guests on a nostalgic trip through the 1950s, 1960s, and 1970s. **Medieval Times** (7662 Beach Blvd., Anaheim; 521-4740) features knights on horseback and a four-course dinner. **Wild Bill's Wild West Dinner Extravaganza** (7600 Beach Blvd., Buena Park; 522-6414) is a fun-filled western hoedown complete with a four-course meal. **Crazy Horse Steakhouse and Saloon** (1580 Brookhollow Dr., Santa Ana; 549-1512) has music with a swinging western beat and often features name country performers. **The Cannery** (3010 Lafayette Ave., Newport Beach; 675-5777), besides its light rock music, is notable for the building itself—an old cannery, with some of the original equipment still in place. It's a good spot for dinner and drinks and attracts a large singles crowd (see *Getting Ready to Go*). A dinner/dancing spot of note is **Peppers** (12361 Chapman Ave., Garden Grove; 740-1333). It features dancing nightly to Top 40 hits, and offers a free shuttle to and from Disneyland-area hotels. **The Coach House** (33157 Camino Capistrano, Suite C, San Juan Capistrano; 496-8930) showcases music of top pop stars.

COMEDY: Improvisation Comedy Nite Club (4255 Campus Dr., Irvine; 854-5455 and 945 East Birch St., Brea; 529-7878) features comedy shows nightly.

menu, including Mexican, Italian, and American dishes. 364 N. Beverly Drive, Beverly Hills; 310-278-7270; 4142 Via Marina, Marina Del Rey; 310-306-3344. Major credit cards. Moderate. L, D, Sunday brunch.

CHIN CHIN: Pot stickers and Chinese chicken salad are among the specialties here. 8618 Sunset Blvd., West Hollywood; 310-652-1818; 13455 Maxella Ave., Marina del Rey; 310-823-9999. Major credit cards. Moderate. L, D.

RJ'S RIB JOINT: Sumptuous spare ribs, seafood, and salads are the specialties. Portions are generous and best accompanied by the steam beer on draft. The chocolate cake is colossal. Reservations recommended. 252 North Beverly Dr., Beverly Hills; 310-274-7427. Major credit cards. Moderate. L (Mondays through Saturdays), D, Sunday brunch.

ALICE'S: Sitting right on the scenic Malibu Pier, this cozy little restaurant offers diners a breathtaking view of the Pacific Ocean and coastline. Seafood is the specialty here, and dishes range from shrimp scampi to grilled king salmon. For the landlubbers, there are hamburgers and a variety of sandwiches and salads. The restaurant also has a full-service bar. Reservations are recommended for dinner. 23000 W. Pacific Coast Hwy.; 310-456-6646. MasterCard and Visa only. Inexpensive to moderate. L, D.

STAGE DELI OF NEW YORK: Located right next door to *Dive* (see below) in the fashionable Century City Mall, it's a bit more pricey than your average deli, but the food is quite good and the sandwiches are gargantuan. The wall-to-wall movie memorabilia also makes this place a fun dining experience. 10250 Santa Monica Blvd.; 310-553-3354. Major credit cards. Inexpensive to moderate. L, D.

DIVE: This nautically themed eatery in the Century City Mall is painstakingly decked out in submarine paraphernalia. The menu tempts with more than 20 gourmet submarine sandwiches such as Chinese chicken salad or Tus-can steak. There is a full service bar. 10250 Santa Monica Blvd., 310-788-3483. Major credit cards. Inexpensive. L, D.

KWGB: Boasting the "World's Greatest Burgers," this festive restaurant in Universal City's outdoor CityWalk Mall has a radio station motif and features a deejay who plays requests that you phone in from your table. Besides its delectable burgers, KWGB also offers a variety of soups, salads, and sandwiches. Universal CityWalk (take Freeway 101 to Universal City exits); 818-622-5942. Major credit cards. Inexpensive. L, D.

MALIBU INN & RESTAURANT: "Take a step back into time" is the theme of this popular beach-house-style eatery, which dates from 1927 and has been at its present location on the Pacific Coast Highway since 1946. Omelettes and burgers are featured on the menu. Dozens of photographs of screen stars from yesteryear and today on the walls. A saloon adjoins the restaurant. 22969 W. Pacific Coast Hwy.; 310-456-6106. Major credit cards. Inexpensive. B, L, D.

MARY AND ROBB'S WESTWOOD CAFÉ: Homey and comfortable, this is the ideal place to come for a home-cooked breakfast, lunch, or dinner. Breakfast specialties include delicious french toast and a variety of omelettes. Among the lunch and dinner dishes are open-face turkey and roast-beef sandwiches, as well as beef and seafood. 1453 Westwood Blvd.; 310-478-3822. Major credit cards. Inexpensive. B, L, D (closed Sundays).

ORIGINAL PANTRY CAFE: A family-style restaurant that has been in business since 1924. Dinner options include thick sirloin or platter-filling T-bones. Lunch tends to be short ribs and beef stews. But the ham omelette at breakfast is truly outstanding—filled with half a pound of chunked pieces of ham steak. The hash browns, cole slaw, and sourdough bread are heavenly. Ninth and Figueroa; 213-972-9279. No credit cards. Inexpensive. Open 24 hours.

Meal by Meal

Breakfast

DISNEYLAND

Main Street: Eggs and Mickey Mouse-shaped waffles at the *Carnation Ice Cream Parlor*; fresh-baked muffins at the *Blue Ribbon Bakery and Yogurt Shop*; character breakfast at the *Plaza Inn**

New Orleans Square: Fritters at *Mint Julep Bar* and *Royal Street Veranda*; pastries and fruit at *La Petite Patisserie*

Frontierland: Waffles and Mickey Mouse pancakes at *River Belle Terrace*

Tomorrowland: Fresh fruit with a yogurt dressing at *Tomorrowland Terrace*

ANAHEIM: Character breakfast at *Goofy's Kitchen* at the *Disneyland Hotel*; Sunday brunch at *El Torito's, Charley Brown's,* and *Marie Callender's*; omelettes at *Tiffy's*; pastries and espresso at *Café Oasis;* breakfast buffet at *Alice's American Grille* in the *Anaheim Marriott*

ORANGE COUNTY: Sunday brunch at *Five Crowns, Chanteclair, Royal Khyber,* and *Angelo's & Vinci's Ristorante*

LOS ANGELES: Sunday brunch at *R.J.'s Rib Joint* and the *Cheesecake Factory*; ham omelettes, hash browns, and grilled sourdough bread at the *Original Pantry Café*; french toast at *Mary and Robb's Westwood Café*

Lunch

DISNEYLAND

Main Street: Sandwiches and salads at *Carnation Ice Cream Parlor*; fried chicken and ribs at the *Plaza Pavilion**; hand-dipped corn dogs from *Little Red Wagon*

New Orleans Square: Pasta primavera salad or chicken Florentine at *Blue Bayou*; sandwiches at *Café Orleans;* fried chicken or french dip sandwiches at *French Market*

Critter Country: Burgers and fries at *Hungry Bear*; hot dogs and sandwiches at *Brer Bar*; seafood at *Harbour Galley*

Fantasyland: Burgers and salads at *Village Haus*; pizza and hot dogs at *Meeko's*

Frontierland: Ribs at *Big Thunder Barbecue**; tacos and enchiladas at *Casa Mexicana*; take-out barbeque chicken at *River Belle Terrace*; burgers at *Stage Door Café*

Mickey's Toontown: Spicy chicken wings at *Daisy's Diner*; hot dogs at *Pluto's Dog House*

Tomorrowland: Burgers and sandwiches at *Tomorrowland Terrace*

ANAHEIM: Mexican food at *Acapulco* and *El Torito's*; ribs at *Tony Roma's*; pizza and pasta at *Sal's Bit of Italy*; Cobb salad or New York-cut steaks at *Mr. Stox*

ORANGE COUNTY: Mexican food at *Peppers*; burgers and fries at *Hard Rock Café*; salads and soups at *Rutabegorz*; salad bar at *Back Bay Rowing & Running Club*; fresh fish and cheesecake at *Los Alamitos Fish Company*; Chinese cuisine at *Wok Inn*; chicken at *Mrs. Knott's*; pizza at *Angelo's & Vinci's Ristorante*

LOS ANGELES: Submarine sandwiches at *Dive*; burgers at *KWGB*; ribs and salads at *R.J.'s Rib Joint*; Chinese cuisine at *Chin Chin*; huge sandwiches at *Stage Deli of New York*

Dinner

DISNEYLAND

Main Street: Sandwiches and salads at *Carnation Ice Cream Parlor*

Adventureland: Mediterranean food at *Aladdin's Oasis**; skewered meat or veggies at *Bengal Barbecue*

Critter Country: Burgers and fries at *Hungry Bear*; sandwiches at *Brer Bar*

New Orleans Square: Fresh salmon or prawns at *Blue Bayou*; jambalaya at the *French Market*

Fantasyland: Pizza, burgers, and fries at *Village Haus*

Frontierland: Ribs and chicken at *Big Thunder Barbecue**; burritos and tacos at *Casa Mexicana*; veggie stew at *River Belle Terrace*

Mickey's Toontown: Pizza at *Daisy's Diner*; hot dogs at *Pluto's Dog House*

Tomorrowland: Fried chicken, sandwiches, and burgers at *Tomorrowland Terrace*

ANAHEIM: Northern Italian fare at *Thee White House*; seafood at *The Catch*; Japanese dishes at *Benihana of Tokyo* and *Keyaki* at *Pan Pacific*; Mexican fare at *El Torito's*; barbeque ribs and chicken at *Richard Jones Pit BBQ*

ORANGE COUNTY: Confit of duck and Dungeness crab at *Bistango*; homemade pasta at *Antonello*; Indian food at *Royal Khyber*; Maine lobster at *Watercolors*; continental cuisine at *La Brasserie, Nieuport 17,* and *Chanteclair*

LOS ANGELES: Exotic pizza at *Spago*; seafood at *Alice's* and *Dante*; ribs and chocolate cake at *R.J.'s Rib Joint*; steaks at *Original Pantry Café*

* Only open during Disneyland's busy seasons.

SPORTS

No matter what you've heard about Southern California's urban sprawl—one town feeding into another and not an inch of land without a freeway or a house on it—there's still plenty of wide-open space for recreation. This is particularly true in Orange County, where more than 10,000 acres of parkland provide a variety of sports facilities. Some have baseball fields and basketball and racquetball courts. Others offer golf, fitness courses, bike trails, and natural areas.

In addition, there are close to 70,000 acres of mountain terrain in the Cleveland National Forest in Orange County. They are ribboned with more than 40 miles of hiking trails and 60 miles of fishing streams.

Anaheim itself has two municipal golf courses and any number of convenient tennis courts. And though the hotels in the immediate vicinity of Disneyland generally don't qualify as "resorts," most do have swimming pools.

Just 15 miles south of Anaheim lie some prime Pacific Ocean beaches, so head south to pursue the California sunshine and find the ultimate wave. In all, some 42 miles of inviting sand lie within an hour's drive of the city.

Even with its urban reputation, this part of Southern California offers such a variety of recreational opportunities that no matter what your sport is, there's someplace here to play or practice it.

(Unless otherwise noted, all phone numbers are in the 714 area code.)

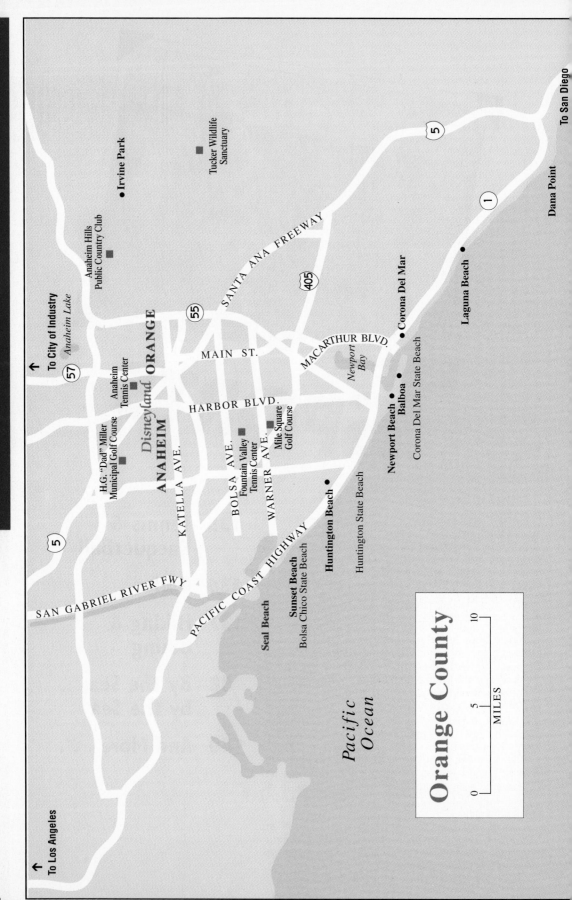

To Los Angeles

To City of Industry

To San Diego

Dana Point

Anaheim Lake

5

57

55

405

U.S. 5

1

SANTA ANA FREEWAY

Anaheim Hills
Public Country Club

• Irvine Park

Tucker Wildlife
Sanctuary

Disneyland ORANGE

ANAHEIM

MAIN ST.

HARBOR BLVD.

Anaheim
Tennis Center

H.G. "Dad" Miller
Municipal Golf Course

KATELLA AVE.

BOLSA AVE.

Fountain Valley
Tennis Center

WARNER AVE.

Mile Square
Golf Course

MACARTHUR BLVD.

Newport Bay

• Corona Del Mar

Corona Del Mar State Beach

Newport Beach •
Balboa •

• Laguna Beach

Huntington Beach •

Huntington State Beach

PACIFIC COAST HIGHWAY

SAN GABRIEL RIVER FWY.

Sunset Beach
Bolsa Chico State Beach

Seal Beach

*Pacific
Ocean*

Orange County

0   5   10

MILES

Tennis & Racquetball

ANAHEIM TENNIS CENTER: About two miles from Disneyland, it has the facilities of a private club—pro shop, Spanish-style clubhouse, computerized practice machines, lockers/showers—but is open to the public. Here they'll try to match you up with a suitable partner, if you put in a request in advance. There are 12 fast, hard-surface courts, all lighted for night play. Singles rates range from $3 to $7 per person per hour, and doubles rates range from $8 to $20 per court per hour, depending on time of day. Ball machine use is $3.50; it's separated from the courts, but still a good place to practice forehand and backhand strokes. Hours are 8 A.M. to 10 P.M. Mondays through Thursdays, 8 A.M. to 9 P.M. Fridays, 8 A.M. to 6 P.M. Saturdays and Sundays. Racquets rent for $3. Locker and shower facilities are free; towels are not supplied. A half-hour private lesson with the pro costs $19. Semi-private and group lessons also are available. Call for rates. Advance reservations (bookable up to three days ahead) are a good idea, especially after 5 P.M. 975 South State College Blvd.; Anaheim; 991-9090.

CANYON TERRACE RACQUETBALL AND HEALTH CLUB: This facility has seven air conditioned racquetball courts. Court fee is $7 per hour for nonmembers; there are no rentals. The club's weight room is open to nonmembers for $4, and aerobics classes are available for $3. Hours are 6 A.M. to 10 P.M. Mondays through Fridays, 7 A.M. to 9 P.M. weekends. 100 North Tustin Ave.; Anaheim; 974-0280.

FOUNTAIN VALLEY RECREATION AND CULTURAL CENTER: Located on the west side of Mile Square Regional Park, the center offers indoor and outdoor racquetball courts and outdoor basketball courts. The indoor court fee is $5 per hour. Outdoor courts are free during the day. From dusk to 8:45 P.M. they are $7 per hour. There are no rentals. Hours are 9 A.M. to 8:45 P.M. Mondays through Thursdays (the three outdoor courts are lighted until 8:45 P.M.); 9 A.M. to 5 P.M. Fridays and Saturdays; and noon to 5 P.M. Sundays. For evening play, book reservations a day in advance. 16400 Brookhurst St.; Fountain Valley; 839-8611.

FOUNTAIN VALLEY TENNIS CENTER: Located in Mile Square Regional Park (see "Hiking & Biking"), facilities are fairly spartan, consisting of 12 hard-surface courts, all lighted on weeknights. Courts are open 8 A.M. to noon and 4 P.M. to 9 P.M. Mondays through Fridays; 8 A.M. to 4 P.M. weekends. A reservation card, which costs $15, is necessary to reserve court time. Reservations may be made up to a week in advance. Court time is $5 per hour during the day; $7 per hour after dark Mondays through Fridays; and $6 on weekends. The busiest hours for play are 9 A.M. to 11 A.M. and 5 P.M. to 8 P.M. You must have your own equipment. Showers and lockers are not available. Near the Fountain Valley Recreation and Cultural Center. 16400 Brookhurst St., Fountain Valley; 839-5950.

INDUSTRY HILLS & SHERATON RESORT: About 25 miles north of Disneyland, the elaborate sports complex here includes 16 hard-surface tennis courts, all lighted for night play, along with one practice court. The rate is $8 per person Mondays through Fridays; $10 per person Saturdays and Sundays. Juniors under 18 pay $5 every day. Hours are Mondays through Thursdays, 7 A.M. to 10 P.M.; Fridays, 7 A.M. to 9 P.M.; Saturdays and Sundays, 7 A.M. to 8 P.M. Racquets rent for $2; lockers cost $2. Instruction is available by appointment for $36 to $38 per hour for pro instruction, $19 per half hour. Reservations are suggested after 5 P.M., and may be booked up to three days in advance. One Industry Hills Parkway; City of Industry; 818-854-2360.

135

Hackers and experienced golfers alike can match their skills to these local courses.

ANAHEIM HILLS PUBLIC COUNTRY CLUB: This challenging course has a hilly, par-71, 6,330-yard championship layout with 18 holes nestled in the valleys and slopes of Santa Ana Canyon. Greens fees are $16 Mondays through Thursdays and $22 Fridays through Sundays. Carts are available for $20 and clubs (matched sets) can be rented for $14. Busiest on weekends; the least-crowded days are Mondays and Tuesdays, but even then reservations are recommended (call seven days ahead for both weekday and weekend play). 6501 Nohl Ranch Rd.; Anaheim; 998-3041.

INDUSTRY HILLS GOLF COURSE: The lure of this place is its two beautifully landscaped, challenging 18-hole golf courses—the "Babe Zaharias" and the "Eisenhower." The former, named after the pioneer professional woman golfer, is a par-71, 5,994-yard layout; the latter, nicknamed "The Ike," is a par-72, 6,287-yard course. The cost to play each course is $42 (including cart rental) Mondays through Thursdays; $25 after 2 P.M.; $57 Fridays through Sundays; $30 after 2 P.M. Rental clubs are $25. Reservations for morning tee-off times can be made three days in advance. One Industry Hills Parkway; City of Industry; 818-810-GOLF.

MILE SQUARE GOLF COURSE: This flat 18-hole, par-72 course runs along the southern side of the same Mile Square Regional Park area that offers such other sports as tennis, baseball, basketball, and jogging. Greens fees are $17 Mondays through Thursdays and $22 Fridays through Sundays and holidays. Carts are available for $21. There are rental clubs (matched sets) for $12. Reservations are recommended; call seven days ahead for weekdays, five days ahead for weekends. 10401 Warner Ave.; Fountain Valley; 545-7106.

H. G. "DAD" MILLER MUNICIPAL GOLF COURSE: "Dad" Miller made a hole-in-one on this course (on the 112-yard 11th hole) when he was 101 years old, and it's still a favorite with senior citizens since the terrain is rather flat and easy to walk. But don't let that keep you away even if you're a tad younger. This is the third-busiest golf course in California, partly because of its convenient mid-city location, but also because it's just right for the strictly recreational golfer. It's a 5,920-yard, par-71, 18-hole course. The cost to play here is $16 Mondays through Thursdays; $22 Fridays through Sundays and holidays. Reservations are a must, and may be made a week in advance by calling the automated tee-time system at 748-8900 or the golf shop; 430 North Gilbert St.; Anaheim; 774-8055 (golf shop).

PELICAN HILL GOLF CLUB: This Tom Fazio-designed, 6,647-yard, par-70 course has great ocean views from just about every hole. The cost to play is $129 Mondays and Tuesdays; and $158 Wednesdays through Sundays and holidays for reservations made one to six days in advance. Add $20 for noncancellable reservations made 7 to 14 days in advance. Twilight rates (after 3 P.M.) are $75 Mondays and Tuesdays and $85 Wednesdays through Sundays and holidays. 22653 Pelican Hill Rd. South; Newport Coast; 760-0707.

Hiking & Biking

Most of the Santa Ana mountain range lies within the boundaries of the Cleveland National Forest, where the Forest Service maintains campgrounds and hiking trails. There are several areas for hiking, horseback riding, picnicking, and biking, but two of the more popular are Santiago Canyon and Modjeska Canyon.

IRVINE PARK: Located in Santiago Canyon, near Irvine Lake, it has plentiful picnic facilities, and hiking and equestrian trails that wind through 477 hilly, tranquil acres and 800-year-old sycamores and oaks. The oldest county park in California, it also offers several miles of bike trails, a petting zoo, playground, waterfall, and lake. The park is open from 7 A.M. to 9 P.M. April through October, and from 7 A.M. to 5 P.M. November through March. On weekends, bicycles-for-two and pedal boats may be rented. The entry fee is $2 per vehicle, which includes parking. 21501 East Chapman Ave.; Orange; 633-8072.

MILE SQUARE REGIONAL PARK: Among the facilities here are four miles of trails for biking, hiking, or jogging; a fitness course; and two fishing lakes, as well as a public golf course (see "Golf") and tennis courts (see "Tennis and Racquetball"). On the west side of the park, the Fountain Valley Recreation and Cultural Center (located at 16400 Brookhurst St.) has indoor and outdoor racquetball courts (see "Tennis and Racquetball"). The recreation center is open from 9 A.M. to 8:45 P.M. Mondays through Thursdays; 9 A.M. to 4:45 P.M. Fridays and Saturdays; and noon to 4:45 P.M. Sundays. The park is open 7 A.M. to 6 P.M. November through March; during the summer months from 7 A.M. to 9 P.M. 16801 Euclid Ave.; Fountain Valley; 839-8611 (center), 962-5549 (park).

YORBA REGIONAL PARK: Located in Anaheim Hills, the park offers picnic areas with barbecues, playgrounds, hiking, biking, and equestrian trails. You are responsible for supplying your own bikes or horses, but the 3½ miles of trails provide a pleasant (and not too demanding) workout. There also are four lakes within this 135-acre park (see "Fishing"). It's open November through March from 7 A.M. to 5 P.M.; during the summer months the hours are 7 A.M. until 9 P.M. You can walk or bike into the park without charge, but driving in costs $2, including parking. 7600 East La Palma Ave.; Anaheim; 970-1460.

SPECTATOR SPORTS

When the urge to become a spectator rather than a participant strikes, Southern California has a wealth of opportunities to watch the pros at work.

FOOTBALL
San Diego Chargers: Jack Murphy Stadium; 9449 Friar's Road; San Diego; 619-563-8281.

BASEBALL
California Angels: Anaheim Stadium; 2000 Gene Autry Way; Anaheim; 634-2000.
Los Angeles Dodgers: Dodger Stadium; 1000 Elysian Park Ave.; Los Angeles; 213-224-1500.
San Diego Padres: Jack Murphy Stadium; 9449 Friar's Road; San Diego; 619-280-4636.

BASKETBALL
Los Angeles Lakers: Great Western Forum; 3900 West Manchester Blvd.; Inglewood; 310-419-3100.
Los Angeles Clippers: Los Angeles Memorial Sports Arena; 3939 South Figueroa; Los Angeles; 213-748-6131.

HOCKEY
Anaheim Mighty Ducks: Anaheim Arena; 2695 Katella Ave.; Anaheim; 740-2000.
Los Angeles Kings: Great Western Forum; 3900 West Manchester Blvd.; Inglewood; 310-419-3182.

By the Sea, by the Sea

Fishing, whalewatching, boating, surfing, and swimming—all popular in this area—are at their best where Orange County meets the Pacific Ocean.

BEACHES: For relaxation or, for surfers, a real workout, head for one of the many free public beaches, listed below as you drive south from Anaheim. Be forewarned that there is a fee to park your car in any of the beach parking lots.

Seal Beach: The Orange County coast begins here and this is its northernmost beach. It's a 1 1/2-mile expanse of sand stretching south from Long Beach to Anaheim Bay. This is a high-density residential area, and not the prettiest spot along the coast, but there are some good boutiques at Old Town Seal Beach, as well as a variety of eating establishments on Main Street in the Old Town area. The city also has a fishing pier. For further information on the beach area call 310-431-2527 (310-379-8471 for surf information).

Bolsa Chica State Beach: A wide and sandy expanse with its own nature reserve, it provides restroom and changing facilities. There is a $5 entrance fee for autos and recreational vehicles ($14 for an overnight stay). The beach is located off the Pacific Coast Highway (Route 1), between Goldenwest Street and Warner Avenue. For further information call 846-3460.

Huntington Beach: This self-proclaimed "Surfing Capital of the USA" hosts annual surfing competitions. It's also been the site of world surfing championships. On any given summer Saturday or Sunday, surfers swarm into the water. Diehards in wet suits are out in winter, too. The pier provides an ideal spot for fishing and a good vantage point from which to watch the surfers catch the waves. Equipment can be rented along Main Street.

Huntington Beach also boasts a long stretch of sand, and it's a rare day when there isn't a beach volleyball game to join. This is also a good beach for jogging. For further information call 536-5281 (536-9303 for surf information).

Newport City Beach/Balboa Beach: This, too, is a popular area with surfers, as well as sightseers, especially since Newport Harbor shelters nearly 10,000 boats, including those of the dorymen who go out in their small, wooden craft each morning at dawn. These hardy souls leave from the pier at Newport Beach and return at about 10 A.M. to clean and sell their catch. The scene quickly becomes a large, open-air fish market, and is quite picturesque.

The Balboa Peninsula juts into the Pacific here, and the beaches—Newport on the mainland, Balboa on the peninsula—are long and horseshoe shaped. They are pleasant and sandy, albeit a bit far from Anaheim if you just want to catch some rays for an hour or so. It's the sightseeing that makes these beaches worth the drive.

For a good view of the harbor, drive along Newport Boulevard to Balboa Boulevard on the Balboa Peninsula. Turn right on Palm Street to find parking for the Balboa Pier. Or stop at Main Street, near the landmark Balboa Pavilion. Adjacent to the Balboa Pavilion is Davey's Locker, where it's possible to rent 14-foot skiffs with outboard motors if you'd like to do some fishing, go parasailing, or just take a tour of Newport Bay. There also are regularly scheduled sightseeing boats that provide a view of local residences, and since Newport/Balboa is Orange County's answer to Beverly Hills, the shorefront houses are quite opulent and fun to look at. For more information contact the Newport Harbor Area Chamber of Commerce (644-8211).

Corona Del Mar State Beach, Laguna Beach, Doheny State Beach, and San Clemente: These beaches farther south are equally as dramatic as the more northerly strands, with high cliffs and sheltered coves, and plenty of tidal pools to explore. If you wend your way south along the Pacific Coast Highway from Huntington Beach to San Clemente, the county's southernmost beach outpost, you'll find these beaches all in a 20-mile stretch, as well as many smaller ones. Signs lead to parking nearby and on the bluffs overlooking them, where it's possible to get the full effect of the Southern California ocean vistas. In general, beaches are open from 6 A.M. to midnight, with lifeguards present in summer.

FISHING: Anglers will find no shortage of action—both saltwater and freshwater—around Anaheim. You can go out for mackerel, whitefish, or halibut in the Pacific; try catching grunion on the beach from March through September; or take youngsters to one of a handful of stocked lakes to cast for trout, crappie, catfish, or bass.

Sportfishing: The Dana Wharf sportfishing fleet, in Dana Point, generally makes four trips a day in season. Prices are $20 for adults and $15 for children 12 and under for half a day of fishing, or $32 for adults and $22 for children for ¾-day. For details and to confirm schedules, call 831-1850. Boats also go out several times a day from Davey's Locker, in Balboa, and the company charges comparable prices. Balboa Pavilion; 400 Main St.; Balboa; 673-1434.

Boats from Dana Wharf and Davey's Locker go out for bonita, barracuda, bass, and yellowtail. Reservations are required at Davey's Locker and can be made a day in advance. The price of a full-day boat rental (which is equipped with some bunks and a galley; food is extra) ranges from $55 to $65 for adults and $40 to $50 for children 15 and under; for half a day, $22 for adults and $14 for children 12 and under. Pole rental is $7. Fourteen-foot skiffs (which accommodate six people) with outboard motors also are available, at $35 for five hours or $50 for a full day, which includes bait, motor, and gas.

Fishing licenses, which are necessary for deep-sea sportfishing, can be obtained at Davey's Locker; $17.35 to $27.60 per year, $6.50 for one day. Dana Wharf boats go out at 7 A.M. for ¾-day fishing (returning between 5 P.M. and 6 P.M.). The cost is $35 for adults, $25 for children under 13. For a half day of fishing, the price is $22 for adults, $14 for children. Poles rent for $7. Licenses may be obtained on the premises. Reservations are advisable, and they can be made up to two weeks in advance.

Irvine Lake: There's no charge for fish caught, and no fishing license required at this stocked freshwater lake. The gate fee is $12 for adults, $10 for children 4 to 12, under 4 free. Fishing poles rent for $7.50 a day. Boats with motors can be rented for $40 a day, including gas. The rate is $20 for half a day, beginning at noon. Rowboats rent for $25 a day (no half-day rates). Pontoons are available for $80 a day and $55 for half a day with a $25 deposit. You can launch your own boat ($6 launch fee), but it must be at least ten feet long. Caution: The five-mph speed limit is strictly enforced. There is a tackle shop and a snack shop on the lake. Pets are not allowed. Hours are 6 A.M. to 4 P.M. daily. 4621 Santiago Canyon Rd.; Orange; 649-2560.

Yorba Regional Park: Three of the four lakes within the boundaries of this 135-developed-acre park are stocked with catfish. To fish you'll need a valid California fishing license, available at most of the local sporting goods stores, but *not* at the park. 7600 East La Palma Ave.; Anaheim; 970-1460.

Bolsa Chica: This is one of the better beaches in the area to try your hand—literally—at catching grunion. From March through September, the tiny fish are swept onto beaches here to lay their eggs in the sand, and they head to sea again on outgoing waves. Best times to get them are on the second through fifth nights after a full moon, about an hour after high tide. You must catch grunion with your bare hands—they're slippery, but easy to see because they shimmer in the moonlight. A fishing license is required if you're over 16 years old. For information call the State Department of Fish and Game at 310-590-5132.

WHALEWATCHING: Each winter, hundreds of California gray whales migrate along the coast to the warm waters of Baja California and western Mexico, then early in spring swim back to feeding areas off the Alaska coast. From December through March, the 50-foot-long leviathans are usually easy to spot from cliffs along the ocean. Boats will take the adventurous out for even closer looks from Newport Harbor and Dana Point Harbor (named after the explorer and author Richard Henry Dana, who wrote *Two Years Before the Mast*) .

And More . . .

NATURE: Bird- and wildlife-watchers will be pleasantly surprised to learn that they can easily spend anywhere from an hour to a full day close to nature in this land of freeways and parking lots.

Bolsa Chica Ecological Reserve: Here you'll find 250 acres of Pacific Ocean marshland in which to observe fish and wetland birds. From the parking lot, cross the bridge and follow the trail that loops through the marsh. Binoculars are useful, but not absolutely necessary. The parking lot is on Pacific Coast Highway 1½ miles south of Warner; Huntington Beach; 897-7003.

Upper Newport Bay Ecological Reserve: During the fall and winter months, this 750-acre reserve at Newport Beach is teeming with birds, great blue herons and ospreys among them. Once a month—usually on the second Saturday—during the migratory season (October through March), Friends of Newport Bay guide groups on walking tours through the reserve and point out the birds, as well as fossils, marsh plants, and fish. But it's easy enough to enjoy the area on your own. To reach the reserve, proceed from the intersection of Back Bay Drive and Jamboree Road by driving or walking along Back Bay Drive for the length of the reserve. Call to confirm tour times and dates: 646-8009. For year-round guided tours, call the Department of Fish and Game at 640-6746.

Tucker Wildlife Sanctuary: Located in Modjeska Canyon in the Santa Ana Mountains, this sanctuary is a beautiful oasis of trees, flowers, plants, and wildlife. Walk along the lovely stream and commune with the birds—more than 140 species have been identified here. Naturalists are on duty to answer questions. The sanctuary is open daily from 9 A.M. to 4 P.M. A $1.50 donation is recommended. Information 649-2760.

AERIAL SPORTS: Parasailing and hot-air ballooning have become popular year-round sports in this sunny clime. From Dana Point, a parasailing excursion runs $45 per person for a ten-minute ride; call 496-5794 for details. Hot-air balloon tours take off at sunrise or sunset, and offer a bird's-eye view of some of the area's most scenic spots, most an hour or two from Disneyland. Above All Balloon Charters (546-7433) features flights over the Perris and Temecula areas of Riverside County, and the Del Mar area of San Diego County. Prices range from $80 to $140 per person, depending on the options chosen. Sunrise Balloons (800-548-9912) takes guests on one-hour flights over the Temecula area for $100 to $135 per person. Brunch at a nearby winery is available for an added fee.

SKIING: Although it's unlikely that you'd come to Southern California solely for the skiing, it is not at all out of the question. In fact, you'll find fine areas like Big Bear in the San Bernardino Mountains, just 90 miles northeast of Disneyland. If you didn't bring any ski gear with you, don't worry. The Newport Ski Company—which has locations in the city of Orange (just a few miles from Disneyland) and in Newport Beach—rents and sells equipment for skiers and snowboarders and also offers repair service. It's open from 10 A.M. to 9 P.M. Mondays through Fridays, and 10 A.M. to 6 P.M. Saturdays and Sundays. 1632 E. Katella Ave., Orange, 633-7100; and 2700 W. Coast Highway, Newport Beach; 631-3280.

CATALINA ISLAND: On this special island, an outdoor enthusiast can choose from golf, horseback riding, snorkeling, scuba diving, and sportfishing. Less-active types can opt for a glass-bottom-boat tour for crystal-clear views of underwater life or an inland tour for glimpses of buffalo, wild goats, deer, and boar. From Orange County, Catalina Passenger Service (673-5245) has a high-speed catamaran, the *Catalina Flyer*, which makes the one-way trip in 75 minutes; call for schedules or to make required advance reservations. Tours leave from the Balboa Pavilion, 400 Main St., on the Balboa Peninsula. From Los Angeles County, Catalina Cruises (800-228-2546) offers daily service year-round from Long Beach, plus weekend service year-round and daily service in season from San Pedro. Catalina Express (800-995-4386) offers daily trips year-round from Long Beach and San Pedro. (**Note:** Those prone to seasickness should take precautions because the ride over can be choppy.) Advance reservations are required for hotels, condo rentals, and campsites; it's best to make these at least a month ahead. Information: Catalina Chamber of Commerce; Box 217; Avalon, CA 90704; 310-510-1520.

ANAHEIM

With a population of about 285,000, Anaheim is Orange County's second largest city. It is an amalgam of apartment complexes, mobile-home parks, graceful adobe residences, and housing tracts. The general landscape is softened and shaded by royal palms, jacaranda, and bougainvillea. And the dry weather claims of the local chamber of commerce notwithstanding, Anaheim is washed clean every once in a while by rain. Then the clarity of vista and line makes even smog-jaded residents take a new look at their surroundings.

Anaheim really doesn't look much different from the cities that surround it. What sets Anaheim apart is Disneyland, whose creation totally changed the concept of amusement theme parks all over the world. It is the number one tourist attraction in California.

According to local legend, everyone thought Walt Disney was more than a little crazy when he broached the idea of putting his pioneer amusement attraction in Anaheim. After all, who'd go all the way out *there* just to shake hands with a mouse?

It turns out that lots of people would—and did. Disney chose Anaheim as the site for Disneyland on the advice of the Stanford Research Institute. Since the park's opening in 1955, Anaheim has become just what the Stanford people predicted it would—a well-developed city that's a pleasant place to visit.

(Unless otherwise noted, all phone numbers are in the 714 area code.)

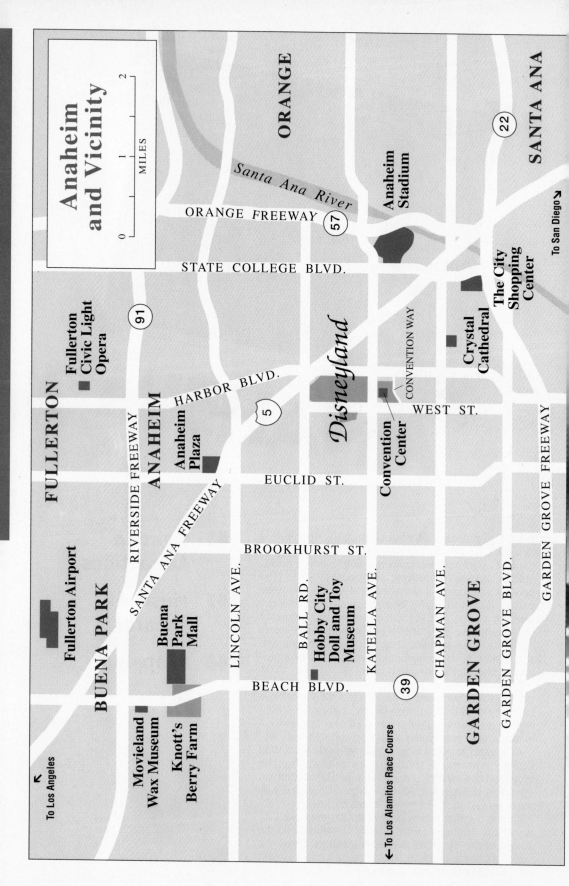

Anaheim
and Vicinity

0   1   2
MILES

FULLERTON

Fullerton Airport

BUENA PARK

To Los Angeles

Movieland
Wax Museum

Knott's
Berry Farm

Buena
Park
Mall

■ Fullerton
Civic Light
Opera

RIVERSIDE FREEWAY

91

ANAHEIM

HARBOR BLVD.

■ Anaheim
Plaza

5

SANTA ANA FREEWAY

STATE COLLEGE BLVD.

ORANGE FREEWAY

57

Santa Ana River

ORANGE

Anaheim
Stadium

Disneyland

CONVENTION WAY

Convention
Center

WEST ST.

Crystal
Cathedral

The City
Shopping
Center

SANTA ANA

22

To San Diego →

EUCLID ST.

BROOKHURST ST.

LINCOLN AVE.

BALL RD.

Hobby City
Doll and Toy
Museum

BEACH BLVD.

KATELLA AVE.

39

To Los Alamitos Race Course

CHAPMAN AVE.

GARDEN GROVE

GARDEN GROVE BLVD.

GARDEN GROVE FREEWAY

Sights & Attractions

ANAHEIM MUSEUM: Exhibits depict the history of Anaheim from its beginnings as a rural society to the opening of Disneyland in 1955 to its present-day role as an important Southern California city. There also is a hands-on children's gallery. Open Wednesdays through Fridays from 10 A.M. to 4 P.M., Saturdays from noon to 4 P.M. No admission is charged, but a donation of $1.50 per adult is requested. The museum is about a mile from Disneyland. 241 South Anaheim Blvd.; Anaheim; 778-3301.

ANAHEIM PIONEER MOTHER COLONY HOUSE: This redwood-frame house, the first residence built in Anaheim, dates from 1857, when George Hansen and 50 German colonists established the town. Artifacts that survive from the families that called it home until the 1920s are on display. The house is open by appointment only. About three miles from Disneyland. 414 North West St., Anaheim; 254-1850.

ANAHEIM STADIUM TOURS: Guided tours of Anaheim Stadium (home of the California Angels and formerly the Los Angeles Rams) take visitors behind the scenes. You can stand at home plate and imagine you're an all-star, and even visit the locker rooms. The tour also takes in the press areas, where radio, TV, and news reporters watch the games. Tours are conducted daily on the hour on weekdays from 11 A.M. to 2 P.M., except during games and other scheduled events. Before heading to the ballpark, call 254-3120 to make sure that there are no scheduled events at the time you plan to tour.

Rates are $3 for adults, $2 for seniors, $2 for children under 17; children under 5 are admitted free. Parking for tour guests is free. Anaheim Stadium is located at the corner of Katella Avenue and State College Boulevard, two miles east of Disneyland.

BOWERS MUSEUM OF CULTURAL ART: Dedicated to the preservation, study, and exhibition of the fine arts of indigenous peoples, this museum is particularly well known for its collections of pre-Columbian, Native American, Oceanic, and African artifacts, as well as early California artifacts. The *Topaz Café* overlooks the museum's courtyard. Hours are 10 A.M. to 4 P.M. Tuesdays through Sundays, until 9 P.M. Thursdays. Admission is $4.50 for adults; $3 for seniors over 62 and students; and $1.50 for children 5 to 12; children under 5 are free. About five miles from Disneyland. 2002 North Main St.; Santa Ana; 567-3600.

CHILDREN'S MUSEUM: Housed in what was the 1923 Union Pacific railroad depot, this is the only children's museum in Orange County. Among the attractions are a model train village, a science area, a Lego city, nature walks, a bee observatory, hands-on exhibits, and special programs. Hours are 10 A.M. to 5 P.M. Mondays through Saturdays, 1 P.M. to 5 P.M. Sundays. Admission is $4; free for children under 2. 301 South Euclid St.; La Habra; 310-905-9793.

CRYSTAL CATHEDRAL: Just two miles southeast of Disneyland, in the city of Garden Grove, is what *Newsweek* magazine called "the most spectacular religious edifice in the world." More than 10,000 panes of glass cover a weblike steel skeleton, so that it seems a cross between a greenhouse and a glass obelisk. The glass lets the outdoors come in, and anyone entering the auditorium is surrounded by nature's beauty.

The Crystal Cathedral's pastor, Reverend Robert Schuller, is often seen on television. He began his ministry in a drive-in theater, and his church has been engineered in such a way that a section of it can be opened up for those who prefer to worship in their cars. Open from 9 A.M. to 4 P.M. Mondays through Saturdays and noon to 4 P.M. Sundays. Tours are generally available; group tours must be scheduled in advance. The Crystal Cathedral presents "The Glory of Easter" and "The Glory of Christmas" annually. See "Special Events" in the *Getting Ready to Go* chapter. 12141 Lewis St.; Garden Grove; 971-4000.

DISCOVERY MUSEUM: A variety of hands-on exhibits recreate life at the turn of the century in Orange County. Hours are 1 P.M. to 5 P.M. Wednesdays through Fridays, 11 A.M. to 3 P.M. Sundays. Admission is $2.50 for adults; $2 for seniors and students; $1.50 for children under 12. 3101 West Harvard; Santa Ana; 540-0404.

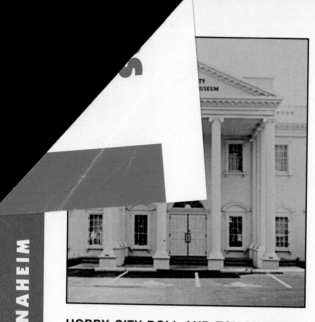

HOBBY CITY DOLL AND TOY MUSEUM:

Bea De Armond has been collecting dolls and toys for more than 60 years. Her collection is displayed here in a half-scale replica of the White House. There are teddy bears, some dating as far back as 1907, and a wooden model of the Kyoto Imperial Palace that was first seen at the Japan Expo, held in Tokyo in 1870 (two of the figures in it resemble the emperor and empress who were reigning at that time). There are 3,000 dolls and other toys in all, easily seen by people of all sizes since some of the display cases run along the walls at floor level. The Doll and Toy Museum is a part of Hobby City, a group of 24 hobby, crafts, and collector shops. Open from 10 A.M. to 6 P.M. daily. Admission is $1 for adults and 50¢ for senior citizens and children under 12. Located four miles from Disneyland. 1238 South Beach Blvd.; Anaheim; 527-2323. **(Note:** Doll lovers might also want to visit Doll City U.S.A., 6,000 square feet of dolls and doll supplies, just two long blocks from Disneyland. 2080 S. Harbor Blvd.; Anaheim; 750-3585.)

INTERNATIONAL SURFING MUSEUM:

Changing displays of surfing artwork and "antique" surfboards and paddleboards are on exhibit. Hours are Wednesdays through Sundays from noon to 5 P.M. Admission is $3 for adults; $1 for students and children 6 to 12; children under 5 free. 411 Olive St.; Huntington Beach; 960-3483.

KNOTT'S BERRY FARM: Not a farm at all, but a themed amusement park depicting much of the history and culture of California, it started out in 1920 as a berry patch (hence the name), where Walter Knott propagated a new fruit that had been started and then abandoned by Rudolph Boysen. Knott christened the succulent berries *boysenberries,* planted a 20-acre crop, and sold his harvest, along with pies and preserves, at a roadside stand.

During the Depression, Knott's wife, Cordelia, started a tearoom to help make ends meet. Her chicken dinners were soon so well regarded locally that visitors had to wait for a seat. Then Walter Knott decided to build a wander-through ghost town, both to honor his mother, who had come to California on a wagon train, and to keep waiting restaurant patrons from getting impatient. The park just grew from there, and today ranks as one of the most visited in the country, after Walt Disney World and Disneyland, which is a ten-minute drive away.

(Chicken dinners and boysenberry pies reminiscent of those that started it all are still available at *Mrs. Knott's Chicken Dinner* restaurant. There's always a line, so opt for an early lunch or dinner and beat the crowds.)

The 150-acre park, still owned and operated by the Knott family, now has 165 rides (including five roller coasters), shows, attractions, restaurants, and shops in six themed areas. Ghost Town (Knott's original park), a reproduction of an 1880s California Old West boom town, includes the Old Trails Hotel (built in 1868 and brought here from Arizona in 1940), a steam train dating from 1881, a stagecoach ride, and a log ride with a final, almost vertical drop guaranteed to inspire screams.

At Camp Snoopy, children can meet and have their pictures taken with the world's most beloved beagle and his friends from the comic strip *Peanuts*. Reminiscent of California's High Sierra terrain, the six-acre "camp" includes a petting zoo, pontoon bridges, a treehouse, the Red Baron biplane ride, and the Thomas Edison Inventor's Workshop featuring hands-on science exhibits.

In Fiesta Village, a recreation of colonial Spanish America, you'll find the park's newest roller coaster, the mammoth Jaguar!, in which the brave-hearted streak across a 2,700-foot route that incorporates a Mayan

pyramid and two 60-foot drops. Fiesta Village is also home to Montezooma's Revenge, a roller coaster that rockets through 600 feet of track, a 76-foot loop, and two spires, backward and forward. The more faint of heart will be happy to hear that Fiesta Village also has a merry-go-round, a throwback to a much slower era.

In Roaring '20s, a replica of a seaside amusement park from the 1920s, there's an entertaining dolphin and sea lion show at the Pacific Pavilion. A time machine transports visitors to the Kingdom of Dinosaurs, providing a face-to-face encounter with 21 fully animated figures, including a 32-foot-long Apatosaurus and a menacing Tyrannosaurus Rex. A roller coaster called Boomerang turns thrill-seekers upside down six times in less than a minute, while Sky Jump, a parachute ride, provides a bird's-eye view of Buena Park before dropping 20 stories in a simulated free-fall.

Wild Water Wilderness, a turn-of-the-century river wilderness park with trees and plants native to California, features Bigfoot Rapids, a wet, wild ride down a "raging" white-water river (with a glimpse of Bigfoot thrown in). Thunder Falls, beautifully landscaped with trees native to the Pacific Northwest Coast, has four waterfalls complete with fog and a light show. Its featured attraction, Mystery Lodge, is a special-effects journey deep into the Native North American West.

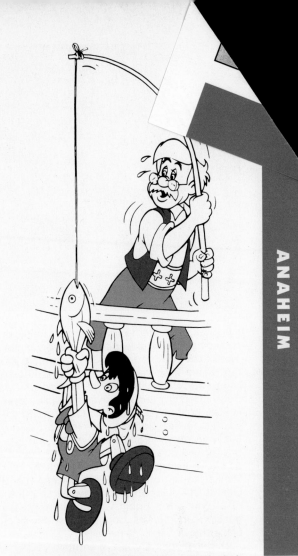

The Indian Trails area honors and celebrates the arts, crafts, cultures, and traditions of Native Americans. Here you'll find an authentic Big House and tepees of the Blackfoot, Nez Perce, Cheyenne, Crow, and Kiowa tribes.

Across Beach Boulevard from the park's main gates, you'll discover Independence Hall West, Knott's exact-size replica of Philadelphia's Independence Hall (look for the entrance through a tunnel from the main parking area near the shops). More than 140,000 hand-finished clay bricks duplicate the original; chandeliers, furniture, and the shape and size of the rooms were precisely reproduced by craftsmen; and there is an exact replica of the Liberty Bell, crack and all.

For more information about the park, including operating hours, call the 24-hour recorded "Knott's Line" at 220-5200. Dining spots and shops in the California Market Place, outside the paid admission section of the park, are open daily except Christmas Day. Admission is $28.50 for adults and $18.50 for children 3 to 11 and for seniors 60 and older and persons with disabilities; free for children under 3. After 6 P.M. in summer, admission is $13.95. Prices include unlimited use of the park's rides and attractions, except for Pan for Gold and the arcade games. Parking costs $5 and is on tree-shaded lots adjacent to several gates and across Beach Boulevard and La Palma and Western avenues.

If you don't have your own wheels, Pacific Coast Sightseeing (978-8855) offers tours to Knott's from most Disneyland-area hotels for about $30 for adults and $19 for children ages 3 to 11. Prices include park admission. 8039 Beach Blvd.; Buena Park; 220-5200.

MOVIELAND WAX MUSEUM AND RIPLEY'S BELIEVE IT OR NOT: The wax museum describes itself as the "greatest gathering of stars," and even if you're not a fancier of sculptures in wax, you'll probably enjoy the

RICHARD NIXON LIBRARY AND BIRTH-PLACE: The extensive library chronicles the life and achievements of the late Richard Nixon, 37th president of the United States. Spanning the years from his boyhood to his work as a political writer until his death, the library features an entire room dedicated to the Watergate scandal, where one can listen to excerpts from the famed White House tapes. The 52,000-square-foot main gallery and archives include a number of film presentations and gifts from world leaders. Hours are 10 A.M. to 5 P.M. Mondays through Saturdays; 11 A.M. to 5 P.M. Sundays. Admission is $5.95 for adults and children over 12; $3.95 for seniors over 61; $2 for children 8 to 11; free for children under 7. 18001 Yorba Linda Blvd.; Yorba Linda; 993-3393.

SHERMAN LIBRARY AND GARDENS: Off the Pacific Coast Highway, in the southeastern Newport Beach area of Corona del Mar, this is a small corner of paradise. The botanical collections surrounding the library building range from desert plant life to exotic tropical vegetation. The gardens are a veritable museum of plants and flowers, displayed amid a setting of fountains and sculptures, brick walkways and manicured grass. They

glimpses of western-movie heroes, musical-comedy greats, and leading men and women. More than 250 movie and TV performers are portrayed in scenes from their best-known roles: Judy Garland in *The Wizard of Oz*, Robert Redford and Paul Newman (blue eyes looking right at you) in *Butch Cassidy and the Sundance Kid*, John Wayne in *Rio Hondo*, Marilyn Monroe in *Some Like It Hot*, and Barbra Streisand as Dolly. Performers recently added to the cast of characters include Tom Hanks (as film character Forrest Gump) and Geena Davis, and a clever two-way mirror display in which Robin Williams is magically transformed into Mrs. Doubtfire from the popular movie of the same name.

The costumes and props in many displays are original, donated by the studios or the stars themselves. And some of the "wax" figures occasionally turn out to be real: Be sure to take a very close look at the Keystone Cop!

At Ripley's there are 10,000 square feet of oddities including the tale of the tallest man in history. Combination tickets are available. The Wax Museum is open daily from 9 A.M. to 7 P.M.; Ripley's is open daily from 10 A.M. to 6 P.M. Admission is $12.95 for adults; $10.55 for seniors; $6.95 for children 4 to 11; under 4 free. Seven miles from Disneyland. 7711 Beach Blvd.; Buena Park; 522-1154.

NEWPORT HARBOR ART MUSEUM: Orange County's premier art museum has expanded its permanent collection in recent years. Post-World War II California art is strongly represented, but major works by New York and European artists also are featured. The museum also houses a bookstore. The museum's hours are 10 A.M. to 5 P.M. Tuesdays through Saturdays and noon to 4 P.M. on Sundays. Admission is $4 for adults; $2 for students and senior citizens; free to museum members and children under 12; free to everyone on Tuesdays. 850 San Clemente Dr.; Newport Beach; 759-1122.

are open daily from 10:30 A.M. to 4 P.M. Admission is $2; free Mondays. The library also should not be missed. It is a major research center devoted to the history of the Pacific Southwest (particularly the amazing changes that the area has undergone over the past 100 years). Its collection includes maps and photographs, more than 2,000 reels of microfilm, about 15,000 books and pamphlets, and about 200,000 papers and documents. While primarily designed for use by students and researchers, the library is open to visitors. Its hours are 10:30 A.M. to 4 P.M. Mondays through Fridays only. The Sherman Library and Gardens are about a 35-minute drive southeast of Disneyland. 2647 East Pacific Coast Highway; Corona del Mar; 673-2261.

Music & Theater

ANAHEIM CONVENTION CENTER: Most concerts here are booked by conventions, but there are some that are open to the public. Check the marquee on Katella Avenue or the concert listings in the local papers. 800 West Katella Ave.; Anaheim; 999-8900 for ticket information.

DINNER THEATERS: The *Elizabeth Howard's Curtain Call Dinner Theatre* offers a sit-down dinner (with a choice of three entrées), followed by a performance—usually a Broadway musical. Shows are presented Tuesdays through Sundays, with both a matinee and an evening performance on Sundays. Prices range from $21.95 on Tuesday nights to $32.95 on Saturday evenings. Drinks and dessert are not included. 690 El Camino Real; Tustin; 838-1540.

Medieval Times, though not a traditional dinner theater, offers a hearty four-course meal and a show that kids, in particular, enjoy, with knights, Andalusian stallions, and swordplay. The admission price of $32.95 for most shows ($22.95 for children under 13) includes appetizers, soup, a chicken or spare ribs main course, beverages, and dessert. Call ahead for show times and special discount programs. 7662 Beach Blvd.; Buena Park; 521-4740.

At *Wild Bill's Wild West Dinner Extravaganza,* you'll enter the lively frontier of the late 1800s, where "Buffalo" Bill Cody leads the cast and assembled guests in plenty of singing, dancing, and audience participation. The filling four-course meal of soup, salad, fried chicken, barbecued ribs, corn on the cob, baked potatos, and apple pie is included in the admission price of $29.50 for Saturday and Sunday matinees, $32.50 for evening shows Sundays through Fridays, and $34.50 for evening peformances Saturdays. Admission for children 3 to 11 is $21.50 for all shows. It's near Knott's Berry Farm. 7600 Beach Blvd., Buena Park; 522-6114 or 800-883-1546.

FULLERTON CIVIC LIGHT OPERA CO.: Specializes in musical comedy and operetta. The season runs from October to early June. The theater is about seven miles from Disneyland. Plummer Auditorium, Lemon Street and Chapman Avenue; Fullerton; 879-1732 for ticket information.

IRVINE MEADOWS AMPHITHEATRE: Open from March through October; normally presents concerts that range from symphonies to heavy metal. There's reserved seating for 10,500 people and seating on the lawn for 4,500. 8800 Irvine Center Drive; Irvine; 855-6111 for recorded information; 855-2863 for the box office.

ORANGE COUNTY PERFORMING ARTS CENTER: This 3,000-seat multipurpose theater hosts regional, national, and international symphony orchestras; opera; dance; and musical theater in an acoustically advanced performance facility. The center is located about ten miles south of Disneyland, across from the South Coast Plaza. 600 Town Center Drive; Costa Mesa; 556-2787 for ticket information.

SOUTH COAST REPERTORY: Two stages—the main stage features large-scale productions of classics. The second, smaller stage is more experimental, showcasing modern plays and new playwrights. The season normally runs from September through July. The theater is across from South Coast Plaza, about ten miles from Disneyland. 655 Town Center Drive; Costa Mesa; 957-4033 for ticket information.

Shopping

Malls may not have been invented in Southern California, but its largely suburban population has refined the phenomenon to a new level. Expect to find three- and four-store malls on just about every street corner. Still others, built on a far grander scale, are just a short drive away.

The equivalent of Middle Eastern bazaars, they provide an all-in-one shopping experience, incorporating stores of every sort and style, along with movie theaters, hair salons, auto-repair centers, fancy restaurants, and sidewalk cafés serving espresso and dessert, along with a vantage point from which to view fellow shoppers.

The shopping malls listed below are within easy driving distance of Disneyland and are generally open from 10 A.M. to 9 P.M. weekdays, from 10 A.M. to 6 P.M. Saturdays, and from noon to 5 P.M. Sundays.

MAIN PLACE MALL: Home to a Disney Store, with its character-conscious toys, videos, books, gift items, collectibles, and clothing for adults and children, the Main Place Mall now houses the first Walt Disney Gallery, which opened adjacent to the Disney Store in 1994. The gallery features four themed areas—animation, contemporary Disney art, vintage Disney, and a gallery shop—as well as an "Inside Disney" exhibit that changes quarterly, the Fantasy Video Timeline, the Interactive Disney Storybook, and the Animation Kaleidoscope. Also at the mall,

you'll find Bullock's, Nordstrom, and Robinson's-May, along with about 190 shops and restaurants, and a cinema complex. A shuttle runs frequently between it and the Anaheim hotels. The mall is at 2800 North Main Street in Santa Ana, near the intersection of the Santa Ana and Garden Grove freeways, about four miles from Disneyland; 547-7000.

NEWPORT CENTER FASHION ISLAND: This parklike mall offers about 150 stores, restaurants, and services amidst a Mediterranean-themed setting of potted flowers and towering palms, plazas with umbrella-covered tables, fountains, and fish ponds. Department stores include The Broadway, Neiman Marcus, and Robinson's-May. The enclosed Atrium Court houses many small shops, plus the Farmers Market. The mall also has an Edwards six-cinema complex. It's located in Newport Beach on Newport Center Drive, about a half-hour drive south of Disneyland; 721-2000.

SOUTH COAST PLAZA: Huge and airy and festive, it houses about 350 shops and restaurants. You'll find Bullock's and Robinson's-May, along with such well-known names as Chanel, Barney's New York, Nordstrom, Mark Cross, Saks Fifth Avenue, and Williams-Sonoma. (Just across Bear Street, another retail complex, the Crystal Court, offers an additional 60 specialty shops; the Orange County Performing Arts Center and South Coast Repertory are nearby, on Town Center Drive.) South Coast Plaza is at the intersection of the San Diego Freeway and Bristol Street in Costa Mesa, about ten miles from Disneyland. Shuttles transport shoppers from Anaheim hotels to the plaza during shopping hours; 435-2000.

WESTMINSTER MALL: This is one of the bigger, better shopping centers in Orange County, with a Robinson's-May department store and—on its upper, lower, and mezzanine levels—enough shops and restaurants to keep you busy and nourished for an entire day. If you get tired of shopping, you can always see a movie. There are two Edwards theater complexes here, one in the parking lot area, one in the mall itself. Westminster Mall is about nine miles southwest of Disneyland off the 405 freeway at Golden West and Bolsa. Be sure to take special note of where you enter, so you can exit through the same door and find your car easily; 898-2559.

IN ALL DIRECTIONS

All right, so now you've been to Disneyland. Is there anything else to do in Southern California? You bet!

It's the sheer variety of things to see—both natural and manmade—that makes Southern California such a great vacation destination. To the east lie windswept deserts. And that doesn't mean just cactus and bleached wastelands: Rich carpets of wildflowers in spring and lush oases of palms are among the many surprises awaiting inland.

Across the map to the north you'll find mountains—the towering Sierra Nevadas. Between the Sierras and the sea lies the San Joaquin Valley, a rich and highly developed agricultural region.

California's Spanish missions deserve more than a passing glance for their beauty and historical significance. And what about the mighty Pacific? That road that hugs the coast to Big Sur (two-thirds of the way to San Francisco) is Highway 1, and it runs along some of the wildest and most beautiful coastline on earth.

But don't forget that just Southern California itself is *big*, and a day trip can mean a very long day indeed. It's best experienced when you explore just one region at a time—Los Angeles, the desert, or the mission trail, for instance. So gather up your road maps, your sunscreen, and your family and friends—Southern California is waiting!

Los Angeles Area

The American dream was invented in Los Angeles—glamour, fame, palm trees, endless sunshine, and incredibly good-looking people lounging around their swimming pools. The myth may conflict with reality just a bit, which tends to include a certain amount of yellowish smog, 500 miles of freeways in Los Angeles County, and 4,000 square miles—imagine!—of urban sprawl.

Yet despite natural and other disasters—everything from earthquakes to brush fires to flash floods to highly publicized court cases—the city and its inhabitants always have demonstrated a remarkable resiliency. Take the 1994 earthquake, when damaged freeways and buildings were speedily repaired.

It's well known that Angelenos (the locals' preferred moniker for themselves) live in their cars, and with good reason. From the rugged ridges of the Santa Monica Mountains to the vast San Fernando Valley and downtown, the city is enormous.

To get a radically different perspective, take a walking tour through downtown L.A. or Old Hollywood. You might discover a few surprises along the way.

DOWNTOWN LOS ANGELES: If you ever wondered what the place looked like before shopping centers were invented, work your way into the heart of the downtown area—and abandon your wheels.

El Pueblo: Here's where the great city began, as the tiny Spanish village of El Pueblo

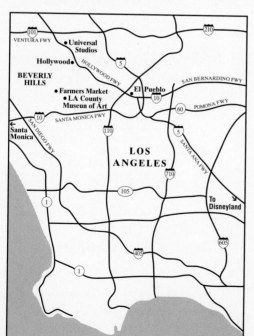

de Los Angeles. Built around a wide central plaza, El Pueblo offers an open-air bandstand, the restored fire station of Engine Company No. 1, the tiny Plaza Church, established in 1822, and Olvera Street, a pedestrian walkway paved in cool brick and filled with colorful Mexican shops and restaurants. Sample the spicy tacos, burritos, and enchiladas at food stalls along your way. The oldest house in Los Angeles is here—the 1818 Avila House, made of adobe. Free walking tours are offered hourly from 10 A.M. to 1 P.M. Tuesdays through Saturdays. El Pueblo de Los Angeles State Historic Park; 845 North Alameda St.; Los Angeles, CA 90012; 213-628-1274. To get to El Pueblo and Olvera Street, take the Santa Ana Freeway (Rte. 5) north to the Hollywood Freeway (Rte. 101), then exit at Alameda Street and head north two blocks. During noncommuter hours, it's a 45-minute drive from Anaheim.

Farmers Market: 150 stalls of American, Mexican, Italian, Chinese, and vegetarian foods, and any number of exquisite bakeries and candy shops. If you don't like to eat standing up, there are tables set up in several locations throughout this indoor market. Open in summer from 9 A.M. to 7 P.M. Mondays through Saturdays and in winter 9 A.M. to 6:30 P.M.; 10 A.M. to 6 P.M. Sundays in summer (to 5 P.M. in winter). Free parking. 6333 West Third St. and Fairfax Ave.; 213-933-9211.

Los Angeles County Museum of Art: The Robert O. Anderson Building houses the museum's distinguished collection of 20th-century art, and there's the Pavilion for Japanese Art. Special exhibits come and go in the Armand Hammer Building while a dazzling permanent collection stays put: See pre-Columbian and African art, tapestries, and paintings from the 18th century to the present. Closed Mondays. Admission charge. 5905 Wilshire Blvd.; 213-857-6111.

HOLLYWOOD—OLD AND NEW: A walk through Old Hollywood will delight lovers of the great era of Hollywood movies, though the area is no longer the physical center of film production and its glamour is, sadly, long gone. While the streets are crowded, bustling, and safe by day, it's not wise to walk down Hollywood Boulevard after dark.

Mann's Chinese Theatre: Better known to movie fans around the world as the old Grauman's Chinese Theatre, this is probably the most visited site in Old Hollywood. But if you wander down Hollywood Boulevard toward Highland Avenue looking for the Grauman's sign, you'll never find it. When Ted Mann took the theater over in 1973 he replaced the famous old sign with his own and it caused considerable local controversy. The Chinese Theatre's forecourt is world-renowned for its celebrity footprints and handprints immortalized in cement. If you buy a ticket to get into the original theater (rather than one of Mann's adjacent new twin cinemas), you'll see one of the world's most impressive and elaborate movie palaces. The ornate carvings, high decorative ceiling, plush seats, and the enormous screen itself are all part of a Hollywood that no longer exists. 6925 Hollywood Blvd.; 213-464-8111.

El Capitan Theatre: This Hollywood Boulevard landmark (formerly the Paramount) has been completely restored to its original elegance. Built in 1926 as a legitimate stage house, it was remodeled in 1942 and became the Paramount movie theater. Thanks to a joint effort by Pacific Theatres and Buena Vista Pictures Distribution, moviegoers can enjoy first-run motion pictures in an elegant atmosphere with a state-of-the-art projection and sound system. 6838 Hollywood Blvd; 213-467-7674.

STUDIO TOURS: No trip to Hollywood and environs would be complete without a tour of a film or television studio. Each of the ones listed below offers an entertaining look.

Universal Studios Hollywood: Some of the lingering evidence that the local movie business is still alive and functioning. Tours are conducted on SuperTrams by tour guides, with about 175 people per tour. Highlights include a look at some of the production facilities and 34 soundstages, especially the World of Cine-magic, where some of Alfred Hitchcock's best-kept secrets are revealed. You'll also see the parting of the Red Sea, a burning house, a collapsing bridge, an attack on the tour tram by a 30-foot-tall King Kong, and the Doomed Glacier Expedition, in which you plunge down an Alpine avalanche. A popular attraction allows visitors to "experience" an earthquake measuring 8.3 on the Richter scale. This moving experience—ominously called The Big One—may not be suitable for younger children. Other attractions include Lucy: A Tribute; E.T.'s Adventure; and the Back to the Future flight-simulator ride, which takes you on a thrilling trip from the ice age to the future in a souped-up DeLorean. After the

tour, you can visit an area of shops and special shows, including The Flintstone Show, a Broadway-style extravaganza; Waterworld—a Live Sea War Spectacular, featuring a barrage of stunts and special effects; and Backdraft, a realistic firestorm where visitors truly feel the heat. Admission charge; children under 3 get in free. Off the Hollywood Freeway (Rte. 101) at Lankershim Boulevard. 100 Universal City Plaza, Universal City; 818-508-9600.

Paramount Pictures Studio Tour: The only major studio that is still located in Hollywood proper, Paramount offers a two-hour guided tour where you learn about its rich history and get a behind-the-scenes look at daily operations. 860 N. Gower St., Hollywood; 213-956-1777.

NBC Television Studio Tour: NBC is the only television network to open its doors to the public. Among other things, you'll see the "Tonight Show" set and the studio's production facility. You can also get tickets to the taping of one of your favorite shows. (Exit Buena Vista Street off Freeway 134.) 3000 W. Alameda Blvd., Burbank; 818-840-3537.

Warner Bros. VIP Studio Tours: Limited to approximately 12 participants per group, this personalized tour takes you throughout the Warner lot, where you'll see the actual shooting of film and television projects. Note: Unlike some of the other studio tours mentioned here, this one is not open to children under ten. 4000 Warner Blvd., Burbank; 818-954-1744.

OTHER TOURS: If you want to see more of the city, including the posh homes of movie stars in mansion-studded Beverly Hills, contact VIP Tours; 310-641-8114.

DISNEY'S BEAUTY AND THE BEAST, THE MUSICAL: The Tony Award–winning musical fills the stage of the Shubert Theatre with the timeless story and the memorable music from the film, along with six new songs. Evening performances Tuesdays through Sundays, plus weekend matinees. Shubert Theatre; 2020 Avenue of the Stars, Century City; 800-447-7400.

L.A. SHOPPING: From Melrose Avenue to Rodeo Drive, Los Angeles boasts a collection of perhaps the most eclectic shopping locales of any city in the country. A trip to one can be an adventure unto itself.

Melrose Avenue: Although this popular thoroughfare, made even more famous by the Fox show "Melrose Place," stretches from downtown L.A. to West Hollywood, it is best known for its one mile of colorful shops and cafés between Fairfax and LaBrea avenues, where you'll find everything from designer clothes to movie memorabilia.

Rodeo Drive: Pronounced "ro-DAY-oh" and located in the heart of the Beverly Hills business district, this exclusive street contains some of the most expensive shopping in the world, most of it in just three blocks between Little Santa Monica and Wilshire. Fred Hayman, Ferragamo, and Chanel provide a few of the temptations.

Beverly Center: This mammoth indoor mall, which lies in the center of Los Angeles, is a tourist attraction in its own right. Home to the *Hard Rock Café*, 14 movie theaters, and over 200 shops and restaurants, it's a wonderful place to shop, see a movie, or do some star gazing. 8500 Beverly Blvd., Los Angeles; 310-854-0070.

Century City Mall: If you prefer to get a suntan while doing your shopping, then this elevated outdoor mall is the place for you. Located in fashionable Century City (not really a city, but a part of Los Angeles that was formerly half of Twentieth Century Fox's back lot), this festive 140-store shopping center sits among several mini-skyscrapers and is perhaps L.A.'s best locale for spotting movie stars. (Yes, they do shop like the rest of us.) Featured shops include Bullocks, The Broadway, and The Disney Store. The Century City Mall also has some of the best movie theaters in town. There are 14 of them, many of which are surprisingly large for a mall. Additionally, the shopping center also has some fun restaurants for the whole family, including *Dive*, a trendy, nautically themed eatery that specializes in gourmet submarine sandwiches; the *Stage Deli*, which offers gargantuan sandwiches; and *Houston's*, where you'll find a wide array of dishes ranging from hamburgers to roast chicken. 10250 Santa Monica Blvd., Century City (note that this is really Little Santa Monica Blvd., which runs parallel to and just south of its sister street); 310-277-3898.

SANTA MONICA: Just west of Los Angeles and overlooking the Pacific Ocean, Santa Monica is world famous for its beautiful beach, eclectic shops, colorful coffee houses, outstanding gourmet dining, and fun nightlife. From inline skaters and joggers at the beach to sidewalk cafés on Main Street and Montana Avenue, there's always a lot of activity in this corner of Southern California. Although Santa Monica is a beautiful place to visit, you can expect to see a fair amount of homeless people around town, some of whom are panhandlers. Although most are harmless, it isn't advisable to give them money. If you do decide to make a donation to those in need, you can deposit coins in one of the dolphin statues that are around town. This money helps to support the city's homeless shelters.

Third Street Promenade: With a plethora of shops, restaurants, movie theaters, and superb nightlife, this three-block-long outdoor mall in Santa Monica has it all, and is even adjacent to a more conventional indoor mall. On any given day, there is always a hustle and bustle on the Promenade, including a variety of street performers. Shops range from avant-garde men's and women's clothing stores to new and used bookstores. The restaurants are also plentiful and run the gamut, from *Johnny Rocket's*, a 1950s-style diner with great burgers and shakes, to *Trilussa*, which offers fine Italian dining. Pubs and nightclubs also abound and include *King George's* and *Gotham Hall*, a funky, upscale pool hall with purple—yes, purple—pool tables.

Montana Avenue: The Rodeo Drive of Santa Monica, Montana Avenue is not quite as pricey as its Beverly Hills counterpart and boasts an abundance of wonderful shops and eateries. Art and antique furniture stores abound, as do a multitude of clothing and jewelry shops. Dining spots range from health-food eateries to trendy cafés. All in all, a wonderful place to shop, people watch, or just browse as you enjoy Santa Monica's delightful ocean breeze.

Main Street: The stretch of this main artery south of Pico Boulevard is just a stone's throw from the world-famous Venice Beach, and it features a wide variety of fashion boutiques, antiques shops, art galleries, and fine restaurants.

Museum of Flying: Located right next door to Santa Monica Airport, this attraction features over 40 aircraft, particularly World War II vintage planes, some maintained in flight-ready condition. You'll also see special exhibits and some classic aviation films. For the kids, there's an interactive mini-museum area. At Santa Monica Airport, 2772 Donald Douglas Loop North; 310-392-8822.

NOTE: There are many other compelling sites and attractions in Greater Los Angeles. In fact, you could probably spend a full year vacationing here and still not see them all. For a more complete sampling, as well as maps, write the Los Angeles Convention and Visitors Bureau; 633 West 5th St.; Los Angeles, CA 90017; 213-624-7300. For additional information about Southern California, call 800-TO-CALIF.

Taking I-5 north and Rtes. 101 and 10 west from Anaheim (depending on where you're headed), you can reach all of the sites and attractions described above. Figure on roughly a 100- to 150-mile round-trip.

San Diego Area

San Diego lies about 100 miles south of Anaheim, a 90-minute drive away on I-5 or (if I-5 is congested) on I-15. The city is known for its delightful weather, its sporting life (you can do everything here from inline skating or surfing to hot-air ballooning or sportfishing), and a multitude of activities as varied as museum hopping, theater going, whale watching, and power shopping.

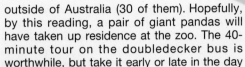

Check out some of the popular attractions described below, and afterward you'll probably be tempted to stay in the area a few extra days. If so, take a look at the lodging suggestions in the *Transportation & Accommodations* chapter. For more information about the San Diego area, contact the San Diego Convention & Visitors Bureau, 401 B St., Suite 1400, Dept. 700, San Diego, CA 92101-4237; 619-236-1212.

BALBOA PARK: Just north of the downtown area, this 1,200-acre park features extraordinary museums that appeal to such diverse interests as fine arts, photography, sports, science and astronomy, trains, automobiles, Russian icons, and Japanese gardens—and that's just for starters. At this writing, the Mingei International Museum of World Folk Art was scheduled to relocate here from La Jolla in late 1996. The park hosts a free concert on the world's largest outdoor organ at 2 P.M. on Sundays, and it is home to the nationally acclaimed Old Globe Theatre. Follow signs from I-5. It's between Sixth Avenue and Laurent St., and Park Blvd. and Presidents Way, San Diego; 619-239-0512.

LA JOLLA: One of the most picturesque communities in Southern California, La Jolla is home to the La Jolla Playhouse, the Mingei International Museum of Folk Art (which moves to Balboa Park in late 1996), the newly renovated Museum of Contemporary Art (scheduled to reopen early in 1996), and the Stephen Birch Aquarium-Museum, with a giant kelp forest, a demonstration tide pool that kids love, interactive exhibits, and a 12-minute simulated submarine ride. Scripps Institution of Oceanography, La Jolla; 619-534-FISH.

SAN DIEGO ZOO: The 100-acre San Diego Zoo is home to 4,000 birds and beasts, and it claims the largest breeding colony of koalas outside of Australia (30 of them). Hopefully, by this reading, a pair of giant pandas will have taken up residence at the zoo. The 40-minute tour on the doubledecker bus is worthwhile, but take it early or late in the day when the animals are more likely to be bustling about. There also are free animal shows and aerial tram rides. Follow I-5 to Park Blvd. Park Blvd. and Zoo Place, Balboa Park, San Diego; 619-234-3153.

SEA WORLD: They glide through the air with the greatest of ease—four-ton killer whales, that is—astounding and splashing their fans in 5,000-seat Shamu Stadium. Bottlenose dolphins, sharks, penguins, sea lions, and otters steal a few shows, and hearts, themselves. Exit I-5 onto Sea World Drive and turn right. 1720 S. Shores Rd., Mission Bay; 619-226-3901; from Los Angeles, 939-6212.

WILD ANIMAL PARK: Hop aboard the monorail here, and let the five-mile, 50-minute ride transport you to the remote landscapes of Africa and Asia, where 3,000 wild animals roam free over more than 2,000 acres. A 1¾-mile hiking trail brings you closer—but not too close—to elephants, tigers, and cheetahs. Wild Animal Park is 30 miles north of San Diego; follow I-5 to Hwy. 78 East to I-15; then take Via Rancho Parkway and follow the signs. 15500 San Pasqual Valley Rd., Escondido; 619-747-8702.

Historic Missions

Scattered along the old Camino Real (sometimes called Highway 101) are 21 historic Spanish missions, 9 of which were founded by Father Junipero Serra beginning in 1769. These structures originally could be seen for miles from the sea and from inland valleys. They employed thousands of native Americans—so-called "heathens"—in agriculture and livestock raising. When California became a part of the United States in 1850, the influence of the Spanish missions waned and several of the abandoned structures have quietly crumbled. Others have had their Mexican/Moorish architecture and lush gardens meticulously restored. Many of these are open to visitors. The missions are spaced about 40 miles apart, so a good strategy is to concentrate on those in a narrow region, keeping away from the ones in major urban centers.

San Juan Capistrano: Today, the mission is no more than a collection of crumbling structures with a wistful air of decayed grandeur. Its church, once the most remarkable of the entire mission chain, was shattered by a powerful earthquake in 1812, though the four bells of the tower and a small sanctuary called Father Serra's Church were miraculously spared. The other miracle is the swallows, which return to Capistrano every year on March 19 (Saint Joseph's Day) with clockwork regularity. Many Christians take

this as a sign of the holiness of the church, while ornithologists explain it as no more than a predictable natural phenomenon.

On the premises are a 300-year-old gilt altar, gardens, ancient pepper trees, the remains of tallow vats and an iron smelter where mission Indians did the Lord's—or somebody's—work, an Indian cemetery, a *calabozo* (jail), the quarters of the early padres, and Spanish soldiers' barracks. The mission tour is self-guided, or, for $5 per person, groups of 15 or more can get a docent-guided tour.

The church and grounds are open from 8:30 A.M. to 5 P.M. daily. Admission is $4 for adults; $3 for seniors; and $2 for children 3 to 11. Take I-5 south to the mission; about 80 miles round-trip. San Juan Capistrano Mission; 31815 Camino Capistrano, Suite C; San Juan Capistrano, CA 92675; 714-248-2048.

San Fernando Rey: Working your way north along the coast, you may want to skip San Gabriel Archangel, which is almost totally lost in the hornet's nest of suburbs around L.A. The next mission along the trail is San Fernando Rey—seven acres of grounds, featuring the Convento, the largest adobe building in California. The museum here is perhaps the best of all the mission museums. It displays hand-carved, 17th-century gold-leaf altars; a library of priceless volumes; and art treasures of Mexican, Spanish, and Indian origin. The famous Bells of San Fernando faithfully ring "Cantico del Alba," an ancient Indian melody, every hour from 10 A.M. to 6 P.M. Admission is $4, or $3 for senior citizens and children 7 to 15; under 7 free. The mission is open 9 A.M. to 4:15 P.M. daily; the gift shop stays open until 5 P.M. Take I-405 north; about 110 miles round-trip. San Fernando Rey; 15151 San Fernando Mission Blvd.; Mission Hills, CA 91345; 818-361-0186.

NEVADA

SAN FRANCISCO

Carmel

San Luis Obispo

Pacific Ocean

Santa Barbara

San Buenaventura
San Fernando Rey
LOS ANGELES
ANAHEIM
San Juan Capistrano

SAN DIEGO

San Buenaventura: Its church is beautifully preserved, though less striking than San Fernando. The surrounding beaches of coastal Oxnard are superb, and the inland Ojai valley is a favorite haunt of artists and writers. Admission is $1 per adult, 50¢ per child. The mission, which has a museum and a gift shop, is open 7 A.M. to 6 P.M. daily, while the museum and gift shop are open Mondays to Saturdays 10 A.M. to 5 P.M., Sundays until 4 P.M. Take I-405 north to Rte. 101; about 200 miles round-trip. San Buenaventura Mission; 211 East Main St.; Ventura, CA 93001; 805-643-4318.

Santa Barbara: The town of Santa Barbara prides itself on preserving its Spanish heritage—wide sidewalks lined with flowering trees, hybrid Mexican/Moorish architecture, and not a neon sign, billboard, or mailbox in sight. By contrast, the mission (completed in 1820) offers a Roman temple facade, gleaming white walls, and graceful towers; it still is used by the parish of Santa Barbara. The mission has a good museum and beautiful grounds. Lush expanses of lawn are adorned with flowering trees and shrubs and a lovely Moorish fountain. (For more of the same, the town's Botanical Gardens are about 1½ miles north.)

A $2 donation is requested; children under 16 free. Open 9 A.M. to 5 P.M. daily. Take I-405 to Rte. 101; about 210 miles round-trip. The Old Mission of Santa Barbara; 2201 Laguna St.; Santa Barbara, CA 93105; 805-682-4713 or 805-682-4151.

San Luis Obispo: The Los Padres Mountains of Central California harbor one of California's best-kept secrets—San Luis Obispo. This picturesque town, midway between Los Angeles and San Francisco, is close to some of the state's best beaches. Restaurants, shops, and boutiques encircle Mission Plaza, dominated by the Mission San Luis Obispo de Tolosa. The mission boasts a colorful chapel and a superb museum, as well as a garden of brick paths and benches along a sleepy winding creek.

Again, the nearby beaches are splendid—Avila offers deep-sea fishing and perhaps the best swimming in the area; Pismo is dotted with caves, cliff-sheltered tidal pools, and old pirate coves, as well as year-round clam digging; and Morro Bay is a winter and early-spring sanctuary for thousands of wild birds, including the peregrine falcon.

San Luis Obispo also is the home of San Simeon (see page 157) and the *Madonna Inn*, one of California's most famous and unusual hostelries. It is a gingerbread castle with winding outdoor staircases, a shingled roof, turrets, and 109 rooms, each decorated around some idiosyncratic theme—such as the Love Nest, Yosemite Falls, Victorian Gardens, and the Safari Room. *Madonna Inn*; 100 Madonna Rd.; San Luis Obispo, CA 93405; 805-543-3000.

The museum asks a donation of adults. Open year-round from 9 A.M. to 4 P.M. daily. Take Rte. 101 north; the ride is about 400

miles round-trip. Old Mission of San Luis Obispo; 782 Monterey St.; San Luis Obispo, CA 93401; 805-543-6850.

Carmel: The coastal town of Carmel lies about 15 miles west of Rte. 101 and El Camino Real, but getting there via Route 1 is half the fun. The coastal drive is one of the most famous scenic roads in America, with dramatic cliffs skirting vertiginous ocean vistas, shoals of wild birds, seals and sea lions sunning themselves on rocks, and migrating California gray and humpback whales. The forest village is serene and isolated and has long been a haven for artists and writers.

The Carmel mission was one of the largest and most important in the group founded by Father Serra (who is buried here). Today it is one of the best preserved, presenting a complete quadrangle of authentic mission architecture. The splendid exterior tower, adorned with

a star window, is Moorish in design. An elegant fountain, olive trees, and a hanging flower garden further enhance the site.

The mission requests a $2 donation per adult, $1 for children 6 and older. Open Mondays through Saturdays from 9:30 A.M. to 4:30 P.M., Sundays from 10:30 A.M. to 4:30 P.M. To get there, take Rte. 101 north to the junction with Rte. 1, which doubles back to Carmel; about 640 miles round-trip from Anaheim. Carmel Mission Basilica; 3080 Rio Rd.; Carmel, CA 93923; 408-624-3600.

The Coastal Pacific

NEVADA

SAN FRANCISCO

Big Sur

COASTAL PACIFIC HWY

Morro Bay

Lompoc

Ventura
Oxnard

LOS ANGELES

Malibu
Santa Monica

Seal Beach
● ANAHEIM

Sunset Beach

Huntington Beach

Newport Beach

Pacific Ocean

The Pacific Coast Highway (Rte. 1) winds along the California coast for over 400 miles from Los Angeles to San Francisco. For much of this distance, it clings to the water's edge, twisting and dipping through towering, spray-battered cliffs, silent groves of pine, and those legendary electric-blue glimpses of the wide Pacific. The coastline is truly one of the world's most dramatic, and the Pacific Coast Highway is the best way to see it. But drive carefully—"twisting and dipping" is not an exaggeration, particularly along the 115-mile stretch from Morro Bay up to Carmel, which convict chain gangs spent 20 years carving out of solid rock. If you have the time and strength, this is the stretch of road that's likely to be the most dramatically satisfying. Portions of Route 1 are prone to damage during the winter. For highway conditions call 800-427-7623.

Starting from Anaheim, your route begins well south of Los Angeles (generally in Newport Beach). Along the way, you'll pass fine swimming and surfing beaches, and any number of scenic—though rather densely developed—coastal towns.

The beaches: As you head up Rte. 1, you'll pass Huntington Beach, Sunset Beach, Seal Beach, and so forth. The beach towns blend into one another; the houses—generally weatherworn wood or condos built to look like weatherworn wood—are interspersed with surfing shops, fishing piers, fast-food stands, and broad stretches of classic sand.

Farther north: Drive up through Santa Monica, Malibu, Oxnard, and Ventura to charming, Spanish-flavored Santa Barbara (see "Historic Missions" in this chapter). By now it's almost certainly lunchtime, so pause for a picnic by the sea.

For the next 100 miles, the highway tends to drift away from the coastline. Unless you are urgently moved to see Lompoc, stay on Route 101 and cover the distance swiftly, picking up Route 1 again in San Luis Obispo and making your way another 10 or 12 miles to the coast.

Montana de Oro State Park: Just south of Morro Bay, this park has dunes and headlands that are perfect for short but scenic seaside hikes.

Morro Bay: At the harbor entrance to this seaport town is Morro Rock, a 576-foot volcanic dome discovered by Juan Rodriguez Cabrillo in 1542. A large commercial fishing fleet sails from here, and many boats are docked along the Embarcadero. Morro Bay State Park, a 2,500-acre tract with hiking trails, picnic areas, and campsites, also has an interesting natural history museum that primarily focuses on local marine biology.

San Simeon: About 25 miles north of Morro Bay, William Randolph Hearst's fabled castle contains decorative elements (and even whole sections) of castles shipped to this site from all over the world. Stunningly elegant, this treasure house is now a state historical monument set on 123 acres overlooking the ocean. There are four tours available, including an evening tour that runs during the spring and fall and during the Christmas holidays. For reservations call 800-444-4445. Tickets are available

on arrival but reservations are suggested. Open year-round.

Big Sur: The most dramatic piece of shoreline on the continent. About 65 miles to the north of San Simeon, Big Sur's rolling, grassy hills end abruptly in cliffs towering high above the sea. There are many places to stop and watch sea otters, seals, sea lions, and occasionally even whales spouting in the waves far below. You won't need to be told which specific spots on the road are especially scenic—when you round a hairpin curve and find yourself gasping at the view and simultaneously reaching for your camera, you'll know you've found one.

Pfeiffer–Big Sur State Park, a deep forest of redwood and other trees, provides a change of scenery from the grassy hills of Big Sur. It has hiking trails, fishing spots, picnic areas, campgrounds, food service, and a lodge. At Jade Cove, about 20 miles south of the park, you can hunt for pieces of jade at low tide. Pfeiffer–Big Sur State Park; Big Sur, CA 93920; 408-667-2315.

Thirty-Mile Drive: The 30 miles from Big Sur to the Monterey-Carmel area include some of the most dramatic scenery in the country. Though you've driven about 300 miles by now, push on for the extra hour to cover this coast-hugging, twisting road. Here's where the Santa Lucia Mountains meet the sea. Bixby Creek Bridge, just south of Carmel, is a 260-foot-wide observation point where you can park, watch the ocean pound the beach, and gaze hypnotically at the Point Sur Lighthouse, which flashes every 15 seconds.

Ever northward: It's quite possible to let this route get out of hand—you're not too far from San Francisco, and before you know it, a fired-up imagination may lead you even further, to Seattle and into the majestic blue pines of British Columbia. But that's really terrain to tackle on another trip.

Instead, turn your eyes and your heart to the mild, dreamlike paradise of Southern California, the ocean, the highways, the sports, the oil wells, the sun. This may be your first visit here, but it needn't be your last. Take in as much as you can reasonably enjoy, but no more. For there's always more to see and, after all, Southern California never goes away. Come back and catch it next time.

Desert Landscape

The deserts of Southern California have two things to offer—one is a certain quantity of sand, and the other is Palm Springs. Either is worth a look, but don't try to do them both in one day. The best times to visit are in winter, spring, and fall, when temperatures are a bit less mind-baking.

Joshua Tree National Park: Created in 1936 over howls of protest from mining companies, it is a haven for the Joshua tree and other desert wildlife and plants. The tree was given its name by early pioneers who felt it resembled the prophet Joshua raising his arms in supplication to God, or at least pointing the way for them to go. Nature trails and good major roads provide access to 870 square miles of park. Split Rock, near Pinto Wye, one of the park's best-known landmarks, is a giant split boulder more than three stories high, with a natural cave underneath. There also are rocks carved into weird shapes by the wind, an impressive view of the San Bernardino Mountains, and the distant waters of the Salton Sea. Work your way out of Anaheim via Rte. 91 east to 60 east to I-10 east; about 240 miles round-trip. Joshua Tree National Park; Attention Superintendent; 74485 National Park Dr.; Twenty-nine Palms, CA 92277; 619-367-7511.

Anza-Borrego Desert State Park: It's loveliest in the spring, when the willow and tamarisk trees, wildflowers, and pine groves are at their best (call the wildflower hotline at 619-767-4684 for recorded information). The desert ranges from 100 feet below sea level (near the Salton Sea) to 6,000 feet above (in the Santa Rosa Mountains), and sprawls across half a million acres. See bighorn sheep (*borregos*), jackrabbits, coyotes, gray foxes, mule deer, and round-tail squirrels.

There are hundreds of miles of vehicle trails. Self-guided auto and hiking tours describe the region's geology, while ranger-guided tours are available on weekends and holidays from November to May. Check at the visitors center for schedules.

Camping sites offer tables, wood stoves, shade ramadas, toilets, and running water. Reservations are recommended for any day of the week from November through May, and for weekends and holidays the rest of the year. Reservations can be made using MasterCard or Visa, and information can be obtained about the locations of walk-in reservation outlets throughout the state by calling 800-444-7275. The Visitors Center at 200 Palm Canyon Drive (619-767-4205) is open daily from 9 A.M. to 5 P.M. October through May; Saturdays, Sundays and holidays from 9 A.M. to 5 P.M. June through September. Take I-5 south from Anaheim to Rte. 78, which rambles east into the park; about 260 miles round-trip. Anza-Borrego Desert State Park; Box 299; Borrego Springs, CA 92004; 619-767-5311.

Palm Springs: The sun shines here only about 350 days a year, the days average 88° (delightful because the humidity is so low), and the nights average a perfect 55°. In summer, though, daytime highs often reach 105°.

The spot was discovered centuries ago by the Agua Caliente Indians, who considered the hot water (*agua caliente* in Spanish) springs to have miraculous healing powers. While Palm Springs was a spa for many years, people today are more interested in it for its warm, dry climate, its desert scenery, and its superb resort facilities.

Golf is very big here—on more than 40 courses, with tournaments just about every week from September through May, including the Bob Hope Desert Classic. Don't miss the Palm Springs Desert Museum, a multifaceted cultural center featuring art exhibits, a history museum with unusual Indian artifacts, and outstanding facilities for the performing arts (101 Museum Drive). The San Jacinto Wilderness State Park, which can be reached only by aerial tram, is nearby, as is the larger San Bernardino National Forest. Take Rte. 91 east; about 200 miles round-trip. Palm Springs Desert Resorts Convention and Visitors Bureau; 69930 Highway 111, Suite 201; Rancho Mirage, CA 92270; 619-770-9000 or 800-96-RESORT.